Ronald Fino

THE TRIANGLE EXIT

Ronald Fino

with Michael Rizzo

The Triangle Exit

Senior Editors & Producers: Contento De Semrik

Editor: Sherrill Layton

Layout and Cover Design: Ivan Bogod

Historical assistance by James McGough

ISBN: 978-965-550-193-3

International sole distributor:

Contento De Semrik

22 Isserles, 67014 Tel–Aviv, Israel

Semrik10@gmail.com

www.Semrik.com

The Triangle Exit

RONALD FINO

with MICHAEL RIZZO

CONTENTO DE SEMRIK

Table of Contents

Preface

FOR YEARS I HAVE BEEN LOOKING forward to writing my story but every time I was ready a new undercover project commenced and that became my priority. I received offers to appear on the Larry King Show, among others, but the *Federal Bureau of Investigation* (FBI) and others felt my appearance would place me and the new projects in jeopardy.

I received calls from author Tom Clancy as well as celebrities such as Charlton Heston. I obtained a literary agent and the thought of the money, which I desperately needed, kept tugging, as well as telling what really happened, the true story, correcting the fabrication and spin that was being dished out by the mob, its lawyers, and lackeys.

On the other hand there were ongoing matters, court cases and the unfinished business that the bureau wanted me to complete. After much thought and many book starts I decided to postpone any publications. Well, here it is 2013, and even though there are ongoing investigations that I am involved in, I feel it is the right time to tell my side.

I say that you can no longer tell a mobster by his fedora hat; today they try and portray themselves as helpful citizens, popping up at charitable events and public functions. The children of Cain have mutated and now even pay their taxes. The bosses and leaders try to avoid any illegal communication with most of their underlings and leave the dirty work to trusted Cosa Nostra (LCN) members. My story does not just cover the Western New York Mafia, it goes well beyond that.

Because of my unique position as the son of a made man (fully initiated member of the Mafia) and a union official I got to know numerous made men from New York, Chicago, Cleveland, Newark, Philadelphia, Pittsburg, Los Angeles, Miami, New Orleans, St. Louis and more. I learned how they were able to control members of our Congress, as well local officials and their ties to presidents, politicians and law enforcement officials.

After I completed most of the mob cases, I worked with the exiled democratically elected government of the African nation of Gambia in an effort to see if we could restore them to their rightful offices. I then started to infiltrate the Russian Mafia which I found even more terrifying than La Cosa Nostra. That activity brought me in contact with many Muslim terrorist groups as well as illegal arms smuggling, child porn, narcotics and money laundering.

In this story I name names, including some quite well known. I feel that it is important to point out that no one, including high-level political figures, as well as celebrities, is immune to the power of the underworld.

I will say up front that I have great respect for the FBI and the *Central Intelligence Agency* (CIA), and the other federal and state agents and officers were always professional. Canadian Security Intelligence Service's, Criminal

Intelligence Service Ontario (CISO) officers and agents were a tremendous help to their United States counter-parts.

Even though there were procedural disagreements and arguments, I never once found them to abuse their respective power bases. No one ever told me to fabricate a story or expand beyond the truth; this includes the *Department of Justice* (DOJ). There were agents and officers I did not get along with, but only a few. Many became close friends of mine and remain close friends.

During my life I have uncovered too many corrupt union and government officials and it makes me doubt just how this country of ours can even function. Like they say in the bureau, "If the public ever put this all together on how their tax dollars are misused, there would be a revolution." I have tried not to paint myself as a victim or more than I really am. Don't get me wrong, I have lost quite a lot at the expense of the Mafia but I equally used what I learned to fight this arcane pestilence as hard as I could.

It is not my intent to in any way condemn all our elected officials. They, too, know that in order to get elected it takes money and lots of it. They are victims, as well as we are, to a system that favors companies, people, and special interests that have the financial resources to hold sway to compel a well-intentioned office seeker to favor their desires. Without needed funds for campaign advertising, the well-intentioned almost always lose. Let's face it, publicity works and it works well. Those individuals who seek offices that involve positions that pass judgment on us all are another matter. They should be guided by their *conscience* and the principles of ethics and moral virtues. Those judges and law enforcement officials who cast aside ethical behavior and use their position for political, egotistical, financial, and personal gain are the lowest of the low and should be admonished. Labor union officials are elected to their respective positions as fiduciaries representing the needs of the membership. As you will see in my story, this is not always the case. Not all unions are bad, but when the mob gets involved with one, membership freedom is expunged and discarded.

It has been written that my life as an undercover operative has been riddled with sadness and of having to go it alone. Sure, I have had my bad times, especially not seeing my children as much as I wanted, or visiting my friends and relatives who remain dear to me and our always in my heart. But going it alone? Never. My country and its intelligence and law enforcement agencies never once let me down. The officers and agents not only became dear associates but stood by me in my darkest hours. I cannot say enough about these brave men and women who put their lives on the line so the rest of us have a better world to live in. It was, however, no free ride. I was required to go far beyond my role as a witness against the Italian-American Cosa Nostra. I had to attend in-service classes and pass the grade just like anyone else. I had to hone the skills I did possess and develop new ones so that I was equipped to deal with non-traditional criminal activity that had befallen us. It was not easy and I spent many a sleepless night in boning up on what would become a new way of life. I did and do think that this midstream change of life gave rise to my feeling, a sense of purpose, and my being an asset to the United States and its people.

Has it been worth it? Yes, by all means! I may have had my down moments but overall it has been a hell of a ride. I have been around the world a couple of times. I have seen the ruins of Egypt; the steps that Jesus walked; the cliffs of the Aryan Isles; the ruins and devastation caused by the Chernobyl meltdown; ridden a gondola through the canals of Venice; walked the 32nd parallel separating North and South Korea. I could go on and on. Many still think of the former Soviet Union as a cold, dark place. This is so far from the truth and I consider it a must for any Westerner to see, the people are absolutely wonderful and a joy to be around. The nightlife, the restaurants and pleasures are second to none. Sure, they have their problems, but let's face it, so do we.

I have met and befriended world leaders, ambassadors and representatives from hundreds of countries; I obtained more insight than most and just how others feel about America and what we can do to correct the misgivings.

I have also been asked (!) if I committed a crime, would I turn informant to beat a jail sentence. I have never been in that situation and what I have done did not involve any arm twisting or saving someone, nor myself for that matter, from a jail sentence. I acted out of conviction; I acted because I believed that something had to be done to stop all this damn garbage that hurts us all. If I was in that predicament, I would never try and beat a rap by becoming an informant. Personally, I don't like the practice. I understand the need, but I would rather see the decent victims of this outmoded nonsense reach down deep inside and have the courage to act. Believe me, I know it's not easy and a price has to be paid that most people dread. It is, however, the only way; if enough people raise their voices to a daring level, then, and only then, can we expunge this yoke and become free of the mob and its control.

Would I do it all over again? Yes, without hesitation. There are other jobs I would like to have practiced, a medical doctor, or maybe an investigative reporter; and if it wasn't for the limited visitations with my children, operating as a gatherer of potentially needed information for our country remains right up there.

Acknowledgments

I dedicate this book to my wife Alla; her mother Tatiana, sister Svetlana and their families; my children, Joseph, Danielle and Daniil. My sisters Diane, Joanne, and Angela and their families; my brother Richard and his family. Stanley Penn, *The Wall Street Journal*, Joe Ritz, *Buffalo News*, Dan Moldea, author and investigative reporter. Jack Platt, CIA officer; Philip R. Manuel, Chief Investigator of the Permanent Subcommittee on Investigations for the United States Senate.

In Memory

Reverend Herb Reid; James "Tex" Smith, just an ordinary man who became my best friend and a person I believed in. Former Buffalo Mayor, James Griffin. Reader's Digest Senior Editor Eugene Methvin. Norman Goldfarb, State University of New York at Buffalo. CIA/Organized Crime Strike Force official Alphonse Hartel, CIA Officer Richard Stolz, and New York City Detective Jack O'Connor. FBI agents Gene Bedsole, Stanley Ronquest and Stanley Nye; Col. James R. "Jim" McDonald, USAF; Israeli Defense Forces Chief of Staff "Motta" Gur; Gary Wall, Georgio Adrimis, who left Italy to become a communist only to become a capitalist; Robert Goulet, Daniel Domino, who may have been a tough mobster, but also saved my life; Ugo Rossini, Robert Powell and Rollin "Bud" Vinall, Laborers' International Union vice presidents who valued the welfare of the union's membership, and Patrick J. Sullivan; Longshoremen George Wessel, AFL-CIO; Danny Fulcher, and Laborers' Local 210.

FBI Agents

Larry G. Ankrom, Andrew G. Arena, Andy Bell, Jules J. Bonavolonta, Andy Bringell, Michael Buckley, Wendy Brower, John J. Burke, Kenny Callahan, Carlos Costa, Anthony E. Daniels, James B. Darcy, Linley DeVecchio, George L. Dysico, Roger Edens, Steve Edwards, Ronald Eowan, Louis J. Freeh, Lawrence Frisoli, David A. Gentile, Gerard D. Galbreath, Jan Galbreath, Tom Gancarz, Richard Genova, Joseph Griffin, Robert Hargraves, Van Harp, Donald Hartnett, Ronald Hettinger, Kristi K. Johnson, Michael V. Kogut, Karl L. Grouse, Charlotte Lang, G. Robert Langford, Ernest T. Luera, David G. Major John M. Mallul, Charlie Mauer, David Gentile, Gregg O. McCrary. John "Jack" McDonnell, Thomas McDonnell, Jeff, McLaine, James E. Moody, Paul Moskal, Jack Moughan, Harry A. Mount, Greg Naples, Dean G. Naum, Steve J. Naum, Don North, John J. O'Rourke, R. Gerald Personen, John Pistole, Joseph Pistone, Jack Porstel, Ervin L. Recer, Oliver "Buck" Revell, and R. Douglas. Rhoads, Todd I. Richards, Daniel R. Romanzo, Michael Ross, Richard C. Ross, Glen Rukoff, Larry Schneifer, Phil Smith, George Sturm, Roger P. Tardie, Robert Ulmer, Mike Wacks, Peter J. Wacks, Duncan Wainwright, Robert Watts, Arthur "Dave Webster, F. Ronald Webb, David Weigand, and Thomas M. Woodby.

United States Attorney Staff Members

Samuel A. Alito, Dan Braun, Anthony M. Bruce, David D. Buvinger, Michael Chertoff, Keith Corbett, Richard D. Endler, Joel Friedman, Janet Lynn Goldstein, J. Kenneth Lowrie, Manvin Mayell, Richard P. Maigret, David Margolis, Mitchell Mars, Kevin E. McCarthy, Paul J. McNulty, Craig A. Oswald, Ann Rowland, Cynthia Shepherd, Robert Stewart, Mary Jo White, Stanley A. Twardy Jr., Sam Wohlbrandt, James R. Wooley, Fred Wyshak.

United States Senate and House Committee Investigators

Amelia DeSantis, Lisa Odle Kaufman, Philip R. Manuel, Bill McDaniel.

Department of Labor Members

Ronald Chance, John Grande, Gilbert Heighert, Brian Hitt, Melinda Long, Raymond Maria, Stephen J. Willertz.

CIA

Richard Stolz, Mary McCarthy, Jack Platt, William Long, Christopher Page, Michael Roy, Harry Rositzke, Philip Stone, Ben Wickham

United States Air Force

Capt. Doug Brock, Colonel George "Buster" Barksdale

United States Army

Colonel Keith A. Detwiler, SSG Christopher Braman

United States State Department

Stefanie R. Altman

Defense Intelligence Agency

Colonel Donald Hukle

EPA

David W. Wilma

United States Customs – ICE

Wayne A. Day, Gregory C. Nevano, Edward G. Salvas, James Scott, Jim Raferty

International Monetary Fund

Owen Evans

United States Congress

Hon. Howard Coble, North Carolina, Hon. William McCollum, Florida, Hon. Robert Barr, Georgia, Hon. John LaFalce, New York Hon. Jack Kemp, New York, Hon. Henry Nowak

New York State Organized Crime Division

Ronald Goldstock

New York Police Department

Joseph W. Zamboni

National Labor Relations Board

Frank Novak

Drug Enforcement Agency

Shannon Pinto, Scott Johnson

Ambassadors

Valery Tsepkalo, Belarus; Ousman Sallah, Gambia; H.E.

Mr. Le Van Bang, Vietnam; Yuri Ushakov, Russia; Mikhail Khvostov, Belarus

Labor

Tom Fricano, UAW; Bob Brown, Laborers' Union, Rochester, NY; *Ed Asner, Actor- Screen Actors Guild;* Jack Wilkinson, Laborers' International Union; Gene Adams, IBEW.

Reporters

John Mulligan, RI Journal; Ed Barnes, *Time Magazine*; Viveca Novak, *Time Magazine*; Dean Starkman, *Wall Street Journal*; Michael Beebe, *Buffalo News*; Joseph Ritz, *Buffalo News*; Bill Dowell *Time Magazine*; Peter Edwards (author of 'Unrepentant'), *Toronto Sun*; Byron York, *American Spectator*; Mike Orfelt' *Hardhat Magazine*; Kenneth F. Boehm, *National Legal and Policy Center*; Rael Jean Issac, *National Review*; Mike Stanton, *Providence Journal*; Joanne Kimberln, *Virginia Pilot.*

Literary Agents

Frank Weimann, Netanel Semrik.

Authors

George Anastasia, Dick Billings, Jerry Capeci, Linda Chavez, Tom Clancy, Robert Fitch, Sam Giancana, Kathy Maxa, Dennis King, Danny Moldea, (great friend) Joe

Pistone, Rick Porrello, Selwyn Raab, Mike Rizzo, Robert Ernest Volkman, Robert "Bob" Woodward.

Actors

Carol Burnett, Robert Davi, Gavin O'Connor, Robert Goulet

Sports Figures

Whitey Ford, Conrad Dobler, Paul Guidry, Daryle Lamonica, Lou Saban

My Associates and Friends

Colonel George "Buster" Barksdale, Timofey S. Borodin, Carol Linnan Burke, William Connell, Irina Krakovskaia, Anatoly Massiuk, Joseph May, James McGough, John Kenton, Dennis King, Laura Moon, Alexander Orlov, William Rogers (who was always there for me), Anton Romanovsky, Abraham Rosenthal, James Sawh, Wadell Smith, Gerard Snyder, Ruth Tavss, Valery Tspekalo, Thomas Turbeville, Alexander Vanshin, Christopher White, Kenneth Yoffy.

Prologue

DRIVING AROUND THE CITY OF BUFFALO in plain view with FBI Special Agent Jack Porstel was quite common and I don't know if it was because of our ignorance, or that we did not believe that we would be seen that caused us to continue this reckless way of passing on information.

This modus operandi came to a screeching halt one morning when Porstel and I were noticed by two Buffalo mobsters who, by sheer dumb luck, were stopped at the same red light on the opposite side of the street. Billy Sciolino and Nick Rinaldo gazed at us, their facial expressions revealing their astonishment and I knew I was in trouble and almost panicked by opening the passenger door on the bureau car and bolting. I was so confused and befuddled by this sighting and I didn't have time to think of a way out, let alone how really stupid Porstel and I were by allowing ourselves to be exposed like this.

Porstel could only utter, "Fuck!" Regaining my composure and attempting to exhibit an air of I-have-nothing-to-do-with-it, I slumped in my seat and made it appear that I was the target of an FBI inquiry. Porstel dropped me off and said, "Call me if you need help, take care, Ron."

What stupidity, I thought, *we must be brain dead to take these kind of chances!*

Rinaldo, being the spiteful Mafioso he was, knew of Porstel and considered him an aggressive punk with a sarcastic approach to the mob, and who would go to great lengths to put wiseguys behind bars. I knew word would get back to higher-ups and I knew it would happen quickly.

I then headed back to the Local 210 Union Hall to await the mob's response. As I walked into the Union Hall, I could tell that the sighting had not yet been revealed to Dan Sansanese or the secretaries. I quickly asked secretary Jennie DeAngelo to contact Dick Lipsitz, the union attorney, right away. I decided I would tell him what had happened and make it sound like I was being hassled by the bureau.

With Lipsitz on the phone and Dan Sansanese right next to me, I started making up a tall tale to get my ass out of hot water.

I started by saying I was picked up by *two* FBI Agents. I gambled that Sciolino and Rinaldo did not notice whether there was anybody in the back seat. Telling the lawyer, "Two FBI agents pulled up in front of the Union Hall and asked me to get in the car. Figuring that I was under arrest, I got in. One of the agents got in the back seat and as we drove away the agent in the back seat told me, 'Ronnie, you're a good kid, you don't have to be with these people and we would like you to cooperate with us.'"

Lipsitz was listening intently, as was Sansanese. So I told them, "After hearing that, I asked the feds if I was under arrest and they said, 'If you don't cooperate, you will be; if not today, then soon.' They were driving close to the federal building on Delaware Avenue and I thought they were going to bring me into the FBI office. I told them, 'I want to speak to my attorney; if I am not under arrest I would appreciate being dropped off.'"

While on the phone, Lipsitz said that there was nothing that I could do, that they were just harassing me. As I hung up the phone Angelo Massaro (the administrator of the benefit funds) walked in and told me that he had heard about the incident and that I must immediately travel to Angola, New York and see the boss of the Buffalo Mafia, Sammy Frangiamore, also known as "Sam the Farmer."

As I drove to the Farm (the Frangiamore home) I tried to think if I should add any additional information to my story and if I had made any mistakes in the fabrication.

After I arrived and he greeted me, the elderly boss asked me to take a walk with him and inquired about what had happened. I explained the story and also let him know that I was angered and felt it was an insult for Sciolino and Rinaldo to have those kinds of suspicions about me and that they should be ashamed of themselves. I sensed that he believed me because no agent or source would ever be that dense to be seen on a highly traveled thoroughfare in downtown Buffalo.

After leaving the Farm, satisfied that I had explained myself out of the dire situation, I questioned my future as a conduit of mob activity. Was it really worth it? All this jeopardy, and for what? An outside chance that the mob would be excised from the union? That right always wins? By October, 1974, the compromise was history. As a memento of that fateful day I also learned to stay away from public places while meeting agents.

Growing Up

TODAY WHEN PEOPLE MENTION BUFFALO, NEW York they always seem to connect it with snow, bad weather, rusting factories, and industrial plants. Sure, it's had its share of bad weather and like most of the cities of the so-called "Rust Belt," it has only memories of an economy. For me, growing up on the streets of Buffalo convey only fond memories that seem to occupy a portion of my everyday thoughts. I loved the city and treasure most of that part of my life I spent living there.

I was born in 1946, to Joseph Fino and Arlene Burkard. I really didn't know my father as a child and I was told that he was in the Army and would eventually some day be returning. My mother was a feisty German-Irish gal that seemed to be more like a sister and I truly cherish those moments we spent together. As I sit here in front of my computer trying to compile and put down on paper those obscure but not totally forgotten moments, I reach back to my subconscious recollections that take me to a time and place of the city called the Fruit-Belt. It was considered one of the poorest sections of Buffalo, occupied by houses that had already seen their day.

While being raised by my mother and grandmother, I

did not know that my father's army stint was in reality his incarceration in the New York State penitentiary located in Attica, New York, and home to some of the hardest criminals in the state. To me, the prison was an army fort where my father worked as a soldier in defense of his country.

I recall telling my mother one time, "I see Uncle Danny is in the army too, Ma…" after seeing Danny Sansanese Sr.a close mobster friend of my father, immersed in gardening on the perimeter of the prison walls.

The times my sister and I spent with my mother were moments to be treasured, but the one problem that we had was the lack of food; there was never enough. The welfare handouts were welcome except for the contents of the plastic bag that had a red glob in the middle that would have to be worked into the goo called *oleo.* To this very day, I refuse to eat margarine.

My mother always seemed to be mad at my father's family especially my father's elder brother Jimmy for not helping us more during our time of need.

The house we lived in was owned by my mother's father and even though he allowed us to stay there rent free, his assistance did not go beyond that. He was quite well-to-do and owned numerous properties, as well as stocks of food stuffs and everyday necessities.

"The old kraut," as my mother would call him in a fit of despair, or when she would call him for additional assistance, but to no avail. He would tell her to divorce my father and, "find a man with a job if you need help, Arlene."

I made a few pennies from my lemonade stand that was perched in front of my home and my skill as a food and coal thief was renowned in our neighborhood. At seven years old

I was the best thief around. I would raid my grandfather's fruit cellar by removing the screws from the locked door, and carefully take away only items that were in abundance then replace the screws and rub a little dirt into them to conceal the marks left by the screwdriver. Our wonderful neighbor would plant his tomatoes close to the fence that separated our two properties so that I didn't have to climb over and trample all his fruits and vegetables to get at them.

On my forays I was only caught twice, once when I raided a chicken processing center and thought I had made my get away— only to be coughed up by the two cackling chickens I held. The other time, I was trailed over fences and through back yards by the tracks that the heavy Christmas tree had left.

The winter brought a new source of revenue, to the father-in-the-army family, in shoveling snow and its removal. I would crisscross, going door-to-door and clean walkways and driveways of those willing to pay a quarter for my services. My mother assisted me every now and then, and as youthful as she was and looked, I would insist that I do the talking and for her to remain out of sight.

One time a lady saw that I was struggling with the snow removal and feeling sorry for my "brother" George (the name that I had given my mother) and me, so she grabbed a shovel and started assisting us.

"That's all right Madam, we'll take care of it," I said. Not listening to my plea, she started to help anyway. "George," I yelled, "stay in the front and finish that area!" hoping that this kind woman would not notice that my brother George was really my mother.

Every month or so my father's older brother Jimmy

would drop off a box of produce, eagerly awaited by us; even though it was old, moldy, and sometimes rotten we would try to savor the desirable vegetables and fruit.

Outside of the lack of food, I knew little about the effects of poverty and its impact on us and our neighbors. A child normally doesn't think of these things and for me our home and way of life was just like that of everyone else's, nothing more!

I did relish the days when my father's friend Marshall Miles would pick me up and take me to the Buffalo Zoo, Delaware Park for a boat ride; The Museum, Humboldt Pool, or the YMCA located on Ferry Street near Jefferson, where I would go every Saturday. I didn't know that Mr. Miles was one of the largest numbers racket operators in the area, as well as the manager of heavyweight boxing champion Joe Louis, and a criminal associate of my father.

To me, he was my dear friend as well as my first teacher. His taking me to the wondrous places and discussing how I should make sure that education came first, had, and continues to have, a place in my heart. He always smiled and treated me as he would his own son.

One day Mr. Miles came by unexpectedly and spotted me outside playing near the street with no shoes on. "Where are your shoes, Ronnie? There's broken glass near your feet and you are going to get cut."

I explained that my shoes were old and falling apart. "Where's your mother?" I pointed to our home and told him she was inside. He then went into our home and discussed the matter with my mother, who informed him that she did not have the money to buy me new shoes.

"Arlene, what happened to the money that Freddy [Randaccio] and Vito ["Buck Jones" Domiano] gave you?" My mother later told me that she said to him, "What money, what are you talking about, Marshall?" He then explained, "Money was put aside for you and the kids, Arlene, and I'll look into why you're not getting it."

On leaving he told me, "I will see to everything." I didn't know what he was talking about, but that evening, Marshall's brother Percy and Joe Occhino (also an associate of my father and a member of the mob) came by our home and dropped off steaks and boxes of food. I am not sure, but this was the first time I remember ever eating a steak, which was an experience I will never forget. They also gave my mother $100 to help us out. My mother, my sister Diane and I were overjoyed and could not believe our good fortune. New shoes for me and my sister, the taste of quality food and my mother recovering from despair.

We didn't know at the time, but $5,000 was put aside for us by my father's associates and, instead of giving it to my mother, they gave it to my uncle to pass on to her. Later on I learned that Stefano Magaddino (the Godfather of the Niagara Falls/Buffalo Mafia family), Freddy "The Wolf" Randaccio (the underboss) and other made men learned of this and wanted to kill my uncle.

Joe Occhino, my uncle's boss, and mob member Rocco LaPenta found my uncle (who drove a taxi, which was a front for his gambling business, and worked at Bethlehem Steel). My uncle immediately admitted taking the money, using it for himself and there was nothing left.

On learning this, father was shocked and disappointed and wondered why my mother didn't tell him of our plight. (Later in life she confessed to me that she did not want to burden my father with the knowledge that his family was in trouble while he was in prison.) My father immediately sent word back to The Boys, as they were referred to, not to harm his brother and he would straighten it out when he was released. From that time on, until my father returned, Joe Occhino and Marshall and Percy Miles made sure that we had food, clothing and a better life.

Right before my father came home, Vito Domiano drove me to nearby Niagara Falls to attend a party. I remember many people were there and I was introduced to Stefano Magaddino. Even though through the years I had numerous get-togethers with his son Peter, this was the only time that I ever remember meeting the "old man" as he was sometimes referred to. Unfortunately, I cannot recollect what he said to me. But I do remember him handing me a $5.00 bill. When I returned home that evening and showed my mother the money, she called Magaddino "a cheap bastard."

I was eight years old when I greeted my father, the "war" soldier, and within days started enjoying the companionship and affection that my father showered on me. He was in quick possession of a car and I started "making the rounds" (as he would refer to it) with him, meeting with his friends, associates and fellow bookmakers. We would visit the men that sat behind barricaded doors and windows and answered the constantly ringing telephones. After leaving we would stop for lunch and be joined by other Mafiosi members whom I was told to refer to as my "uncles."

I was somewhat naive, but I was also aware that the activity I witnessed was illegal. One afternoon, while my father was visiting a bookmaking operation, two police detectives walked in. "Hi, Joe," they said, their smiling faces revealed to me that this was not a bust, but only a payoff for turning their backs on the gambling activity.

As my father would cruise the streets, the well-liked "Ebe" (his nickname) would be warmly greeted by many of the people gathered on the street corners. I couldn't believe that my father knew so many people and was so popular, especially after being gone for so long.

One afternoon I learned the hard way that my father's absence was not because he was in the army, but because he was in jail. Friends of mine, Jack and Mike Floyd, told me that they could not come over to our house and play with me anymore. When I asked them why, they responded, "Your father is an ex-con and our parents want us to stay away from you." I yelled back that it was not true and even a barrage from my fists didn't change the reality of it and the truth that had come from their lips. Still, I welcomed the presence of this man that I vaguely knew, from the moment he was not allowed to reach over the Attica Prison wooden barrier to fix a bandage on my finger that was too tight.

With the birth of my brother Alan, the contentment that my mother enjoyed spilled over to my sister Diane and me. Never again needing hand-me-downs or Goodwill clothing was something we savored. My thieving and our huddles under the blankets on a cold night were becoming a passing memory. The enjoyment of travel became the norm every Easter, and during the summer holidays as we would hop in the car and take off for places unknown; a trip undiminished in the least by my constant throwing up as a result of motion sickness.

Religion played a deep part in our upbringing and my mother brought us to church every Sunday and on religious holidays. Outside of only one Christmas Mass that he slept through, my father never joined us. My mother was a wonderful piano player and while she played she would teach my sister and me the words to Christmas carols. Many a December night we would join her in singing them while we eagerly awaited Santa Claus and the toys and gifts that lay beneath the tree.

The ignorance of my father's brother regarding our plight occupied my mother's memory for many years and she was not afraid to point out this unsavory act toward my father. In defense of his brother, my father always came up with an excuse for his brother's behavior. Her dislike of the Mafia was repeatedly voiced and reflected in her attitude toward the Mafia members and my father's cohorts. Congenial, but reserved, she would tell me, "What phonies your father's friends and their wives are! They sit around all day and only talk about their money, clothes and hairdos."

My mother did like my father's brother Jimmy's wife who was always nice and helpful. She would pick us up and drive us to a friend's farm for a day of fun for us kids.

During weekdays my father would come home around 5:00 p.m. and after dinner, like clockwork, he would leave again at 8:00 p.m. Where he went I never knew. All he would say was, "I have to meet some friends."

I remember one time being woken up as my father was struggling up the stairs with two bushel-barrels full of coins. Sometime right after that, I was awakened again, but this time by my mother who was somewhat panicked. "Ronnie, wake up and help me." Only half-awake she wanted help taking some of the coins from one of the bushels and sliding them under the living room couch.

"Why?" I asked my mother. "Because I overheard your father telephone his brother Nick and tell him to come over and he could have the change." We waited until my father was wrestling with the first bushel barrel and its journey back down the stairs to where his brother was waiting.

Seizing the moment and dragging me to where the other barrel of money was placed, we quickly started shoving the mostly fifty-cent pieces and quarters under the couch. The sound of my father coming up the stairs sent us scurrying to our rooms and beds. After he finished the task, my father came in and kissed me on the forehead and tucked me, pretending-to-be-asleep, in. I heard him go into his bedroom and move quietly, so as not to disturb my mother, who I'm sure was pondering over the score she had just made.

Our life was good and we truly enjoyed the money my father had access to, even though he was not wealthy and we seldom had any cash for ourselves. My father never made much money, and the only cash that was available came from his bookmaking operation headed up by his brother, Nick, and his six for five loan shark operation run by Frank DeNisco. That was basically it.

"Dad, can I have a dollar?" was usually answered with, "What do you need it for?" and "Is it important?" Every now and then he would let us have a little money for a movie and a box of popcorn.

I am sure, at least in part, that my mother's feelings and the treatment that we received during my father's incarceration led me to repudiate the Mafia and everything it stood for.

Boxing

I was only 12, but like most children of that age, school and education were secondary and not as important as playing and having some spending money. Without my father's knowledge I started visiting a boxing training center called Singer's Gym. I did not have the money to join but they let me train while I worked as a gofer.

I took the bus back and forth every day and my presence at the gym introduced me to the sport of boxing and the role the Mafia played in it.

Richard Fumerelle was my father's son from his previous marriage, and as a result of his having to spend time "going to jail" he gave parental custody of his son to his sister Josephina and her husband, Louis Fumerelle. He also had a daughter, Joanne, who kept the Fino name and was raised by her parental mother.

For as long as I can remember, Richard was called Rocky. This was probably because my grandfather's name was Rocco, but I am not sure.

Rocky was good boxer who could hit as hard as anyone his size and he could equally take a punch. He was nicknamed "The Blonde Bomber" because of his light hair, a Fino trait. Rocky rose in stature and became a top-ranked middleweight fighter, headlining in Madison Square Garden and elsewhere. Our father did not like Rocky's involvement in the boxing business and his constant attempts to stop him went ignored. Rocky did not want our father, or the mob, to get involved in fixing any of his bouts and our father assured him that it would never happen.

My locker at Singer's Gym was next to that of heavyweight fighter Dick Wipperman and near to the fighters that Bernie Blacher, Frank "Chops" Alberti, Johnny Suddac and Salvatore "Sammy" Cardinale were managing and training. Boxers, such as Tony LaBarbara, Poncho Padilla, Vinnie Calla and "Irish" Jackie Donnelly befriended me and always showed kindness.

I could see that Sam Cardinale, a made member of John Cammilleri's crew, held power at the gym, and walked around as if he owned the place. One day Cardinale came up to me and asked if my father knew I was there. I told him, "No, but I don't think he would mind."

I was wrong, dead wrong. The very next day while sparring in the ring with Vinnie Calla, I spotted out of the corner of my eye an irate, with blood in his eyes, Joe Fino. He was pissed and I mean pissed. He quickly grabbed me and said, "Get your bag, you are leaving with me." The ride home was quite uneasy and I was ordered not to ever see Singer's Gym again. "It's bad enough that I have to put up with Rocky, but not you! Ronnie, that's it, period." This may have ended my stint as a boxer but it was only the beginning of my education in the boxing industry and just how corrupt a sport it really was.

In July of 1961, Jackie Donnelly was scheduled to fight the highly talented Paola Rossi in a nationally televised fight for the title of New York State Lightweight Champion.

Fixing fights was big business and I had previously met Lucchese crime family member Paul "Frankie" Carbo, who brought the national Mafia more money from the boxing industry than anyone else. Carbo and his comrades could arrange for just about any fight to be rigged.

At the time, Carbo was on trial for conspiracy and extortion, yet remained active in arranging rigged fights. The heavily favored Rossi agreed and then proceeded to lose in a ten round battle with Donnelly. It proved to be a winning night for the mob and even the public wanted a rematch.

The rematch took place in Boston in September 1961, but this time the outcome of this unfixed bout was different. Jackie Donnelly suffered a technical knockout in the 2nd round. We put our television in the garage attached to our home so more than 20 guests could watch it.

Buffalo boxing manager Phil Gliosca was there and said that he told Donnelly not to get involved in any rematches with Rossi. I am quite sure that Jackie didn't know that his first battle with Rossi was fixed. He didn't have to know, what mattered is that Rossi knew and went along with it. I don't remember if Phil Gliosca had any involvement with Donnelly, even though I think he did. Gliosca was connected and would have known that the second fight was not prearranged. I liked Donnelly a lot and was extremely upset with the mob's involvement with him. Later on, after he left the boxing business and worked as an ironworker, he would always go out of his way to say hello to me.

One spring day in 1963, after coming home from school, my father told me, "Don't eat, we're going out to dinner, there's someone I want you to meet."

It was around 6:00 p.m. when we left and after picking up my uncle Nick, we drove around, so as not to be followed, and eventually ended up at the Hackney House, a restaurant located in the Buffalo suburb of Williamsville. The restaurant was secretly owned in part by Jimmy Williams, the uncle of future garbage and hazardous waste king, James H. "Harry" Williams.

Jimmy was a player who became extremely tight with the mob and local entrepreneur (and owner of Sportservice) Louis Jacobs. The Syrian-Lebanese business and criminal players were always around and maintained good ties with my father, Freddy Randaccio and Stefano Magaddino. Later in life, Jimmy Williams and I would frequently go golfing and I would get my butt kicked by the scratch player.

Jimmy Williams directed us to a private room and I noticed many of my father's friends: Sammy Pieri, Roxy Gian, Sam Cariola and others I cannot remember. I went to my father and said that the one guy looked like a small Rocky Marciano. He replied, "That is Marciano! Do you want to meet him?"

Marciano was talking to Gian and as we walked over to the former boxing champion, Gian asked Marciano if he knew my father, to which Marciano replied that he did. "Joe, how are you doing? How is Danny?" (He was probably referring to Danny Sansanese Sr., another Buffalo mobster.) I was then introduced to the champ, who seemed very affable, but not as big as I expected.

After dinner, on the drive home, I asked my father why Marciano was here and how did he get to know him? "He is going to lend his name to sponsor a sport or recreation center or something like that being developed by Freddy

Randaccio. I was introduced to him early in his boxing career through some friends from Boston."

During those early years of my life, my father was always quiet and rarely spoke about *this life of mine*, as he would refer to the mob. He told me not to tell anybody about meeting Marciano or his being in Buffalo, because it might cause problems for the former champ.

Another boxer, James Ralston, was born May 2, 1941, and grew up in the Riverside section of Buffalo. He started boxing in 1960, and for a time Sammy Cardinale was his manager. On September 6, 1969, he was suspended, along with his manager Pat Giordano, for pulling out of a fight.

Ralston was retired and Linda Cardinale, the daughter of Sammy Cardinale, wanted Ralston to be her boyfriend and she stalked him constantly. After his numerous rejections she decided to get even with him for not wanting her. She went to her father and lied that Jimmy Ralston tried to rape her. Sam was furious and wanted Ralston killed but the family told him it would bring too much heat. It was agreed that a beating was in order and the assignment was given to Danny Domino. Domino took a knife and cut the boxer's scrotum as a warning.

Broke and in need of spending cash was the norm for me so during the summer of 1963, I asked my father to see if he could help me find a job. He said that he would find something for me to do. A couple days later I was working as a groom for horses that were owned by my Uncle Louie Fumerelle. I hated it, up every morning at 4:00 a.m., and the cleaning of stalls took its toll, but I needed the money and somehow managed to make it through my summer vacation and had some cash to see me through that fall and winter.

School Years and Working as a Laborer

It was during my last year of grammar school when I first became aware of my father becoming a *Mafia Capo* (captain) and in control of his own crew. My Uncle Nick received his induction into the Mafia around that time and oversaw the bookmaking operation. Together they wanted to have all their brothers and sisters move into new homes neatly arranged at the end of a dead end street. My aunt had previously purchased property in West Seneca, a southern suburb of Buffalo and my father and uncle bought up the adjoining property, financed and built homes for their brother Jimmy and their sister Antoinette.

Bishop Timon High School was located in South Buffalo and it was here that the breeding of my future was redirected into the eventual allegiance and cooperation with the feds. My freshman year was greeted with a firmness and education that I needed. I'm not saying that my parents weren't concerned about my upbringing, but Bishop Timon was good for me and I probably needed the Franciscan friar's firm hand and discipline.

I was waffling back and forth between the forces that would decide which path I should take. While attending

Bishop Timon I was introduced to a group of guys who were concerned about their future success. We did our fair share of pranks, beer drinking and mischief, but were careful enough to weigh and balance our good times with proper reservation.

The Franciscan priests and my classmates were aware of my father and his being a high-ranking member of the Mafia; however, they never threw it in my face or held it against me. The cruelty that I had previously experienced by the Floyd brothers was an isolated case, still remembered, but quickly faded. My classmates and new friends were sons of working class parents and openly friendly to me and their parents never thought any less of me when I visited their homes.

I also had a new passion, Girls! I was so taken with the opposite sex and the girls I fancied, that I let my grades slip to mediocre. Even though I never had less than a 90 in history, my math grades seldom rose above 70 which did not change until my senior year when I made the honor list.

After graduating from Bishop Timon in 1964, and trying to decide just what I wanted to do with my life, I received a baptism into just how powerful the mob is and its control of organized labor.

Outside of a beat-up 1958 Ford, I really didn't have much and with little money available I couldn't even take my girlfriend Margie to the drive-in movie theater or the beach. Margie meant everything to me and we wanted to eventually get married. Her house was not far away from ours so I could walk over and not have to worry about finding some gas money or other means of transportation. At least three nights a week she would babysit for a wild divorcee named Vivian Sacco, who was previously married to Rudy Sacco, owner of the famous Bocce Club Pizza. She didn't seem to mind my frequent jaunts to join Margie in watching her three children. Vivian would stay out until the wee hours of the morning and by the time she did return I was usually home in my bed asleep. This was a great time for me and our romance became more than just holding hands.

In June of 1964, I again asked my father if he could assist me in finding a summer job in construction or some type of work where I could obtain a needed paycheck. He said that he would check with Freddy Randaccio and see if he could find me employment with the Teamsters or the Laborers' Union. Randaccio was at the height of his power and about a week later my father asked me to take a ride with him to see Freddy. We arrived at an auto dealer (whose name I cannot remember) and I immediately spotted Randaccio, Freddy Mogavero and Pat Natarelli.

After I got out of the car, Freddy walked over and told me to fill out a couple of membership applications for Laborers' Local 210 and after completing them he told me to change my birth year from 1946, to 1943; why? I didn't know, but I went along with his request. He then handed me a work slip that showed the name of the employer "S.J. Groves" who at that time was building the New York Thruway Interstate 290. Randaccio told me that I should report to the Local 210 Union steward Leonard Territo (his nephew and a future Laborers' Local 210 president). I was delighted! Here was an opportunity for me to make a few bucks and enjoy fruits of the life that went with it.

The next morning I went to the work shanties where I

met up with Territo who acted somewhat arrogant and very aloof! He introduced me to the general foreman, Charlie "Bones" Cicero. Immediately, I could see that Cicero knew the construction industry and how to handle the workers, their needs and complaints. Cicero said, "Because you are so new, Ronnie, I am going to have to place you as a flagman for a short time until you learn the ropes a little." I can tell you a flagman's job may be physically easy, but is very boring and I hated it.

It didn't take long for me to recognize the haves from the have-nots and that some jobs, such as the one Danny Sansanese Jr. had, were basically non-working positions. Show up, then disappear for a while, and then show up again.

An S.J. Groves superintendent who took a liking to me asked me if I would like to assist him with what, in the industry, is referred to as grade work. It involved surveying, directing heavy equipment, bringing the road and slopes we were working on to the right height. Eagerly, I said, "Yes, but would I need permission?" Cicero allowed it, but told me to be very careful, because in directing the heavy equipment, it could be very dangerous.

Becoming a grade foreman was exactly what I was looking for. Not only did it bring in more pay than the $3.39 an hour I was making, it offered me an opportunity to learn. With the arrival of late autumn came the traditional layoffs as a result of lower temperatures and the start of Western New York's inclement weather period.

Most of the laid off workers would collect unemployment insurance from the state if they had worked 20 or more weeks. Some of the younger guys would venture off to the various universities and colleges in the area to complete their education. I was tired of school but I had enough sense to know that to get ahead, it was a necessity. Like most 19-year-olds, I dreamed of the pleasures of having more; a boat, new car, clothes, going to parties, money and Margie. She became my constant companion and at least in my desires, she was the focal point of all my projections and schemes.

It is hard for me to reflect on that time and the way I felt when she broke off our relationship. I was deeply hurt, feeling lost and abandoned. I wallowed around in my pity and sorrow for quite some time and it took me a little while to get over her. Eventually I did, and girlfriend after girlfriend became the norm. My thoughts of marriage were over and replaced by the desire to get ahead and continue my education.

During the summer breaks I kicked around a number of construction projects and in the summer of 1967, I was assigned to Peter Kiewit and Sons Construction Company as a grade foreman. The company had the contract to build a new expressway near the village of East Aurora, New York. I further developed the skills I had previously been taught and plunged headlong into my new position. It may have been hard, and you needed eyes in the back of your head at all times, but I truly did like this type of work and the employer supervisors' praised my efforts and wanted me to stay with them for future endeavors as a supervisor.

Rarely did I get to see other mob-connected laborers who were working on these jobs, but when I did, they seemed quite puzzled by my wanting to do the arduous work that many workers considered quite difficult. They would say something like, "Ronnie, you can have any job, why do you take such a responsibility-filled, difficult job like this?" We did have our share of non-working laborers, or as they were commonly referred to, "pinky rings," on the job, but it was not as widespread as it would later become.

I could have stayed with the company, and when autumn arrived, they were sorry to see me go. I did consider staying but after much thought decided that the required travel to different areas of the country was not what I wanted, at least at that time.

After working on a few other jobs with periods of schooling mixed in, a change took place in 1969. The Buffalo/ Niagara Falls Mafia realm was about to be transformed into an area of immediate benefit for me, but also an area of wanting purpose, and something else out of life.

The Buffalo Family Coup

IN NOVEMBER OF 1968, THE BOSS of the Western New York Mafia, Stefano Magaddino, was arrested. Almost $500,000 was found hidden from the crime family and the Buffalo, Montreal, and Toronto factions of the family had had it with Magaddino and his keeping all the proceeds for himself and his relatives in Niagara Falls.

With Stefano Magaddino's underboss, Freddy Randaccio, in jail and Magaddino's son Peter ineffective, my father was placed as the leader of the revolt. He didn't discover he was just a pawn in the charade until much later.

Magaddino was a member of the Mafia's New York City-based Commission, but lost his power after the arrest. A bloodless takeover took place and even though it was resented by the Commission, my life was changed forever.

I noticed the workers' attitudes change immediately. Not being privy to my father's limited authority, they started treating me with warmth, or as the Mafia likes to refer to it, with *Respect.* While working as a laborer, I had become used to the buttering up that would be showered on the Randaccio relatives and the siblings and friends of the Cosa Nostra.

I remained somewhat naive and sheltered from the mob, but I knew of its power and dominance, the names of many of its members and associates, as well as its illegal activities. Still, it perplexed me why so many political and community leaders, and the people who knew them, would bow down and humble themselves to this mysterious gang.

In early 1969, the Buffalo and Rochester factions of the family decided to break away from the iron grip of Magaddino and his son Peter. Meetings were held in Fort Erie, Ontario; Rochester, New York; at Sammy Spano's home (the brother of Buffalo-made member Benny Spano), and at our home.

At one of the meetings that took place at our house, I was introduced to Joe Colombo, the boss of one of the New York City families, and Joe Aiuppa (Joey O'Brien), who later became the boss of the Chicago Family (even though the real power lay with Tony Accardo). Both were very close to my father and he would meet with them on a regular basis. I was present at many meetings but was usually asked to go into the other room, not allowed to listen in, except for only a few.

By April of 1969, it was agreed that the breakaway faction would stop paying tribute to Magaddino and that my father would head up the breakaway faction with Danny Sansanese Sr. as his underboss and Salvatore "Sammy" Frangiamore would be the *consigliere*, or adviser. What my father did not know at the time, was that, if by chance, the rebellion was opposed by the Magaddino loyalists, then my father would be a main target if shooting broke out.

With the wheels in motion, the coup took place and the Magaddino-run empire was no more. Frank Valenti and Rene Piccarreto of Rochester, Sammy Frangiamore, Roy Carlisi, John Cammilleri and Danny Sansanese Sr. were constant companions to my father. Secret meetings were held in Batavia, New York, in Pittston, Pennsylvania with Russell Bufalino, and other locations. Numerous trips were taken by my father, Joe Colombo and Roy Carlisi to Chicago where they would get together with Tony Accardo and Joey Aiuppa. Mostly, these meetings were held to discuss, and gain support for, the new *Buffalo Borgata* or Mafia family.

Danny Sansanese Sr. extolled his new position and the power it brought him. His girlfriend, Vivian Sacco, was no longer the wild child and her aloofness toward others showed the change that power brings. Vivian became a pain in the ass and nobody liked her anymore, even Victor and Danny Jr. disliked their father's choice and avoided her when she was around. Incidentally, I never heard of my father cheating on my mother, never once. If he did it was surely the best secret ever kept.

My father brought Billy "The Kid" Sciolino into the family. Sciolino was a thief who worked for years under master burglar Tommy Gascoyne and I always felt it was a mistake and as much as he was around us, I neither liked him, nor trusted him.

My father never had a bodyguard and he always left the house alone and would pick up my Uncle Nick, then venture off to his daily get-togethers with The Boys. Every now and then I would go with him to meet with the Valenti faction of the family. Like my father, I liked Frankie, Rene Piccarreto and Rene's son, Loren. Unlike me, however, Loren wanted to enter the life and our many talks together always revealed just how he and his father wanted to bring the family into the new Mafia way. He would talk about how they wanted more secrecy than what was currently going on, as well as limiting membership, delving into the stock market, and other new fields of opportunity. Like I said, I liked Loren but this did not change my feelings about the secret society. I knew I would never join them. I thought to myself, *If I was a guilty party then I was guilty by birth, not by choice.*

I still had my desires and wanted money and like most of us, this elemental yearning was a constant thought that occupied my mind in everyday life. Even back then, my conscience seemed to always get in the way of my crossing the line to join in on the opportunities that lay before me. To this very day, I still cannot think of a good answer as to why I was, and am, this way. It was surely not that I consider myself a good person, nor was it because of any religious merits I may have instilled in me. I don't think so! But I just don't know. I did not like the Mafia because of the harm it caused innocent people and I did not like my family being involved in it. The stories I was told about how it became a necessity for the Italians to combat the forces of other nationalities just didn't jive with me. Hell, these people reaped a good portion of their profits off of the hard-working innocent Italian workers who became victim to this sly group of men. Even though I was only in my early 20s and with my father as the boss, I could have financially benefited tremendously. People who had previously treated me with arrogance were now 'humbly' trying to associate with me. I knew they were phonies and I would not allow this kiss-ass stuff to venture into my life or change me in any way. I wanted to do what I could! Change it all. I, in no way, wanted to hurt anyone in my family, I just wanted the Mafia out of my life and I wanted the Fino family free from its control.

The CIA

In 1969, with my father as boss, a former classmate, Anthony Waszkielewicz (who became a Buffalo fireman and was later killed by a propane explosion), contacted me and said that he wanted me to meet with a CIA official who was close to his family and wanted to discuss something important with me. Like most of us, hearing the name CIA or someone associated with it was something out of an Ian Fleming novel. I, of course, was curious why he wanted to talk to me and what about. I asked my friend Tony but he did not know the reason. I asked myself, *Does it have something to do with my father and the mob?*

A meeting was arranged that would take place in the Student Union cafeteria at the University of Buffalo. As pupils flowed back and forth from lunch to waiting classrooms, and while I was looking around, I was approached by a man who appeared to be in his late forties. The casually dressed man introduced himself as Phil Stone. To me he looked more like a professor than a spy and thought that maybe he was. Another man with gray hair and more rumpled look immediately joined us. After introducing himself as Al Hartel, the reserved man pointed to an area where we could sit. Hartel explained that he recently was transferred to the Organized Crime Strike Force with a cover as an investigator for the Department of Labor.

With Hartel doing most of the speaking, he asked me if I could assist them with some important, pressing issues. They both assured me that what was needed would have no impact on my father and, if I decided to help, that my cooperation would never be revealed. They both said that in the future, if I agreed, Al Hartel would be my contact. After a few remarks to show they knew quite a lot about me and also attempting to play on my allegiance to my country, Hartel stated that he knew that I had access to information that they wanted. Still not knowing what they were up to, I asked, "What information and why me?" I ascertained they were trying to make me feel important and/or lure me in when Stone said, "First of all, before we tell you what we need you for, we would like your assurance that you will not speak of what we are about to ask of you, and you must agree to maintain utmost secrecy."

After assuring them, Hartel said, "Not even your wife, okay?" After assuring them that I would keep my mouth shut, Hartel addressed Stone and said something in German and Stone's response was in German.

Interested to find out what they wanted me to do, Stone then said, "That's enough for today; we won't ask anything of you just yet. Al has your home number and in the near future he will call you." I was confused; did I say or do something to turn them off? I thought, *What a strange meeting.* I never expected to hear from them again, but a couple weeks later Hartel did call and asked me if I could meet him at our previous meeting place the next day.

The next afternoon I found him patiently waiting. He

greeted me with a smile and a handshake and after he asked me to sit down he started in with questions that would require honest answers. He asked me how I felt about the mob and many other questions to see how much I knew about them. I thought that he must think I was evasive, or that I was not telling everything, because my answers were quite limited.

He was very interested in an old friend of mine, Arnold Stanton, who previously held a position with the *Students for a Democratic Society* (SDS) at the University of Buffalo. I told Al, "I know Arnie, but haven't seen him for quite some time." Al then told me that Stanton and others were suspected of breaking into a CIA operation facility located in the Buffalo area. I remembered reading or seeing something about a break-in that took place a few years back that involved Stanton. Hartel stated, "Some of the documents stolen by Stanton, and possibly other members of the SDS, included some undercover student involvement with a Soviet Union operative working in the Toronto, Ontario area. The documents contained information on an enterprise to export weapons to the *Irish Republican Party* (IRA).

Hartel was also quite interested in Buffalo Capo Roy Carlisi. I told him that I knew Roy and that he was quite successful. He went on and said that Roy spent a lot of time in Canada, to which I responded, "He has a cottage near Crystal Beach, Ontario." After asking me about a number of people, which included some that were Spanish sounding whom I never heard of before, he then pointed out, "Your father is a pawn of Roy's and even though he is the boss, your father's future is in doubt."

Startled by this exposure, I quickly reeled off a number

of questions and concerns. He talked as if this was not hypothetical or conjecture, but from a person in the know. Without revealing any sources he mentioned that the takeover of the Magaddino Family that was led by my father was really a sham and that my father's use was up and he may already be in danger. This really caused me to sit up and listen to his every word.

Hartel stated that Fidel Castro had allowed a portion of the mob's money that was seized during the Battista takeover to be returned to the families via Canada and other countries, that Roy Carlisi was one of the contacts through whom part of the transfer was made, and then he asked if I knew anything about it. I uttered no and that he was telling me something I knew nothing about.

The main purpose of the meeting with Hartel was that he wanted me to see if my father could tell me about Roy Carlisi's activity in Canada. After giving me a telephone number where I could reach him, he asked, "Think of a cover name that you would like to use as the caller." After thinking a couple of minutes I said, "Mike Stitt," the name of a high school classmate. "Okay, from now on when we communicate, use the name Mike Stitt." Our meeting ended and we went our separate ways.

That night I visited my father and with Hartel's words eating away at me, I asked him if his position as boss was in jeopardy. "What makes you ask that, Ronnie?" I didn't have an answer and thought for what seemed an eternity, finally saying, "I'm concerned and maybe I'm reading too much into Vic Randaccio's attitude" (which ran hot and cold).

His answer did not reassure me, nor did it make me think that Hartel was lying, when he said that the changeover was not complete and that he was traveling to New York City for a meeting with 'friends of ours' because it was still a question of who was running the family. I figured it was a good time to ask him about Carlisi because he was very seldom in a talkative mood when it came to the Cosa Nostra and its members.

I started by asking him if he thought the mob was behind the Kennedy killing and before I had a chance to finish my question, he said, "Where is all this shit coming from, who's filling your head?"

I told him I was watching a television show about the shooting and it brought back memories to something that was said in school about the mob hating Kennedy and their possible part in his death.

For the next hour he went on about the mob's connection to Joe Kennedy and how he had gone to the Mafia for its assistance in his son's presidential election. The elder Kennedy assured some of his old partners (who were involved with him during Prohibition) that the favors would not go un-rewarded. The Cosa Nostra families went all out in the primaries and in the general election and more than likely carried the day for Kennedy.

Once he was in office, President Kennedy's father Joe had convinced his son that the mob could assist the new president with the "Cuban problem" by destabilizing and possibly killing Castro. Government officials, together with the mob's assistance, developed different plans that would soon be implemented. From what I was told, everything went wrong and many of the families backed out of the precarious venture. It was an embarrassment for Joe Kennedy and some Chicago Family members who tried to stay the course. In reference to mob involvement in the Kennedy killing my father answered, "I don't know if they played a part, but I doubt it. His death made many mobsters happy because they had connections with Vice President Lyndon Johnson and he was too smart to fall into the pitfalls like the one made by the Kennedys." The mob's reward for not helping more with the Castro problem was that an irate Attorney General Bobby Kennedy wanted to go after and incarcerate all those mobsters who turned their back on his brother. Not only did I hear my father's version of what happened to turn the Kennedys away from the mob, later Arthur E. Coia echoed the same set of circumstances.

By this point I was afraid to ask him about Roy Carlisi and I felt a sense of betrayal in asking him the questions and picking his brain. This man trusted me, I was his son, and I loved him. How could I take what he told me in confidence and turn this information over to the feds? I hated myself for what I was doing and, at least for the moment, decided to keep my father's information to myself and not be dragged into the ring of cooperating with the enemy.

The next morning I called Al and told him that it was important that I see him. That afternoon I informed him that I had changed my mind; I was violating my father's confidence and I felt that I would not be capable of finding out what he was interested in anyway.

His expressionless face revealed his disappointment and after what seemed like an eternity, he said, "I understand, Ronald, but before you make up your mind let me tell you a little story. During World War II my assignment with the OSS was to assist with the destruction of Germany and that included not only the Nazis, but also much of the German population. I was assigned to work out of Moscow as an assistant to Averell Harriman and do what I had to do to bring this war to a successful conclusion. It even included the killing of relatives of mine who were in Germany aiding the Nazis. Our country is still at war, Ronald. The enemy may be different but it is still a war."

Even though I had a sinking feeling in my gut, I felt I had a responsibility; after all, what he was asking me to do could bring about the same conclusion I desired.

"This may not be World War II, but it is still a war and like it or not, there are many innocent people that will die and suffer if those of us who happen to be in the right place, or chosen to defend the innocents, do nothing. Think about it for a while, Ronald. If you could save the life of one decent person, would you do it? Or if you could feed one starving family, would you do it? We're not asking you to betray your father; we wouldn't ask that of you. Besides, I assure you that any information that may relate to him or your family will not be used, nor will it even be considered.

"The mob... where is the betrayal? You're not part of them. These are serious matters in serious times, and the choice is yours. Think about it, don't answer me today, but I am sure, after you have time to think and with the conscience and concern that you have already shown me, that you will assist us."

I was moved by his words, which tested me. An attempt to respond was met with, "Don't answer now, Ronald, I want you to think about what I just said."

I knew what my decision would be, his patriotic speech may have been just window dressing, but I was moved by it. As much as I visualized this fight as a needed one, it was, at least to me, no World War II and that comparison didn't mesh with my thought process. However, the truth of the mob taking advantage of the impoverished and unsuspecting worker did. I knew that I would call Hartel back and let him know that I was on board.

I started to look for Arnold Stanton, and when I did find him he was totally incoherent from his years of drug abuse. There was just no way could I even begin to question him. When I asked the stuporous Stanton how he was, I was met with a totally unintelligible response. A few years later, Stanton visited me at Local 210 and, still incoherent, he asked if I could give him some money. I reached in my pocket, which only contained around $40, and gave it to him. He rambled about being followed and he had to get away. I never saw him again and I do not, to this day, know whatever happened to him.

Wilputte and the Union Steward

THE BETHLEHEM STEEL MILL IN Lackawanna, New York was vast and there was always ongoing construction activity that utilized many members of the Laborers' Local 210. In 1969, the steel plant was in the process of building new coke ovens. It was an immense project and the Wilputte Coke Oven Division of Allied Chemical had engaged close to 400 workers and Local 210 had 148 employed on the project. I was assigned to a brick crew that would bring the fireproof silica bricks to the installation area and the waiting brick layers.

One Saturday I visited my father at one of the many gambling clubs in the area and after the stopover I decided to join his friend, Joe Moses, who wanted me to go to the race track with him. "The Moe," as he was called, told me that his daughter, Donna, did not have a car and needed one. After hearing this, I said that she could have my old one. I had just purchased a very beat-up used Jaguar XKE for $1,700 that I loved, at least when it ran.

Gambling was not a vice whose lure had befallen me, but I needed a night out and visiting the racetrack sounded like fun. While driving to the raceway, the Moe asked me if we could stop by his house first and inform his daughter about her new car. I was quickly taken by her beauty, and felt quite attracted to her. I felt it would have been quite awkward for me to let my emotions show, so with a reserved smile I offered my greetings. A couple of weeks later, Moe invited me to his home again, this time for dinner. I quickly said yes, remembering my attraction to his daughter.

I not only knew Joe and Rose Moses well, they were like family to me. The Moe was a childhood friend of my father and when he married Rose Martino my parents were their Best Man and Matron of Honor.

The dinner was congenial and with the exception of childhood remembrances and small talk, quite reserved. A couple of months went by when a chance meeting at a Buffalo night club brought me and Donna Moses into a relationship that would blossom into marriage and the birth of two children.

Even though the Moe came from a conservative background, his desires and his companionship with a number of future wiseguys led him into a life of gambling and all its consequences.

One evening my father asked me if I wanted to be the union steward at the coke oven project. I responded, "Danny (Boone Domino) is the steward there, Dad, I couldn't take his job."

My father acknowledged that he knew that, but explained, "The Boone has exhausted his appeal and will have to spend some time in jail. I arranged a deal so that his family will keep the bookmaking operation and the two concession stands, do you want the job?" I remarked, "Yes of course," knowing that the pay and all the overtime would more than double my earnings.

I liked Danny Boone, even though he was a made guy and an enforcer for Sam Pieri. He was always warm and genuinely concerned about me. Unlike other mobsters, The Boone was deeply preoccupied with the welfare of the workers and that included the unconnected ones. I knew I didn't have his ability, nor was I even close to acquiring it. I was a green kid and this job would involve me having to publicly speak to the workers, a fate that I dreaded. The Boone had to put up with the other mob guys and I was aware that he was bothered by their comings and goings, but he was able to somehow make it work. The Boone was a good leader and respected by all.

Although I was inexperienced, I had many ideas, but concluded that it would be best to keep them in check, at least for the time being. I decided to follow the agenda established by the Boone; except for the dining procedures. For some unknown reason it was segregated. The black workers did not eat in the main area with the white workers. I was met by subtle resistance, and some of the wiseguys didn't want the "melanzanes" (eggplant in Italian) or "garbunes" (as they would refer to black people when they couldn't hear them), eating with them. My insistence was eventually accepted, even though I sensed that they thought I was some kind of crusader who should stay out of their way of living.

I also set out to try to correct the problem of wiseguys and their refusal to do any work. I politely asked if they could help a little bit, and even begged Frank "Chicky Botts" Grisanti to do me a favor one day and stick around when we were going through a routine inspection by Wilputte overseers. Visiting the area where Grisanti was supposed to be, I noticed two elderly workers toiling and The Botts was nowhere to be found. The floaters and no-shows were ingrained into the work system; there was just no way I could get rid of their practice and bring them back into the fold.

One day, Donna surprised me by informing me she was pregnant. We immediately set out to get married and in April of 1970, we tied the knot. Because my father was boss of the Buffalo Family, more than 1,000 guests attended our wedding reception, a who's-who of mobsters from Chicago, Cleveland, Detroit and New York City attended the reception. Most of the Buffalo Borgata members and associates were there and showed their respect.

My father asked for the envelopes, which contained over twenty thousand dollars. After I handed them over to him, he ventured to an area where he could not be observed, counted the money, then handed me back $5,000, telling me that he would save the remainder. It would be placed in the family bookmaking operation. Even though my father was the boss, he was never able to really reap the financial benefits of his position; Dan Sansanese Sr. and Roy Carlisi were the benefactors. I would never see the $15,000 again. I didn't care, he was my father and I truly loved him.

After I returned from a Las Vegas honeymoon, I was contacted by Al Hartel and asked if I could meet a man named Bill for a cup of coffee at restaurant located in South Buffalo.

Bill was looking for my assistance regarding two laborers that were working at the steel plant project. Bill mentioned that "Dingy" LaPaglia and Tony Balls (I cannot remember his last name) had a Cuban connection and were seen on numerous occasions visiting with Fidel Castro-connected Cubans in Toronto. I asked what they were doing and was told it was not smuggling cigars or heroin. I suspected that he knew more than he was imparting and I voiced, "Why me?" repeating my constant worry; if my father or any of my relatives were targets or suspects. He affirmed they have no interest in my father and his activity. He also assured me that I had absolutely nothing to worry about and would never be asked any questions related to my family. I told him that I would try to find out what I could. Little did I know that these so-called "innocent" meetings would place me on the path of dancing in the fire and on the back of the tiger, a "hang-on-for-dear-life" ride that would eventually become my way of life.

LaPaglia and Tony Balls were small-time players and mob associates of Victor Randaccio and his brother Freddy. Even though LaPaglia and Tony Balls were employed by Wilputte, they very seldom spent much time on the job. Using the excuse that the company was starting to inquire about their absenteeism, I learned that they were continuously making trips to the Fort Erie Race Track, just over the border in Canada. Learning from my father that the sneaky twosome was involved in something to do with gold, and without making it look obvious, I ceased my inquiry. I reported this information back to Al Hartel and he said it was helpful that he, too, didn't want me to look suspicious.

The pay from Wilputte was welcome, and even though I enjoyed my life and my family, I still despised the mob and questioned my status as a mob-run union steward. If it weren't for my father and his position, I could very well be digging a ditch or pumping gas. This turmoil inside me was constant and I kept telling myself that all glory and fame was fleeting and to never forget my frailty. Being the union steward on a big job like this was only a gift because of my father's status in the mob.

Becoming a Laborers' Union Business Agent

Mike Rossiter, the titular president of Local 210, had died and the vacancy left Vic Randaccio with a position that needed to be filled. In an effort to ingratiate himself with my father, Randaccio asked that I be hired as a business agent for the union.

Besides the union's business manager and secretary-treasurer, the business agents were the most cherished and sought after positions in the union.

The pay was unbelievable and included a new Lincoln Continental and an open expense account. No matter how I felt about the mob, this was something my dark side wanted. I felt ashamed, and wondered if I had contaminated myself with the "get the money" disease. I contacted Al Hartel and asked him what he thought. His response made me feel better. "Go for it! You must, don't be stupid; this is a big opportunity not only for you but for us as well." Al wore two hats and my role and information aided him in both, the intelligence and law enforcement fields.

Eager to make a good impression at the union, I arrived early on the first day. Secretary Jennie DeAngelo, who I vaguely knew, welcomed me and asked me to wait in the coffee room for Sam Bongiovanni, the business manager, to arrive. I knew of him, but we were never formally introduced. He knew the business and was in charge of the field reps which included his son Carl, Sam Pantano (a longtime associate of the Randaccio Family), Leonard Territo (Randaccio's nephew who was the steward on the S. J. Groves job and whom I disliked; he must have owned hundreds of shirts because I never saw him wear the same shirt, tie or suit more than two or three times), and Joe Latona who also doubled as a business agent and as the newly appointed president, replacing the deceased Mike Rossiter. But it was Vic Randaccio (a made member of the Cosa Nostra and secretary-treasurer) who was the real power and controlled the union, carrying out the bidding of the mob.

In 1934, the Buffalo HOD Carriers International Union (later renamed Laborers' Union) was organized by Irish workers led by the late Mike Rossiter and the long-deceased John McNamara. The Buffalo Mafia was previously aligned with the employers and at that time was responsible for busting many strikers' heads. The inability of the union to organize employees and their mob supported employers led Rossiter and McNamara to ask for assistance from the wiseguys. The price was high and soon they lost control of the union. Mafia-controlled John Termini was appointed secretary-treasurer. By 1955, the Randaccio's were a power to be reckoned with and with mob boss Stefano Magaddino's approval, Victor Randaccio replaced Termini. Rossiter and McNamara were allowed to stay, but any power or leadership role they may have had was relegated to the Mafia. The mob and its control became absolute; there was no room for input from the membership and any outspoken opposition was dealt with harshly.

This was the atmosphere that I entered, and after welcoming me into the mob-controlled union, Sam Bongiovanni made clear that my role would be limited to a reporting only role; I was not allowed to think or take any action without his or Vic's approval.

Geographically, Local 210 took in all of Erie County and a small portion of Cattaraugus and Niagara counties. I was assigned the southern portion that included the heavily industrialized waterfront and extended to the Indian reservations, 40 miles south of Buffalo. My schedule was to stop at the Union Hall in the morning then visit at least two job sites in the afternoon, only executing a visual scan and questioning the union steward to see if everything was all right. I was only allowed to report on non-union activity and not to talk or raise questions with union or non-union workers or company representatives. I did enjoy my country rides, but checking the jobs very seldom took longer than an hour or two. Having nothing else to do, I would travel back to the Union Hall, but rarely did I see anybody there, outside of the secretaries.

One afternoon, while taking a ride with Joe Latona, he asked me what I thought of the way the union was being run. I figured he wanted to hear the truth and would hold my answer in confidence; I told him that I couldn't believe how things were being handled. I couldn't understand why more organization was not taking place. He patted my thigh and told me that he had been there a long time and as much as he agreed with me, he said, "Leave it alone and don't make any waves. Ronnie, you are a smart kid, and you know who makes the decisions and why they are made and for whose benefit. Just try to enjoy the wages and benefits and talk to your father, he will answer you the same as me."

In the autumn of 1973, Joe "Pizza" Todaro Jr. (who stood up for me at my wedding), asked me to travel to New York City with him to buy clothes and meet with some close friends. Pizza was always extravagant and we stayed in the finest hotels and enjoyed steaks and seafood served at New York City's top restaurants.

The first meeting we had included Anthony "Guv" Guarneri, a Magaddino Family Capo who handled operations in the Binghamton and Utica, New York area. Later that same day I was introduced to another member of the family, Louis Marcone, a soldier under Guarneri who was also involved in racketeering activities in Utica, as well as in Montreal, Quebec.

That night we went to dinner with New York City-based Louis Giardina, the business manager of Laborers' Local 23 and a member of the powerful Carlo Gambino crime family. Together with his sons, Joseph and Lawrence, they joined us at the restaurant. Also present was the authoritative underboss of the Gambino Family, Aniello Dellacroce.

Pizza introduced me to all of them and Dellacroce told me to give his regards to my father. Pizza asked me to join Joey Giardina and sit at another table while they discussed activity not meant for our ears. Over an hour went by before we were told to rejoin the Cosa Nostra figures and finish our dinner. The next day Pizza and I shopped on Orchard Street where I purchased a coat at a mob-controlled shop while Todaro was given a car load of clothing for free. From our conversations and what I saw, it was quite apparent that the Todaros and their uncle, Sam Frangiamore, were tight with the Gambino Family.

Vic Randaccio and Sam Bongiovanni would have the business agents join them when they attended the New York State AFL-CIO Convention held each year at the Concord Resort Hotel located in Kiamesha Lake, New York. I drove to the convention with Local 210 President Leonard Territo and Carl Bongiovanni. Unlike Territo and his hang-ups, Carl was always more at ease, much smarter, and more interested in the welfare of the workers.

While at the meetings, I met more then 50 mobsters and controlled union leaders from New York City and other regions of the state. One of them was Joseph Pagano who asked me to join him and chat a little. We took a couple of chairs in the hotel and Pagano asked me if I wanted to go golfing. I told him that I did not bring any clubs and that I didn't think I had the time. We exchanged mostly small talk and he whispered what became a usual mobster line, "Always be careful Ron, because the feds are watching our activity."

Later on, Vic Randaccio came up and asked me to tell him what the conversation I had with Pagano was about. After telling him, he warned me to be careful of him because Pagano had some serious problems. Sometime after that I was told that Pagano was shot and killed. Mike Lorello, the Laborers' International Vice President who handled New York and New Jersey, was introduced to me. Mike Pagano and Sam Caivano, Lorello's assistants, were on hand to watch over the old and frail Lorello (who was not very bright and downright incapable of managing a position such as the one he held).

Back in 1971, the Justice Department openly identified four unions as being controlled by organized crime. They included the Longshoreman, Teamsters, Hotel and Restaurant Workers, and the Laborers'. I was rapidly learning about the dominance of the Laborers' and Teamsters unions. The conventions I would go to would include introductions to union heads from other cities. I would always be introduced as the son of Joe Fino, asked how my father was, and to tell him so and so said hello. The whole impetus for their involvement in the union movement was threefold: First being the perpetuation of the family; second, the political strength and ability to control or break elected officials; and third, the riches and financial rewards from the ripped off union dues and benefit fund contributions.

Where other organized criminals would have collapsed under the weight of prosecution and internal bickering, the Cosa Nostra continued to flourish. It became important to maintain an air of legitimacy and an ability to have input and control.

The Commission

In 1972, my father, as acting boss of the family, was ordered to appear before the Mafia Commission, comprised of the bosses of the five New York City families as well as the bosses of Chicago, Detroit, and Buffalo (under Magaddino). Most of the families, such as Chicago, Cleveland, Detroit, Philadelphia, Pittsburgh, St. Louis, Kansas City, Dallas and Buffalo, were tied to the Genovese Family. Even though they controlled their own areas and decision making, they still had to respect the Genovese Family's opinions. I was told the only family that did not have to answer to them was the New Orleans, Carlos Marcello Borgata. Traveling with my father was his underboss Dan Sansanese Sr., his consigliere, Salvatore Frangiamore and the influential Roy Carlisi. Prior to going to the meeting, they were all in agreement to defy the Commission if, by chance, it decided not to approve their request.

Tom Eboli, the head of the Genovese Family at that time, was the spokesman. He said that the takeover by the renegade faction was wrong! The representatives from Buffalo would have to abide by the Commission's ruling on who should head the Buffalo Family. My father was the first to speak and told them that he would not go along with the ruling.

Eboli then went down the line, starting with Carlisi first and then with each of the other Buffalo mobsters. To a man, they said that they would respect the Commission's ruling, leaving my father alone in his opposition. Eboli again posed the question to my father who had been left with no choice but to agree to the request or face the consequence of being killed.

When they returned home my father didn't have to tell me of the outcome, Vic Randaccio's attitude told me that my father had lost his power. Randaccio was riding me constantly and quickly limited what little latitude I did have. He made me stay away from all mob-controlled jobs and I was not to talk to any of the stewards about their problems. My new duty would be limited to filing papers and accompanying Sam Pantano by stopping for a cup of coffee and shooting the bull with the old timers.

While giving an account to my father about my Randaccio imposed Union Hall status, he never once told me about the debacle in New York City. He only told me to go along with Vic's requests. I was not at all comforted by his remarks and wondered how long I could take this chiding and subservient role.

I never did find out why Sam Frangiamore was named the new boss of the Buffalo Family instead of Peter Magaddino. Frangiamore's underboss would be Joseph Todaro Sr., whose name was rarely mentioned. When a made guy was talking about him they would make a hand gesture by touching their lips with a finger and then pulling it away for about 6 inches in reference to his constant cigar smoking. The new consigliere would be Joseph Pieri Sr.

I liked Frangiamore and through the years he became

very close to my father and would break bread with our family on a regular basis. Todaro Sr. was a different story, a successful businessman whose nickname was "Lead Pipe Joe" because his victims would suffer the agony of having a lead pipe shoved up their rectum. Todaro's dislike for my father was well known and as the nephew of Frangiamore, he was being prepped to be his successor. I didn't know Joe Pieri that well, having spent most of his life in Youngstown, Ohio, he only recently moved back to Buffalo with his family. He had a reputation as a thinker and strategic planner that knew the history of the Mafia and would bring the Buffalo Family more in line with the basic principles and the format that they should follow.

By January of 1972, I was meeting Al Hartel on a regular basis, and some of those meetings were held in public places, such as the cafeteria in the federal building as well as at his Department of Labor office. I never thought about being discovered, I really do not know why I was so flagrant and took the chances that I did. I was not only feeding information that could be beneficial to the Agency, but also the Organized Crime Strike Force.

An affinity grew between us and we liked each other. I was learning quite a lot about the feds and the various enforcement agencies. Al did not like the FBI; they were given the ball and fumbled it. Former Director J. Edgar Hoover was afraid of contaminating his agents and would not allow them to investigate areas that could expose them to bribes and corruption. Hartel would go on about the elderly commie-hunter and his focus on celebrities and their frailty instead of America's real enemies, the Mafia.

Running for Office

Vic Randaccio was on me voraciously and without mercy would chastise me in front of strangers and visitors to the Union Hall. I couldn't take it anymore and I made up my mind to either quit or fight this tyrant.

"Ronnie, are you crazy?" my father responded after I told him that I was thinking about running against Randaccio in the next election. He hinted that I would be killed and even if I were allowed to run, the mob controlled the membership and ballot box.

One afternoon in February 1972, Vic told me that if I didn't listen to his nephew Leonard Territo, he would fire me. With anger and aplomb I told him to go ahead and that I would run against him for the position of business manager that would be vacant as the result of the retiring Sam Bongiovanni.

After leaving the tyrant's presence and the hall, I went to the new gambling club where my father hung out and told him what I had said to Victor Randaccio.

"Now you've done it, you have really cooked your goose this time," was his response. I told him that I thought that I could win the election.

"Win? Win? You'll be lucky to stay alive. Ronnie, you

don't know this business, they're not going to allow you to run, let alone win."

Overhearing our conversation was John Cammilleri, a Mafia Capo and a close associate of my father, and my father's brother Nick. After explaining what I had done, Cammilleri and my Uncle Nick thought that this disclosure could prove beneficial and they told my father that they would like to talk to him alone, directing me to wait while they conversed about my actions, its ramifications and potentials. They entered a private room, while I nervously paced the floor, wondering just what the outcome and their recommendation would be. After about 15-minutes they came back and asked me if I honestly thought I could win. I strongly responded, "Yes! A lot of the members dislike Randaccio, who controls the union, with an iron fist, and if they get a job or not."

"Go home and don't go out until I let you know that it's safe…" my father said.

"I am not afraid."

"Please listen to me, damn it. Listen for once."

"Okay, Dad."

That night he came over and explained that the only way that we could pull this off was with the help of the Sansanese faction. To me that was like shaking hands with the devil. He remarked, "If you do not accept these terms I am prepared to go to Sammy Frangiamore and beg for his forgiveness. Even with the Sansanese faction on board, you still might not win, but it might be enough to prevent them from killing you." After hearing the mandate, I was left with little choice but to accept Dan Sansanese Sr. and his sons, whom I had little respect for.

The next morning, accompanied by my cousin Michael, I ventured into the lion's den (the Union Hall) to pick up my belongings. I was met by an incensed Leonard Territo, who proceeded to knock all my papers off of my desk with an odious leer and watched without saying a word. After I gathered them and departed, some Randaccio supporters, who waited outside, began to jeer and belittle me.

By the evening, the Sansanese faction was on board and agreed to join me. I learned much later that my running for office was to be a vehicle in which Cammilleri and my Uncle Nick would lead my father into joining a breakaway faction of Buffalo and Rochester mobsters that wanted to separate from the Frangiamore-Todaro leadership.

With the Buffalo Mafia split into two camps, with my father, John Cammilleri, Dan Sansanese Sr., and their soldiers on one side; Frangiamore, Randaccio, Pieri, Todaro, Carlisi and their soldiers on the other, the battle lines were drawn.

Frangiamore asked Vic Randaccio if he could foresee any problems if an election were held. Vic's arrogance visualized a routing victory; chiding Frangiamore for even questioning the outcome. Frangiamore could have easily stopped it anytime. To this day, I cannot fathom why he did not.

High-strung as could be, I often fell asleep nights, my mind racing with thoughts of *why the hell am I doing this*? Deep down inside I knew I wanted to help innocent workers and bring them a better life, but I also knew I liked the idea of having a good paycheck. It wasn't my ego; at least I did not think so. I have desires and wants like most of us do, but I did not want to be controlled by, or fall victim to, my dark side. I was totally confused inside, *Am I a good guy or bad?*

I guess this will always be an unanswered question for as long as I live.

When I informed Al Hartel of my decision to run for business manager, he said, "Ronnie, you're nuts. They have been there for so long and many of the members were either related or bestowed with a union card and job and would never change their allegiance."

"That doesn't mean that they cannot be roused to action," I said. I told him that there were 3,000 members and many of them had not had a job in years or only worked on the bust-your-ass jobs. They never took part in any of the rubber-stamped union functions.

Shaking his head and doubting my ability, Al left bewildered and probably thought, "This nut is going to get killed."

Procuring the membership list from Randaccio was not easy and the election race became the focus of the Buffalo media. If Frangiamore was thinking of stopping us from running, it was too late. Many Buffalo citizens awaited the outcome. Sammy Frangiamore was not a stupid man, and I was sure that he weighed the consequences of killing my father and me.

Frangiamore did not seem worried about the outcome of the election or that a possible war would break out. Whatever the reason, he stopped at my father's club and spoke to John Cammilleri. Frangiamore spotted me, walked over, wished me the best and said, "Keep it clean." That was it, the last obstacle was overcome and the fight was on. I selected my cousin, Mike Burke, to run for the position of auditor with the promise of becoming a business agent later on. John Cammilleri selected Sam Caci for the position of president. Sammy was well liked and the unassuming brother of Cammilleri mob soldiers Jimmy and Albert Caci. Anthony Panzarella, who I did not know that well, except that he was honest and interested in the workers' plight, was chosen as vice president. Jack Giancarlo, the nephew of Joe Latona (my friend who had recently passed away) was selected as a member of the executive board and an eventual business agent's position. Donald Panepinto, a crony of the Sansaneses (later, a made man), was selected to run for the sergeant-at-arms position. Jack Panczykowski and Robert Hollie as auditors rounded out the slate.

We rented space in taverns, VFW halls, churches and any place that we could utilize to spread the word. We told the members that without their support they would remain consigned to the last-person-on-the-job and first-one-to-be-laid-off state of affairs that they knew all too well. I was amazed by the turnout and support we received, especially from the black and American Indian members that overwhelmingly supported us. Vic Randaccio rarely went out of his way to assist them in procuring a job and they became disenfranchised. I constantly listened to their plight and it must have touched a nerve because they volunteered their support in any way they could to help me win without me ever asking them. Cecil Ruskin got down on his knees and begged God to help me get elected.

At times, violence came close to rearing its ugly head and both sides had difficulty in controlling their aligned members. Relatives and friends of Mike Rossiter and John McNamara had waited a long time for the opportunity to take back their union, and I had a difficult time keeping their tempers in check. A day didn't go by that a physical fight was averted. The election was near and to avoid potential fraud at the polls, I called a school pal of mine, Steve Banko, who was a highly decorated soldier during the Vietnam War.

Banko worked as an assistant to Democratic Party Chairman Joe Crangle and was a rising star in the Democratic Party. I had voiced my concern about ballot fraud and requested the use of Erie County's voting machines. Banko gladly remarked that he would see what he could do. The Pieris and Todaros were involved with both political parties and had placed workers in the county and the electoral vote-counting process. Banko contacted Elections Commissioner Ed Mahoney, who I knew quite well, and they readily agreed to make sure that the voting machines were available.

One of the problems we sought to cover was that many of the laborers who lived in Erie, Cattaraugus, and part of Niagara counties had no means of getting to the Union Hall to cast their votes. Years of unemployment and having to fend for themselves created a confinement to their farms, and for the American Indians, their reservations. We opted to rent eight large buses and shuttle the workers back and forth. Many of them had never been involved in an electoral process and had to be taught how to enter a voting booth and make their selection.

Randaccio and his team were downright cocky and boasted about how badly they would defeat us. My previous night's sleep was spent tossing and intermittently waking up to visions of vote rigging and of workers threatened with physical violence. That fateful day was upon us and hordes of union members filled the parking lot and the surrounding neighborhood. The long line of voters stood very silent and many avoided eye contact with me.

Was this their way of their telling me that we would not have their vote? I didn't know and later on we learned that they were afraid of being seen as friendly to us. After all the votes were in and counted, a solemn Vic Randaccio exited the front door and without saying anything to anybody walked to his parked car. Joey Todaro Jr. yelled to Randaccio, "What's wrong Vic? What's wrong with Vic?"

The margin of victory was unbelievable, with a more than a two-to-one landslide for each and every one of our candidates. I didn't wade into the celebration as much as I thought I would. I thought to myself that victory is truly bittersweet, especially since we divided brothers and friends to bring about this victory. I thought about this opportunity that lay before me and the ability to finally reform the union. My first objective would be to heal the wounds the election caused and try and create an atmosphere of unity.

June 1 was not only my birthday; in 1973, it was also the day that held the start of what I believed would be the total transformation of the union. The membership had spoken loud and clear and we had to avoid the sins of the past by not forgetting that we were an instrument of the membership and it was their needs that must come first. Aloof attitudes and greed must be eradicated and not have a place in this new administration.

A secret meeting took place at the home of Dan Sansanese Sr.'s girlfriend, Vivian Sacco. He looked mean and unfriendly and his remarks revealed that he wanted the union controlled by his son. Danny Senior, who really was a tough guy even though he was quite small in stature, was well known for his sexual appetite and exploits with celebrities such as Marilyn Monroe, Jane Mansfield (whose picture with the elderly Sansanese was proudly displayed on his son's desk at Local 210). He also had a tryst with the 50s pin-up model Bettie Page and I am sure there were others.

It didn't take me long to realize that even though our team had won, the real win belonged to the Sansanese's. My father would take my side, but John Cammilleri, Dan Sansanese Sr. and his sons took offense to each and every idea I presented. I wanted to get rid of the Lincolns and bring in quality laborers to become business agents. They were opposed to both. Finally, they agreed to get rid of the luxury cars and buy Plymouths. Of course, they would be purchased at a dealership owned by the brother of mobster William "Billy" Sciolino.

When Sciolino started his criminal ways as a master burglar he, together with Tommy Gascoyne (who later became an informant) formed the 2nd Story Crew, which included Ronald Carlisle, Gregory Parness, Frank D'Angelo, Dennis Borden, and Stanley Seneca. At one time or another I met all of them. D'Angelo and Seneca would later both be murdered.

I was permitted to name Jack Giancarlo, Michael Burke and Sam Caci as business agents. The position of president of the union was not a full time job and paid very little, so Caci needed the business agent's position.

I was compelled to appoint Dan Sansanese Jr. and Ralph "Baggy Eyes" Velocci, partner of Nicholas "Sonny" Mauro, a well-to-do bookmaker and part of the Sansanese Family operation, as business agents as well. My idea for a training program was accepted and my choices of instructors, which included Thomas De Nisco, Robert Hollie and Jack

Panczykowski, had a price, I would have to appoint Mafia member Steven "Flattop" Cannarozzo as a training instructor. Victor Sansanese (who became a made man in 1970) corralled the desired position of Director of Training. "Snidely Whiplash," as he was called when he wasn't around, lacked formal education and did not have any teaching or management skills and was the last person I would place in a position like this. He knew absolutely nothing about the laborers and the type of work they do. It was agreed to keep Joseph LoTempio (the nephew of Vic and Freddy Randaccio) as the administrator of the benefit funds, and remove him sometime in the future.

Concerned about the Sansanese's, I expressed to my father that they had much too much input and that it would lead to their eventual control of the union. He reassured me, "This will not be the case and their only interest is in their jobs, not the running of the Union Hall." I soon learned that my father's words were hollow, even though I am sure that he believed them and trusted the Sansaneses at the time he said it.

I traveled to New York City and met with Mike Lorello, the regional manager and a vice president of the *Laborers' International Union of America* (LIUNA). Lorello looked like a chicken and when he spoke he sounded like someone that never spent an hour organizing or learning the business. This New Jersey native was elevated to this prominent position because of his allegiance to the Genovese Family and its New Jersey cousin, the DeCavalcante Family.

The DeCavalcante Family maintained close relationships with the New York City-based Genovese, Gambino and the other families. In his younger days Lorello was noticed by a New Jersey mobster from the Genovese Family who brought him under his wing and introduced him to the ways of the Mafia. Richard "The Boot" or "Ruggerio" Boiardo was a potent force and with Lorello's servitude to the Genovese Family, he was elevated to prominence in the soon-to-be totally controlled Laborers' International Union. In an effort to keep the peace, Lorello was allowed to help the other families with their union takeover needs. I was not at all impressed by Lorello and his suggestions. Especially that I clear my every move with the Buffalo Family.

Lorello introduced me to his assistants, Sam J. Caivano and Mike Pagano, both connected to the Genovese Family. Like their boss, they did not seem to know much about labor relations either. Later on, while at a meeting with Lorello, Caivano asked me to attend a pre-season football game with him at the Meadowlands in New Jersey. We had plush box seat tickets from the connected and mob-protected Terminal Construction Corp. of New Jersey. During the game I was introduced to John Riggi who was the business manager of Laborers' Local 394 and the boss of the Elizabeth, New Jersey-based DeCavalcante Family. This was the beginning of a long friendship and the first of many meetings Riggi and I would share together. Nearby were the box seats of mob-controlled Schiavone Construction. All three of us walked in and were greeted warmly. I was introduced to Ronnie Schiavone and Ray Donovan (who later became Secretary of Labor under President Ronald Reagan), and many others.

After leaving Lorello, I flew to Washington, D.C. for a meeting with the LIUNA President, Peter Fosco. His claim to fame was his relationship with powerful Anthony Accardo, boss of the Chicago Mafia who would have to be consulted on every important family decision. Accardo signed the death warrant of many unsuspecting victims, even Sam Giancana (the past so-called boss of the Chicago Family.) It was the Chicago Family that held sway over who would be the president of the Laborers' and many of its elected and appointed positions. The New York City families and the rest of the Borgatas in the United States and Canada would abide by their decision provided they were given their fair share and could maintain absolute control over their own respective territories, positions, and kickbacks.

For Peter Fosco to make a decision that affected the United States and Canada, he was required to get approval from the mob families and act on their approvals or rejections. Some decisions would require a Mafia Commission meeting and input before any decision was reached.

At the time Chicago wanted control over all national *Political Action Committees* (PAC) and all national agreements. The New York region, which also included New Jersey and the New England region comprising Connecticut, Massachusetts, Rhode Island, New Hampshire, Vermont and Maine, did not want to lose control in their respective areas to the Chicago Family. New England, under mob boss Raymond Patriarca, did not want Chicago to have any say over these important areas. An accord was reached whereby the New England and New York regional geographic areas were not included in any national agreements.

The International headquarters was strategically located next to the AFL-CIO facility on 16th Street in Washington, D.C., not far from the White House. Fosco's office was located on the top floor and I was greeted by a tiny Italian man with a thick Italian accent, Peter Fosco. After welcoming me to the union, Fosco asked how his longtime friend Roy Carlisi was. I thought to myself—*Mafia, Mafia, that's all these fucking people are concerned with.*

While conversing, Fosco did his best to avoid any mention of the membership and their rights, the very thing I was concerned about. I was looking for advice regarding worker's jurisdiction and all I heard was, "Be sure and heed The Boys." He went on about problems with the government and warned me not to talk on the telephone because it had cancer (in reference to eavesdropping and wire taps, weapons of the Justice Department and its recently declared war on the Mafia-controlled unions.) I was quite surprised by the candor that Fosco and Lorello had exhibited when talking about the Cosa Nostra, even though those words were never mentioned. Cosa Nostra connotations such as, *The Boys*, *Our Friends*, or *you know who I mean*, were always used.

Mike Lorello also flew down to Washington to visit headquarters. Peter Fosco introduced me to other International Union vice presidents, organizers and employees who worked or were visiting the facility. It became quite apparent they also heeded the unseen force and most of them were minions of the omnipotent power that lurked behind every spoken word. Lorello would tell me, "This guy is a friend," or "This guy is someone to be careful with."

Fosco asked if I could spend the night and go to dinner with him at the restaurant located in the Hay Adams Hotel, across the street from headquarters, near the White House. I imparted that I would. That evening we joined Lorello and Vernie Reed, the well-liked general secretary-treasurer who I was advised not to say more than hello to. Four unconnected, but controlled, vice presidents were also at dinner with us. Reed asked the unconnected international vice presidents to join him at another table while Fosco and Lorello talked to me. I wondered why so many of our union leaders were swept up in the Cosa Nostra's path and joined in the servitude. Was it because of the money and greed? Was it that these people were wannabe's, or was it because that in a moment of ignorance they asked for help and their loyalty and subjugation was the price?

Unlike them, I was born into it! They chose this life, or at the very least, acquiesced to it; they allowed themselves to become mediums of its spread and influence.

I wasn't in office more than two months when I was told by Danny Sansanese Jr. to attend a sit-down with some of the family at the Turf Club Restaurant, a hangout of Roy Carlisi. Those present included Roy, Sam Frangiamore, Dan Sansanese Jr., Victor Sansanese (whose star was on the rise) and Nicky Rinaldo, (who was appointed as the caretaker of the Sansanese crew while Danny Sansanese Sr. chilled out in jail for a previous crime).

Unsure as to why I was there, Carlisi took the lead and informed me that I would not be allowed to make any moves without the approval of the family. I would need the okay of Danny Sansanese Jr. before I acted on anything related to the union. I argued and told them that I had made promises to the membership. Rinaldo and Sansanese Jr. laughed and told me to ignore my promises, that I had nothing to worry about and feel grateful that I was able to remain in the business manager's position and all the benefits that went with it.

Angrily, I responded that this election came about because change was needed and I was given prior assurances that I would be allowed to have a free hand with the union and its operations. Carlisi stood up from the dining room chair and approached me, poking his finger in my chest, ranting and raving, "Don't you ever use that tone with me, who the fuck do you think you are? You had better talk to your father about your arrogant attitude and behavior or you are going to find yourself in deep shit."

Knowing I had gone too far, but still defiant, I told him that I felt that the laborers had lost too much work to the other trades and if corrections weren't made there might not be a union and membership to fight over.

"I don't give a fuck, Ronnie," Carlisi snapped, "I don't give a good fuck. You are going to listen, do you understand?" I humbly got up from my seat and asked if I could be excused; that I would like to talk to my father about these requests. Trying not to show weakness, yet aware of the seriousness of my position, I communicated that I would abide by their request, but I hope they understood my dilemma.

My father was angered by their demands and how quickly control was wrested from me and my associates. He told me to go along with their demands for now and not to discuss this with anybody. He was going to talk to Cammilleri and they would come up with a plan.

For the remainder of 1973, and the early part of 1974, there was fading hope for change. Limited to the role of a spectator and adviser, I learned that there were ways in which I could utilize their lack of education and blindness by creating channels that could justify some of my ideas. Their paranoia with the law left them vulnerable. I told them that they would be in violation of the Taft Hartley Act and other federal laws if they didn't allow contractors to bring their employees into the union, prior to signing an agreement and any other creative means that I could think of.

I would stretch my imagination and even make up some of my own laws such as the Mitchell-Moore Act, or utilize laws that had nothing to do with labor unions, such as the Bolton Act. I couldn't believe how well it was working so I told Dan Sansanese Jr. that the feds had enacted a new law that made our hiring hall and our hiring procedures illegal. The only way we could correct the hiring hall practice was to incorporate modifications and changes that would allow the employer to circumvent the need for the hiring hall by hiring employee with special skills.

"Danny," I said, "we are laborers and our people don't possess special skills, so the language in our agreements with the employers is not in compliance with the law." I also noticed that he didn't always go back to the family for permission and that all I had to do was convince him and no one else.

I started regularly meeting with my good friend Norm Goldfarb, a professor at the University of Buffalo, to discuss the International Laborers' setup and that of Local 210, plus the problems I was having. Goldfarb was a very decent guy who was always fighting for the little guy; and he would listen intently. He knew from our previous meetings that I wanted to try and help those members who were relegated to perform the hardest and most dangerous and dirty jobs. There were quite a few minorities in the local union, but, by design, to the best of my knowledge, they were never once placed in a steward's or foreman's position.

When it came to placing members on a job, the local mob had a process that was also used by the mob-controlled LIUNA. The union stewards, foreman positions and the plush work would go to Mafia relatives, wiseguys and relatives of politicians. Regular work, which did not include difficult or dangerous work, usually went to mob family distant relatives and mob wannabes. When construction projects started to wind down, the unconnected were the first to be let go and rarely enjoyed as many hours as those who were connected. Not only were the unconnected members of the union, who almost to a member supported me when I ran for office, they were people who just wanted to take care of their families and have enough to eat. I thought about this quite a lot, and like any normal human being I was disturbed by their low status.

Little by little I devised schemes that would afford them a better chance to obtain quality jobs. Not all the mob, but most of them, had a strong dislike for minorities and in private would call them low-life's or other demeaning names. Norm Goldfarb knew that my task was difficult but encouraged me to follow my beliefs, continue to try and not to quit.

My father was not a racist and never once in my life did I ever hear any derogatory remark about minorities. I do not know if I got my values from him or my father and mother in concert with Marshall Miles. I am not trying to paint myself as lily-clean! Hell, I had my share of performing wrong deeds, but when it came to helping the little guy or gal, I knew how I felt and still do. I tend to think of it as my saving grace.

By April of 1974, my father and Cammilleri were ready

to implement their game plan; they would refuse to recognize the Buffalo Family, led by Sam Frangiamore. They would create their own breakaway faction and aligned themselves with the already-defiant Rochester group and create a new Borgata. Little did they know that Frangiamore and the remainder of the family had anticipated their move, or had inside knowledge, and had already swung some of my father's and Cammilleri's soldiers away. Billy Sciolino, Charley Cassaro and Danny Sansanese Jr. joined John Cammilleri turncoats. Albert "Babe" Billiteri, Angelo Massaro, and Sam Cardinale who also agreed not to join my father, John Cammilleri and Rochester in supporting the Bonnano Family and starting their own Borgata.

On May 9, 1974, as he was returning to his birthday celebration at the Roseland Restaurant on Rhode Island Street in Buffalo, John Cammilleri was gunned down by Todaro loyalists. That same night, my father was scheduled to meet up with Sammy "The Priest" Cardinale at a coffee-shop bakery located in South Buffalo. Cardinale was called The Priest because he would regularly wear black clothing and would utter the word "Amen" over the bodies of his many victims. Cardinale, together with William "Billy" Sciolino and Danny Sansanese Jr., was scheduled to gun down my father. If my father wasn't warned beforehand, he would have met the same fate. They were ready to greet my father with a bullet instead of a kiss and a handshake.

The chilling effect of the Cammilleri killing had not only clued me in that change from within was an effort in futility but that the only solution available would have to be an operation by the feds to get rid of this affliction that had been allowed to fester over organized labor.

Cooperation with the Bureau

One afternoon I was invited by a friend to play tennis. Having tried the game before and enjoying the exercise that went with it, I decided to give it another try. The court next to ours was occupied by two men who exhibited the same ineptitude that I inflicted on the sport. The haphazard shots were met with laughter and humility. This display of waywardness brought about our conversing on our lack of ability.

One of the men remarked, "I see you are also a beginner, Ron." It didn't catch me totally off-guard; I just thought it was someone to whom I was previously introduced and had forgotten. Extending my hand in response to his remarks and his greeting, he responded by saying, "Ron Hettinger, I'm with the FBI. How are things at the Union Hall?"

I was leery of the FBI, they were still the enemy and even Al Hartel held them in low esteem. Still, I was inquisitive and I wanted to chastise them for their lack of interest in aiding the labor movement.

I started berating the bureau and pointed out their lack of effort with organized crime and labor union corruption. I was kind of surprised when he showed no emotion at my outburst. Here I was, the son of the ex-boss of the Buffalo Cosa Nostra Family, publicly speaking about it and my own misgivings. I could tell that he knew quite a lot about me and he voiced his concern about my future at the Union Hall.

I started to wonder if this was a chance meeting or some prearranged overture that was concocted by the FBI. I was ripe and I knew it. I told him that it was a shame that more was not being done to address the union and the membership. Hettinger said, "Ron, I am aware of your feelings and believe me, I know quite a lot about you. You are a decent guy and I know your father quite well and even he does not want you involved with these criminals."

I thought to myself, *Was my father secretly talking to the bureau? Did this revelation come from a wiretap or overhead conversation?* I would eventually learn the answer. Hettinger went on, "Ronnie, you can be of a tremendous help to the membership and to the FBI if you help us." After pondering his request I expressed my willingness, provided that no information be used against my father and family. Hettinger assured me that neither he nor the FBI would ever place me in a position of having to endanger my family and avowing to never disclose my cooperation. Without hesitation I agreed to cooperate and become a conduit of information for the FBI.

Al Hartel was guarded upon hearing the news about my covenant with the agent. He considered it a big mistake; one that would not bring about the change sought and would not serve his plans and procedures and that of the Organized Crime Strike Force. My own naivety had always led me to believe that there was cooperation between federal agencies; even though I remembered Al's previous cynicism of the FBI, I felt that they too wanted to eradicate the disease. I trusted Al, and I kept him up-to-date with my movements and thoughts, which by now were more constrained.

I considered Hartel my most trusted confidant, but Hettinger moved quickly. I started to feel that Al's suspicions of the FBI were nothing more than that of a competitor and the best approach would be to have both forces equally involved in the eradication of the Cosa Nostra.

I received a call from Hettinger who asked me if we could get together. We met in Springville, New York, far away from the mob and Buffalo. At this meeting Hettinger inquired if I knew about the history of the Magaddino Empire. I replied that it would take more than a meeting like this to relate what I know. Even though I did not know much about the early years outside of what my father told me or what I gleaned from others, I briefly discussed some of what I knew. One thing that was not general public knowledge was the vast number of political figures, such as former Buffalo Mayors Steven Pankow and Frank Sedita, police commissioners and numerous Buffalo businessmen, who were all tied to the mob in one way or another. We talked for about three hours and agreed to meet again.

We continued meeting regularly and about six months later Hettinger informed me that he was being transferred. This would be our last Buffalo Mafia get-together. He introduced me to Special Agent Jack Porstel, who would be my new handler. Through the years Porstel and I worked quite closely together and we must have had more than 200 meetings in his car and safe houses. Driving around the city in plain view with Porstel was quite common, and I don't know if it was because of our ignorance or that we did not believe that we would be observed that caused us to continue this reckless way of passing on information.

Chuck Kosich was a hustler from the Buffalo suburb of Lackawanna who had befriended and tipped quite a few beers with my brother, Alan. One evening around 10:00 p.m., my doorbell rang and Alan and Kosich staggered in. Alan told me that they had important documents that I should see. After expressing an interest in seeing what they had in their possession, I asked them to come on in and have a cup of coffee. They placed a ledger book on the kitchen table that was probably acquired by Kosich. After opening it up and paging through it, I soon realized that this rather voluminous book contained the names of over 4,000 ex-employees of the Bethlehem and Republic Steel plants as well as the Ford Motor Company plant.

The cover page said:

The following is a list of employees that we consider to be security risks and who have conducted activity that may be detrimental to us.

Right underneath this heading were the names of the undercover squads and individuals who were secretly monitoring employee activity. They included undercover agents of the FBI, local police, newspaper reporters, as well as co-operating workers involved in looking for any suspicious activity. Most of the ledger was made up of the names of the questionable workers, their home addresses and the reasons that they were fired. The last pages of the journal included the names of organizations and political affiliates that were under scrutiny.

What stunned me the most about this journal was not the witch-hunt mentality it projected, nor the communist-behind-every-corner frame of mind that swept across America from the late 1940s to the 1950s; but that this practice continued into the 1960s, long after it had supposedly stopped. Many of those classified were innocent people fired from their jobs just for being a member of a questionable social group.

Along the left margin in front of the names that were listed alphabetically were dates; they ran the gamut from 1952, to 1966. Hell, I thought that this shit went out with Edward R. Morrow, but here they were. Some were even considered *persona non grata* because they attended a certain church that may have spoken or represented socialistic responses regarding their plight. In some cases, hearsay and reading the wrong newspaper was enough to have the unsuspecting worker discharged from employment. I liked the FBI and I liked the agents who believe that they are acting in the best interest of the people of this country, but this kind of activity was not what our forefathers had in mind when they drafted our Constitution and Bill of Rights.

I paid Kosich the $200 that he wanted for the book and decided to make copies of it. One copy I made was for Richard Lipsitz, the union attorney who previously ran for mayor of Buffalo on the Liberal Party ticket and was accused of being a communist.

The next morning I went to Lipsitz's office and let him read through the book. He personally knew some of the people listed, including an attorney friend of his. He called a lawyer by the name of Griffin and verified that he had worked for Bethlehem Steel. Lipsitz wanted me to keep this information private because it was dynamite and could cause me personal problems as its possessor. I asked him, "What about notifying the people that were listed and having them commence a legal action against the three companies?" "Ronnie, the statute of limitations for such an action has expired and I am pleading with you to avoid any mention of this or you could find yourself in danger's way."

I then visited the United Steel Workers office and showed the ledger to a friend of mine, Joe Benbenek, who echoed the same sentiments as Lipsitz and did not want to get involved.

Louis DePerro, whose name was on the list, was an undercover member of the team and a close friend of my father's and the Fino family. My father and I met with Louie, who was still employed by Republic Steel, and after showing him the book, he was somewhat guarded and taken aback, as if we had discovered his dark secret. My father then assured him that the information would remain confidential.

"Joe," he told my father, "listen to me! I only assisted with the employees of Republic Steel and that was limited to communists and black troublemakers that belonged to the Jefferson Ayd Club." He was concerned that the elder Fino might suspect him of cooperating beyond that and against the mob. My father reassured him that was not the case. He stated that he had never seen the journal before, but that it was quite accurate and that the shakeup, at least as it was reflected in the ledger, was not limited to communists. After our departure my father voiced the same concerns and told me, "Don't get involved and burn the ledger, destroy it, and don't wait!"

I decided that Al Hartel, the understanding voice of reason, was my next stop. "Ronnie, where did you get this from?" he asked. After explaining how I obtained it, he asked me where the original was and who had it. He wanted to know if I had shown the ledger to anybody and whether I had copies. Answering yes, I noticed a *you-stupid-ass* look on his face and he demanded that I bring him the original and copies. Not wanting to get my father in any trouble, I told him only Lipsitz and Joe Benbenek of the United Steel Workers had seen it. The next day I delivered the ledger and the copies to Al Hartel and his impatient hands. What happened with the ledger after that I never did find out.

It was late when I received a phone call from my father who directed me to take a ride with him the following day. The next morning I drove over to his home and asked him, "What's up?" He said., "We have to see the Farmer and I don't know what it is about." After about an hour, we arrived at the Farm.

We greeted Sam Frangiamore with a kiss and hug. He then asked us to take a seat in the kitchen. The house was very small and did not reflect the elderly Mafioso's powerful position. He said to me, "Ronnie, you are going to have to remove Ralph Velocci, Jack Giancarlo, and Mike Burke as business agents and replace them with Dan Domino and John and Joe Pieri."

Desperately, I tried to explain that Jackie Giancarlo was a good agent, as was Mike Burke, but I could tell my remarks fell on deaf ears. My father tried to protect Mike Burke, who was the son-in-law of his sister Antoinette, but he was also unsuccessful. Frangiamore went on, "Ronnie, you must find an excuse for their being discharged and not let them know the real purpose."

On the ride home I told my father this was terrible, how the hell was I going to do this? He was equally shocked but insisted I find a way. When I did let them go, I felt sick to my stomach and the part I was playing in assisting these no-good mobsters.

Unlike the made Pieri brothers, who were not interested in work nor had any desire to learn the business, Danny "Boone" Domino quickly picked up on what had to be done. We became quite close and unlike other mobsters, he really did care about the workers. He was tireless and would also perform all the Pieris' work. Domino previously did some jail time for extortion. While at the Lewisburg federal penitentiary located in Pennsylvania he developed a relationship with a former Teamsters leader and his fellow prisoner, Jimmy Hoffa. He liked Hoffa and considered him a highly qualified union organizer. Hoffa was pardoned in 1971, and wanted his job back. The mob did not want to disrupt the relationship they enjoyed with the current Teamsters president Frank Fitzsimmons and killed Hoffa in July of 1975. The Boone was a good worker and cared for the workers. I also knew he was tough and a prized enforcer for the Pieri Family. Still, he was a breath of fresh air and someone I could confide in without it getting back to the family. I learned quite a lot about the mob from Domino, who never once turned his back or walked away from any of my questions.

More change was in the air. After Angelo Massaro died on September 11, 1980, from a heart attack, Sam Caci became the administrator of benefit funds. Dan Domino replaced Caci as president and Joe "Pizza" Todaro was brought on board as a business agent. Business agent Frank Grisanti was removed, which he accepted without a gripe. The Training Fund also went through a major change. Robert Holle (the one black man on our team) was killed in a knife fight and the vacancy was filled by Sam Todaro the younger brother of Joe Todaro Sr. Nick DiMaggio, Tommy De Nisco and Jack Panczykowski, who were chumming it up with Vic Sansanese, remained unscathed.

The Pieri brothers loved to travel to New York City to get together with some of their Genovese Family cronies. I would have to arrange a meeting with Mike Lorello as a cover so that we could visit the Big Apple under the deception of union business. Accompanied by Dan Domino and the Pieri Brothers, we visited Ponte's Restaurant located in Manhattan and met up with Angelo Ponte, Anthony Salerno, Fred "Fritzy" Giovanelli, Phil Lombardo, Tony Ameruso, Tommy Agro, members of the Gambino Family and numerous other wiseguys; all expenses paid for by Local 210.

Pizza started telling me to use the same "union work" ploy so that he could travel to NYC and meet up with his friends and associates. Most of the time Victor Sansanese accompanied us and I had to put up with his rotten, arrogant attitude. We would get together with quite a few Gambino Family members, Joseph "Joe Piney" Armone, Tommy Gambino, Joey Gallo, Louis Giardina and his kids Lawrence and Joey.

Like always, at many of the get-togethers, I would be asked to sit somewhere else while the mobsters discussed business. There were occasions, (especially during times of trouble), that I was allowed to listen to their wayward connivances.

Tommy Agro had an ownership in a restaurant located on Broadway not far from 57th Street. After eating there he asked us to join him in visiting a mob-controlled private club. Entering the elaborate facility, that on the surface appeared to be very respectable, people were playing backgammon, dining, and just acting normal. It was downstairs where the real fun began. It was a sauna similar to what you would see in Russia. After changing our clothes and putting on white terry cloth robes, we entered a swimming pool area that had more than 30 good looking, partially naked women. One of them asked us what we would like to drink. Over a couple of bottles of Sicilian-made Corvo wine, we conversed and watched other members of the club frolic with some of the girls and then disappear into an adjoining area. Agro asked us to pick out a girl, have a little fun and enjoy the evening. As much as I felt an urge to participate, I told him, in concert with Dan Domino and the Pieris, "No thank you" and declined his offer.

While in the Little Italy section of New York we were met by Genovese mobster Carlo "Collie" DiPietro, a very close friend of Danny Domino who joined us for dinner and discussed some problems he was having with members of the Gambino Family. Not long after that I learned that DiPietro was gunned down by a fellow Genovese member.

The trips to New York with the Pieris went on for quite some time and it was always to meet fellow mobsters or meet with their close friend Jimmy Naples (formerly of Buffalo) who held a prominent position with George Steinbrenner and the New York Yankees. We would eat in the private Yankee Club Restaurant and be introduced to the likes of Reggie Jackson, Sparky Lyle, Ron Guidry, Catfish Hunter and others.

Maybe it's hard for someone to realize how I felt but if you put yourself in my shoes, unemployed workers were begging for a job just to make ends meet and here we were dining, traveling and spending their monthly dues on pleasure trips. It was always interesting and entertaining, but it was all on the union's tab, and something that I really wanted to stop.

Around 1977, or 1978 Buffalo soldier Carl Rizzo and Sam Pieri were introducing a dental program that they wanted Local 210 to participate in. It was headed up by a dentist from New York City by the name of Jesse Hyman. After much wrangling, the Buffalo mob family agreed to it. Together with Danny Sansanese and the fund administrator Angelo Massaro, I was required to implement it. Under the program, the union members were made to utilize the dental clinic for themselves and their families. Like other mob-related schemes, it would become a money maker.

One day while visiting the clinic with Massaro and Danny Sansanese Jr., an envelope was handed to Massaro who was in the front passenger seat. While still parked, he opened the envelope, counted out $2,000 in hundred dollar bills and handed them to me. "What is this for?" I responded, even though I knew it was a kickback. "Don't ask. That is for you and your father." I did not know how much was in the envelope and Massaro also gave a share to Sansanese, but how much I didn't know. From the thickness of the envelope I surmised that there must have been at least twenty thousand dollars.

Danny Sansanese, like his father and later his brother, were absolutely ruthless. Sansanese Sr. was considered a mad killer who liked to cut the testicles off of those who crossed him. Danny Jr. was always trying hard to ape his father and his ruthless ways.

Here was a guy who didn't care whether the unconnected members lived or died, which he expressed on a number of occasions. Joey Todaro Jr., together with the Sansanese brothers, openly disgraced some black members of the union and behind their back they would refer to them as low-life's, making sure that they always had the backbreaking jobs that nobody else wanted. Danny Jr. took every advantage to bring his family on countless vacations under the false front of performing union work. Not limiting his union work expenses to himself and spouse, but for anywhere from five to fifteen relatives, who would enjoy vacation places like Disney World, with meals and all expenses being paid for by the union membership and their benefit fund contributions! The Construction Industry Employers Association, who represented the employer trustees for the benefit funds, never once questioned the mounting cost of these lavish trips. I really could not stand the Sansanese's. I hated how bigoted and arrogant they were.

Later that night I informed my father and Al Hartel about the payoff and arranged to bring Hartel the $2,000 that I received. My father responded, "Good, that's blood money, Ronnie, and I will arrange that you are not to receive any more." I previously told my father about Al Hartel, but I did not tell him all. He never once questioned me about it.

After that I never received any more of the kickbacks and kept the bureau abreast of the dental program activity.

Later on, Jesse Hyman became the target of an FBI investigation and avoided a jail sentence by agreeing to cooperate. The Hyman Dental scandal helped, in concert with my testimony, to convict DeCavalcante Boss John Riggi as well as Tony and Chester Liberatore from Cleveland. But as would become the norm, neither Danny Sansanese nor anyone else from Buffalo was ever brought to justice.

August of 1977 and the Bum

It was August 19, 1977, and the weather was beautiful outside but my thoughts were on the work I had before me. Faced with high unemployment, I, together with the Plumbers and Electricians Union, were in the process of attempting to develop a market recovery strategy plan that could recapture work that had been lost to the growing non-union employers. The biggest problem I had with this: would the mob go for it? Here I was working my ass off and these robber barons were either at home or relaxing somewhere else. Every time I tried to introduce any type of change that may affect wages or make everyone work, including the shop stewards, I was met with mob resistance. They would inundate me with, "What about my son or my cousin; that's so and so's brother," and so on. It was always the relatives or their cronies that came first and fuck everyone else.

The location of my office at Local 210 and its proximity to the secretarial area allowed me to overhear the conversations taking place in the main office. Once I heard Jennie DeAngelo, the very hardworking backbone of the secretaries, telling somebody we didn't have any job openings. Then I listened to the other party say he wanted to see somebody in authority. "Send him in, Jennie," I shouted, sensing she was having a tough time handling this individual.

As he walked into my office it was apparent that he was a street person, in need of a bath and a good meal. I told him to sit down even though my nose was quite offended by the foul odor that started to permeate my office. I inquired about what he wanted and told him that he shouldn't have given the secretary such a tough time. He remarked rather firmly that he wanted a job and that he was ready for immediate employment. I repeated what Jennie DeAngelo expressed and that there was no work available. In order to be eligible for employment he would have to become a member of the union. He affirmatively blurted out that he was in possession of information and documents that I would welcome and that he would trade them for employment. I inquisitively asked him what he had, and if he could show me to what the so-called information relates. Guardedly, he wanted to know if he showed me what he had, would I find employment for him. "Yes," I answered, even though I was skeptical that this vagrant would be in possession of any information that would be beneficial let alone of interest to me. I asked him how he obtained the information that he possessed. He answered that while resting in an alley not far from the Union Hall, he noticed two men in a car actively tracking the movements of everyone entering and leaving the Union Hall. It appeared to me that he was aware, from the newspapers or some other source, that the Union was the subject and the target of federal investigators.

Continuing his story, the bum said that two men got out of the car, leaving the doors open, and attempted to get the license plate of a car leaving the union parking lot. While they were away from their vehicle, he entered their car and stole a briefcase. Apparently it was not noticed missing when the men returned. He then placed a dirty, old brown grocery bag on my desk, reached in and began removing the contents. I immediately knew that these documents belonged to the FBI and SA Joseph Genova. After leafing through some of the documentation and authenticating them, I realized that they were quite important files that related to ongoing investigations, FBI strategy, surveillance photographs, and *names of informants.*

The disheveled old man then said, "You can keep them if you give me a job..." Is there more that is still with the briefcase that he had hidden somewhere? I immediately responded, "Yes! I will find you a job, but you have to get the rest of the files." He said, "They are in a safe place and, oh yeah, I also have the FBI agents ID and a gun." *My God!* I thought to myself, *how the fuck did they screw up like this?*

Explaining that it was Friday and that he would have to wait until after the weekend before I could get him employment, I then told him that I was going out on a limb for him and he would have to give me the remaining documents, gun and ID now. Informing him which car in the parking lot was mine, I asked him to slip the briefcase, gun, and other documents under the car on the driver's side near the front tire. At first he paused but after assuring him about the job, he agreed to my request.

The vagrant then departed and only seconds after his leaving, Pizza Todaro and Vic Randaccio walked into my office. The highly visible documents and photographs were in the middle of my desk and with mouths agape and eyes fixed, the two mobsters listened to my explanation about what just preceded their walking into my office. Having little choice I explained, at least in part, what just took place, avoiding mentioning the additional FBI property that was going to be left by my car. Fortunately, I was able to slip the documents that contained the names of informants in the front of my pants while their enlarged eyes were fixated on the surveillance photos. Todaro started leafing through them with a paper clip in an effort to avoid placing his fingerprints on them. Randaccio said something like, "This may be some ploy by the FBI; they may be trying to set us up."

A third mobster, Angelo Massaro, entered and after viewing the documents commented, "My attorney Bob Murphy can make good use of this shit and the info contained in them." I then said that maybe I should call the union attorney (Richard Lipsitz) and seek his recommendations. "No, don't use the fucking phone, no phones;" shouted Massaro, "I am going to take them upstairs." (He was referring to his office located on the 2nd floor of the building.) Todaro also voiced a concern about it being a setup and told me, "Don't talk on the phone! Ronnie, go over to the union lawyer's office and inform Lipsitz of what has happened." After agreeing, I departed.

The bum was true to his word; the briefcase lay exactly where I told him to put it. I reached under my car, grabbed the briefcase and placed it next to me on the seat. While driving, I removed the file from my pants and inquisitively opened the briefcase and read some of its contents. I wasn't shocked, but I was also concerned to see my name listed as a source of information and how close I came to being discovered. Thoughts raced through my head about the documents that Massaro had taken, never having a chance to fully review the information they contained.

The file with names of informants and sources of information was much larger than I expected and contained information that I must still keep confidential because many of the people on the list are still living and remain highly connected. Two informant names did stand out. One was that of my father and the other was Steve "Flattop" Cannarozzo. I wasn't disturbed about my father. Previous conversations I had had with him pretty much pointed this out, but Cannarozzo's cooperation was something I was not aware of. I had a hard time concentrating on the task before me and my thoughts could not get off the files Massaro controlled. *Was my name in there and do they in any way reflect my FBI cooperation?*

The federal building was only a couple of blocks away from Lipsitz's office and I decided to first go tell the feds what had happened. I didn't like publicly visiting the seventh floor of the federal building on Delaware Avenue where the FBI office was located; there was always a chance of being spotted. Instead, I went to see Al Hartel. His office was located within the Department of Labor where I felt that I could explain my presence if discovered. The secretaries there all knew me and were aware of my relationship with Al. "Hi Ronnie, Al's not here!" one of the secretaries said even before I asked to see him. Pondering for a second or two and thinking who to reach out to, I asked the secretary to contact Bob Stewart for me. Bob was the head of the Organized Crime Strike Force and his office was located in another building. "Not in," she responded. I then told her to call back to his office and tell Stewart's secretary that this was an emergency and for her to reach out to him.

Approximately five minutes later Stewart called me and I explained to him what had happened. Within minutes, FBI SA Jack Porstel rushed in and I could see he was just as shook up as me. I asked Al's secretary if we could use his office which she readily made available. Porstel tried to maintain an air of *everything-is-under-control* that most FBI agents attempt to project, even in difficult situations such as this. After explaining what had happened and turning over all the documents and gun that were in my possession, I expressed my concern about being discovered. He asked to meet me at noon behind the Holiday Inn located a couple of blocks from the Union Hall and to make sure I was not followed.

After departing I went to see Dick Lipsitz. I told the lawyer about the bum and documents story making sure I did not mention the briefcase, additional files, and FBI ID, gun and informant list. Lipsitz strongly instructed me to get the documents back from Massaro and he would arrange for their transfer back to the bureau.

Lipsitz pointed out that if the FBI became aware of our possession of their documents, it could lead to legal problems for us as well as an irate FBI and all the complications that could go with that. Returning to the Union Hall, I informed Joey Todaro Jr. and Angelo Massaro of Lipsitz's concern. A defiant Massaro said, "There is no fucking way I am going to listen to that asshole. I want to talk to my attorney first." A sympathetic Todaro listened and I sensed that he was inclined to heed Lipsitz's wisdom but didn't want to overrule the forceful Massaro.

It was almost noon and I had to meet Porstel. I drove

around for a while to make sure I wasn't followed, and then speedily backing up the one-way alley situated behind the Holiday Inn, I almost ran over one of the agents that was waiting for me to arrive. The normally stoic and reserved Donald Hartnett was a veteran of the war being waged on the Mafia and the supervisor of the Organized Crime Squad but, unfortunately, he now had to contend with hot coffee dripping from his face and clothes. While I was apologizing for almost running him over, the shaken agent wiped his face and asked me where the documents were being kept and if they had been photocopied. I told him that I didn't know what Massaro did with them but thought they would already be in the possession of his attorney Bob Murphy.

As we spoke we devised a plan to recover the documents but I expressed my concern for any plan that would expose me as the source of information. I told agents Hartnett, Porstel, Charles Mauer, and the other two agents present that if they intended to recover the documents by directly entering the building, they had better search all the offices and not just Angelo Massaro's! I explained that if they went directly upstairs to Angelo's office, the mob would know that the bureau had inside information on their location! Furthermore, the only people that knew where the papers were, and who had them, included Massaro, Vic Randaccio, Joey Todaro Jr., Dick Lipsitz, possibly Jennie DeAngelo, and yours truly.

I rambled on about another problem I faced. Come Monday, I am going to be confronted by the bum and his employment request. The possibility existed that some of the mob guys may get to talk with him and he may mention the briefcase, the gun, and the additional documents that I had withheld from them. The agents assured me that they would take care of him and necessary precautions would be taken to avoid my being compromised. I returned to the Local 210 Union Hall and awaited the pending raid and document recovery plot. Hartnett presupposed that the documents were still in Massaro's office and as of yet had not turned them over to his attorney.

Three hours went by, it was 3:30 p.m. and Massaro was getting ready to leave! There was no FBI in sight. *What the fuck is going on?* I thought. Maybe they were going to bust Massaro as he was leaving. As I watched Massaro's car turn the corner out of the union parking lot and his journey down Franklin Street, I speculated that something had gone wrong. *Why are they waiting? Did they change their game plan?* I was trying not to act conspicuous, but it was now after 4:00 p.m. and there wasn't a hint of a recovery operation.

I decided to leave and drive to a pay phone to try and find out for myself. While walking in the parking lot, three vehicles pulled in and ten FBI agents exited the cars quickly scrambling to cover the front and back doors of the Union Hall. SA Charlie Mauer, going through the motions, grabbed me by the arm and escorted me rather forcefully toward the front entrance of the Union Hall and into my office.

All of the other agents, except Mauer, headed directly upstairs and for Massaro's office. My fate ran before my eyes, *Ronnie, you are fucked; there is just no way that they will not suspect someone.*

Once inside the office, and playing my role as business manager, I demanded to know what the reason for the raid was. In front of the secretaries and Dan Sansanese Jr., who had just walked in, Mauer responded, "You know the reason, and we want the documents back." I told him I didn't know what he was talking about and I was going to call the union attorney. It was 5:00 p.m. and by now Lipsitz and most of the lawyers had gone home or for an after-work cocktail. I did reach the Benefit Fund attorney, Paul Birzon, who said he would be right over, as well as Carmen Putrino, an assistant and junior partner in Lipsitz's firm. Putrino asked to speak with one of the agents and I told him that they were all upstairs except for Mauer. Charlie Mauer took the phone, listened to Putrino then said, "This is a matter of national security and we did not need a search warrant; if you have any questions call Bob Stewart in his office."

Putting on a ruse, even though the damage was done, Mauer went into my office and started looking haphazardly through my desk and pulled out an FBI "Requisition For Leave" slip that he must have had in his pocket. At the same time, so that the secretaries and Sansanese could overhear, Mauer said to me, "Pal you are going to jail, unless you tell us where the documents are hidden." I responded, "I will not say a word until my attorney is here."

Agent Porstel came downstairs and asked me to follow him to the upstairs office. Benefit Fund Secretary Dee Giancarlo told me that the agents had requested a key to open Massaro's locked desk or they would go to one of their cars and get a tire iron and use that to open it. I told Dee to not do anything until the attorneys arrived.

At that moment Angelo Massaro phoned in response to a call from his secretary. He asked to speak to me as an agent picked up an adjoining phone to listen to the conversation.

"What the fuck is going on?" Massaro asked. I told him, "I don't know. They kept saying that we possess documents that belonged to them, and that I was going to be arrested if I didn't turn them over. They are going to break open your desk, Angelo, if we don't turn over the key." In trying to aid my dilemma, I also told him, "They rifled through my office as well, and are going to start turning the whole building inside out until they find what they are looking for."

After that, Massaro hung up the phone and I was escorted down the stairs to the main floor. I greeted attorneys Paul Birzon and Carmen Putrino and just as I finished informing them of what the FBI was doing, the agents came downstairs with the documents they found in a lower drawer of Massaro's desk. They then departed, warning us regarding their duplication and if any documents were missing they would be back.

After the agents left, Danny Sansanese Jr. told me that he was glad that they didn't go into his office or they would have found some hot jewels that were still very traceable. Afraid that the place was bugged, Carmen Putrino, Dan Sansanese, and Paul Birzon joined me on the front walkway where we discussed the possibilities of a leak. Was this a setup, or was the building bugged? A setup was quickly ruled out and a leak was more likely. Acting more as a victim of the raid, I kept an open mind during the discussions and suggested that nothing should be dismissed lightly. I suggested a bug was the most logical explanation. Only a handful of people knew we had the documents and no phone calls were placed. Carmen Putrino suggested that Fred Gugino, another lawyer in the Lipsitz firm, immediately make contact with a security firm from Horseheads, New York. "Have them come here tomorrow and sweep the building and phones for bugs and surveillance devices." Dan Sansanese Jr., quickly approved it and told Putrino not to worry about the cost.

I knew I had to move quickly. After leaving, I reached out to SA Don Hartnett and told him of the pending sweep and asked him if they would discover any surveillance devices in the building. He answered, "No, we have nothing in there, Ron." "Well then," I said, "we better plant one or my ass is grass." He told me, "That is impossible." I responded angrily, "Maybe you don't understand the ramifications that I face, if they sweep that building and don't find a bug, I'm fucked."

After receiving little satisfaction, I decided to take matters into my own hands. I went to the nearest Radio Shack and purchased a transmitter, some wire and whatever looked technical. I went back to the Union Hall and started looking for a place to install my makeshift bug. I raised a corner of the drop ceiling and near one of the ventilation openings. I placed the shitty looking Mickey Mouse device; then left for the night.

After arriving home, my wife told me that a Fred Gugino had called; he wanted me to be at his office at 8:00 a.m. the next morning. I called him and with limited discussion told him that I would be there. The next morning I rang the buzzer of the Lipsitz firm and was greeted by Gugino who informed me that the firm from Horseheads would be arriving at around 10:00 a.m. Gugino said, "Once we are at the Union Hall, we cannot discuss anything; if the place is bugged, we will tip off the listeners."

The security experts arrived and they followed us to the

Union Hall, armed with the electronic activity detection equipment they stored in the van utilized for driving to Buffalo. They professionally checked the phones and waved a circular receiver up and down the walls and ceiling. Before long, they discovered my shoddy transmitter. They left it undisturbed and did not respond to my "oohs and aahs" as well as the "ah ha's!" whispered by Dan Sansanese and Nick DiMaggio (the nephew of Roy Carlisi and now an instructor at the Training Fund) who had just arrived. Marking down what they had encountered on a yellow pad, the security men continued. After a couple of hours of sweeping and telephone line checking they asked me, Dan Sansanese Jr., and Fred Gugino to go with them to where the van was now parked.

Upon entering the van, one of the security people pointed out a listening device that looked like a small satellite dish, in the direction of the Union Hall. As we listened, we could hear speaking in the Hall. One of the security people was saying "1, 2, 3, 4," etc. We could even hear Nick DiMaggio on the telephone talking to his wife and telling her he would be home shortly.

I asked if the ceiling device (that I had planted) was what we were hearing. I was embarrassed by his answer; "That is junk and the FBI would never use something like that." They said anyone with half an ounce of knowledge about surveillance would not use it. It was probably put there by somebody whom for whatever reason attempted to listen in. "Even though we didn't take it out or touch it you can bet that it doesn't belong to any government or state law enforcement agency." "But then where is the bug planted that we are hearing?" His answer shocked me when he said that we had bugged ourselves! The front of the Union Hall had a monitoring system used for calling out available jobs twice a day and was left on all the time and near the ventilation duct work. It mimicked a receiver and could easily pick up any nearby conversations.

After everyone left, I drove Gugino back to his office and then went back to the Union Hall myself. I removed the fake transmitter I had placed in the ceiling so as not to have some serial number traced to a purchase that I had made.

When Monday arrived, the bum never came and I was sure that he was whisked away with threats of arrest and prison if he ever followed up and returned for a job. Sansanese told Pizza about our bugging ourselves as well as the shoddy device in the ceiling that both believed was placed there by the Pieri faction. As far as the microphone system that was used for roll call, it was never left on again and they never checked the ceiling again for the device I placed there. But unfortunately, after that day, the television was always on playing loudly and conversations in the hall were limited.

Blizzard of 1977

THE GEOGRAPHIC LOCATION OF BUFFALO, NEW York has made it the snow capital and a victim of many a snide remark about the city and its winter weather. Located on the shores of Lake Erie, it is the victim of many a raging winter storm. The prevailing winds that traditionally come out of the west whip across the lake while absorbing the moisture then dropping it as snow on the city and its suburbs.

Through the years, Buffalonians have become adept at coping with the winter and keeping the snow off the streets and parking areas. I was bringing home a good pay check from the union, but like most of us it wasn't enough, so in 1973, I decided to try to supplement my income with snow plowing. A $300 down payment put me in the seat of a brand new, fully equipped Dodge Power Wagon with a plow.

Knowing very little about business, I thought that my services would be called upon by everyone with a sore back and frozen body! In fact, the opposite happened and nobody called that first winter and even after advertising, not a whisper. Faced with bank payments that I thought would have been taken care of, I started querying snow contractors that I knew to find out what I was doing wrong.

I soon learned that big trucks and heavy construction equipment are required and with plenty of shopping centers, apartment complexes and industries in the area, it would not be hard to find wanting customers. With more borrowed money in hand I set out to purchase the equipment that I would need and quickly secured a few contracts for the 1974, season.

I did encounter a glitch I did not expect. Getting a work crew was not as easy as I thought, even with a great pay check awaiting them. It took a special breed, because no one wanted to be roused from a warm bed at who knows what hour and drive through the inclement weather to start up the equipment in the frigid air. Learning of my need for workers, Roy Carlisi told me that his nephews were good workers and could use some extra money. Unlike the relatives of other mobsters, the DiMaggio's had a reputation for working hard and I agreed to put Joey, Donnie and Nicky on.

When the DiMaggio's first arrived in Buffalo I was required to find good employment for them in the union and construction industry. Nicholas, the oldest and most volatile of the brothers, was given a position with the Buffalo Laborers' Training Fund as an instructor.

They had previously moved to Buffalo from Chicago for some unknown reason and it was suspected that it was over a mob family problem. It was a little surprising to many of us because Roy Carlisi's Brother Sammy "Black Sam" was a Capo (and later Boss) in the Chicago Family and growing in prominence in the national Mafia hierarchy.

Sometime early on my father told me that Roy was as tough as he was smart and was the youngest member of the Al Capone Outfit. After Eliot Ness and the government's disruption of the mob's Chicago operations, Roy moved with his family to Western New York and into the open arms of Stefano Magaddino and the vast empire that stretched from the Canadian Province of Ontario to the outskirts of New York City and Philadelphia. Roy Carlisi's criminal abilities served him well in his taking control of a good portion of the Western New York and Southern Ontario seafood industry, earning him the nickname "Clam Man." Never losing sight of the rewards of illicit activity, and together with "Chicago Joe" Sciales, together they ran the largest behind-closed-doors crap game in the area.

That winter of 1975-1976, proved to be financially advantageous, and I was able to expand my fleet and add additional contracts. The DiMaggio brothers were never once a problem, nor did I have any mob interference.

With my growing business, I set my eyes on an even bigger target, the expansive Eastern Hills Mall located in the Buffalo suburb of Clarence. It was owned by the Edward J. DeBartolo Company of Youngstown, Ohio, and a snow-plowing contract with them would be a great coup for me and my fledgling company, Sno-Go Plowing Service.

After submitting bid request letters which went unanswered, I reached out to see if I could find someone who knew DeBartolo.

Joe "Wolf" DiCarlo was known as the "Sandman" because those who suffered his ire would find themselves in a deep and everlasting sleep. In his youth he included among his female conquests a young Jamestown, New York beauty that later received public prominence, Lucille Ball. He was even once labeled as one of the most notorious and feared mobsters in America, and named as "Public Enemy No. 1" in Buffalo. With a trail of death from Miami, Florida, and Youngstown, Ohio to Toronto Ontario, DiCarlo was a terror and even Magaddino and Charlie "Lucky" Luciano would tread lightly around this violent killer.

DiCarlo was a regular at Santasiero's, a local Italian restaurant on Buffalo's West Side. On any given day between Tuesday and Sunday you would find the local politicians, mob members and even FBI agents seated just a few feet away from each other; enjoying the spaghetti and *Pasta-fazula*. On Mondays, though, the restaurant was closed to the public and was a meeting place for the now aged and somewhat over-the-hill DiCarlo. He would be joined by his nephews, the equally feared Mafia enforcer Salvatore "Sammy" Pieri together with his brother Joseph Pieri Sr., the highly respected consigliere of the Frangiamore Family.

Knowing that DiCarlo had connections in the Ohio area, I asked if he could assist with the snow-plowing contract for the Eastern Hills Mall. He quickly responded, "No problem." The DeBartolo Family was an early recipient of mob assistance and not only did they owe and respect DiCarlo, they were still under the control of the Cleveland Family.

DiCarlo was going to place a phone call, when his nephew Sammy Pieri walked in. The elder Pieri was no spring chicken, but in his 60s he remained as tough as a 30 year-old. Many people even today think he was a boss of the Buffalo Family at one time, but this is not true. Sammy was never the Godfather, but in many ways his power was almost equal.

Even though I knew Sammy quite well, this was our first real get-together. As a Young Turk, he was the Mafia member that induced and enticed my father into joining the Magaddino Borgata. As feisty and outspoken as the old DiCarlo was, he had previously relinquished any authority he had to his nephew's years before.

I didn't know it at the time but with the smell of money in his nostrils and this naive 22-year-old next to him, Sammy Pieri seized the moment. After explaining my request, Pieri responded, "No phone calls are made, especially from here." SP, as I referred to Sammy, said, "Ronnie, let's go outside." As we walked down the street, he explained that Edward DeBartolo was under control and that the best way to handle this was for us to make contact with the family there and let them handle the request.

That September on a rather nice day I drove to Cleveland with Sammy. I was surprised just how open he was about the Cosa Nostra, its structure and its members. Interested in learning more, yet knowing that too much inquisitiveness would lead to an abrupt end in his candidness, I listened and acted like I already knew much of what he was saying. As frank as my father was, he never opened up like Sammy and his unremitting conversing about the mob, its members and historical events. Trying to show me how much of a friend he truly was, Pieri confessed, "John Cammilleri had to go. It wasn't only over his wanting a position in the labor union, this stupid Capo wanted to split the family. Together with Frankie Valenti (of Rochester) they made an arrangement to leave their connection with the Genovese Family and join up with the Bonnano Family, who always desired the Western New York region." (After Magaddino's death, Buffalo did not have a direct seat on the Commission and reported instead to the Genovese Family).

"Ronnie, as I am sure you know, John Cammilleri, Frank Valenti, Rene Piccarreto (the Rochester consigliere) and the Bonnano's could never get permission from the Commission and Joe Bonnano and his kid are sick in the head and everyone knows it." Pieri continued, "It was me that prevented your father's murder. I interceded on your father's behalf, and told the family that with Cammilleri out of the way, Joe Fino would be unable to act and cease to be a threat. From now on you are going to come under my wing," further mentioning the Mafia, their conquests and the role I would play.

Arriving on the outskirts of Cleveland, we checked into a two bed hotel room and while I unpacked, Pieri sat on the bed and made a phone call. He then told me to stop what I was doing and to get ready, "We are meeting some friends." A Cleveland made member by the name of Tommy "The Chinaman" Sinito, met us in the lobby of our hotel and after introductions we left in his car. Sinito drove around evasively constantly gazing in the rear view mirror.

Sammy explained that Cleveland had a mob war going on, and it was quite serious. He went on, even in front of this Cleveland Family member that Capo John Nardi turned against the Borgata and was even using a punk Irishman by the name of Danny Green to wrest control of the family from Jack "Blackie" or "Jack White" Licavoli. Open warfare was taking place so precautions had to be taken.

I did not know where we were going or who we were going to meet up with, but the first stop was a hospital where Leo "The Lips" Moceri, a Capo in the Cleveland Family and a good associate of Pieri, was being treated. After they greeted each other in the traditional way with a kiss on the cheek and a lasting hug, Pieri introduced me as the son of Joe Fino. Moceri asked how my father was and had already heard of me as a bright up-and-coming labor leader. After a rather long meeting, we then left and went back to the car where the Chinaman was waiting. Again, and this time for almost an hour, we elusively drove around until the mobster felt secure in taking us to our next destination.

At a Romanesque restaurant, our host, Jack Licavoli, the boss of the family (who previously was with the infamous Purple Gang) greeted us in the same way as Moceri. Licavoli went on about my father and how well he knew him. He mentioned a historic heist he made with Rocco LaPenta and my father and how they almost got caught.

After our greetings I let Sammy take the lead as I obediently sat and listened. Later, I expressed my satisfaction with the wine and Licavoli said, "I made it, and I am glad you like it. By the way I am aware of your ideas for expanding the Laborers" work jurisdiction, including training and incorporating areas of work not yet performed. After we finish dinner, Ronnie, I want you to meet with Anthony Liberatore and some other union representatives." I already knew Tony Liberatore and his brother Chester quite well from my travels with the LIUNA.

Licavoli and Pieri then spent around an hour talking about old acquaintances as well as the current John Nardi problem. A man attired with a cowboy shirt and a string tie walked towards our table and I could tell that he was important by the way the owner or manager of the restaurant greeted him. Normally wiseguys dress like they had the same tailor: long collars, white on white shirts, "Members Only" jackets, silky suits, and colored shoes to match their outfits. This guy dressed like his horse was tied up outside and looked more like someone you would see in a Roy Rogers movie.

I was introduced to Milton "Mashie" Rockman, who for years had been a Cleveland Family messenger and mob associate. Greeting Licavoli and Pieri, Rockman warmly placed his arms around them and proceeded with the traditional kiss. Rockman then sat down and voiced, "Ed DeBartolo wants to meet you; the snow removal contract will be taken care of. An employee of DeBartolo by the name of Marv Rader will furnish you with the necessary bid information for the project, and do not worry if the price seems low because it will be made up at the end of the year. DeBartolo sent his regrets for not being here, and he gives his regards to Sammy Pieri and Joe DiCarlo." After Rockman finished his report, Sammy Pieri nudged my leg with his leg and whispered, "See, I told you."

After dinner we drove in different cars, but this time with armed bodyguards who were nice, but didn't say much. I noticed that Licavoli walked with a limp and needed a cane. He looked like he was in pain as he dragged his bad leg into the car. I was becoming acclimated to the evasive tactics of our mob chauffeurs and their protective maneuvers. When we reached our destination, a bar in a strip mall, the other mob cars also started arriving. Some of the bodyguards were already there and had already cased the area for suspicious persons and possible hit men. Upon entering the bar and club, screams of "Hi Sammy," were heard from admiring soldiers who paid their respects to Pieri after first acknowledging their Boss and Godfather, Jack Licavoli.

The place was crowded and with so many wiseguys

present, I wondered, "*Who was out there holding off the enemy?* I was affectionately greeted by Tony Liberatore, the Laborers' Local 860 business manager, and his brother Chester, the business manager for Laborer's Local 310. Tony told me to join them at the end of the bar. We stood in the corner next to the bar and were talking about the Laborers' International Union when he remarked to me that he was made or was scheduled to be made (a full-fledged member of the Mafia). I was totally taken aback by his remark. Not being made myself, no one, and I mean no one, discussed this with anyone outside of the Mafia. I could only assume that Liberatore deduced that I was a made guy. Liberatore then went on about having penetrated the Cleveland office of the FBI and that he was getting all kinds of sensitive information. I became uncomfortable when he mentioned this! I wondered if my name would appear. I didn't know how the FBI kept its information and maintained records. I assumed, wrongly, that the information he was getting was from an agent who had gone bad. I later learned that a clerk in the Cleveland FBI office named Geraldine Linhart was providing sensitive FBI documents to him.

Tony was a live wire, telling me about his political prowess and of his ability to have politicians heed his every word. Licavoli then called me over to chat with Mashie Rockman and his nephew, Teamster Boss Jackie Presser, Electrician Union officials Carmen Carpinelli, Pete Zicarelli and others whom I cannot remember. Licavoli told them briefly about me and expressed that they listen to me about my ideas. I was totally unimpressed with Presser and his very limited knowledge about labor relations and thought he seemed more like Angelo Fosco, President of the Laborers' International Union. With all the noise and the many different conservations taking place at the same time, there was little time for labor talk. I informed those present that Buffalo wasn't that far away and I could always come down in the near future and would be more than happy to discuss labor and union activity.

After being introduced to most of the wiseguys and associates that were present, the half-drunk Pieri and I were chauffeured back to our hotel. With a good night's rest, Sammy Pieri and I commenced our drive back to Buffalo. During the ride Pieri said, "Ronnie, it would be a lot easier to introduce you as a *friend of ours* instead of as a relative of a friend." (*A friend of ours* is how the mob introduces one made guy to another, while *a friend of mine* means that the person is not made, and *is a relative of a friend of ours* means that the relative is a made man. I opened up and told him about the Tony Liberatore revelation regarding the leak in the FBI office. He acknowledged that he was also informed and considered Tony a very resourceful man. Pieri then pointed out, "Ronnie, Jack would like you to switch unions. The Cleveland Family has a very high ranking position for you with the Teamsters. This is a golden opportunity for you and a great increase in the money and prestige you receive. What do you think?" I told him, after pausing, "I will consider it." Pieri authoritatively then said, "Ronnie, I want to make arrangements to start introducing you as a friend of ours, instead of a relative of a friend."

Even though my ego enjoyed a boost with all the praise and fanfare I received in Cleveland, it didn't change my views and feeling about the mob, and the last thing I wanted was to join the ranks of them. I responded by telling

Sammy, "Thanks, but you have to talk to my father." On many occasions my father and I discussed the mob and our mutual disenchantment. Even as the boss of a family, he would speak about its downsides, "This is not a lifestyle for you Ronnie."

After arriving in Buffalo and dropping off Sammy at his home, I found a pay phone and called my FBI contact, SA Jack Porstel. Arrangements were made for an immediate meeting at the Regency Hotel in Hamburg, New York. Debriefing Porstel of the Cleveland meeting, I enlightened him about the FBI leak. Even though I don't remember my exact words, I probably said that an FBI agent was leaking the information. He brusquely responded, "I don't believe it. Liberatore was probably exaggerating and lying." Porstel was more interested in Pieri wanting to have me "made." His disgust changed to an expression of anticipation, moving closer, he said, "What a great opportunity this would create."

When the debriefing finished I called my father and let him know that I wanted to get together with him. Sitting next to me in my backyard, I let him know about the Cleveland meeting and Pieri's request for my induction. He didn't seem worried about it and related that he would handle it. He was more concerned with Pieri getting close to me and said Sammy was going to want something in return. "I regret letting your relationship with him go this far."

Not defending Pieri, but still appreciating in his openness and his candor, I responded by telling my father that Pieri didn't ask for one dime and didn't even allude to any needed favor. Even before I had finished my response, he interrupted me by saying, "Just wait. Just wait, Ronnie, you don't know this life," his favorite response about the mob.

He went on to tell me, "Sammy's brother Joe was a reasonable man, and as the consigliere, with his two kids working as no-show business agents at Local 210, he may be able to keep his brother, Sammy, off your back."

The Edward DeBartolo Company reacted quickly. I was contacted by Sammy Pieri, who mentioned that Eddie DeBartolo Sr. wanted me to travel to Youngstown, Ohio and sit down with him. I flew to Pittsburgh and then drove a rental car to their Youngstown, Ohio Market Street corporate offices. I didn't even have time to open a magazine when a man by the name of Gus Regis, the director of all of DeBartolo Mall Operations, introduced himself and ushered me to the office of Edward DeBartolo Sr. DeBartolo started the conversation by telling me how the building trades had screwed him on the Eastern Hills Mall project, if it weren't for our mutual friends, this project would have floundered. For whatever reason, he then told me to underbid the other snow removal companies that had an interest in the plowing project; that arrangements would be made to have additional funds sent to me at the end of the season. He also wanted to know if I wanted to remove the snow at other malls owned by him in Northern Pennsylvania and areas too far away for me to handle. I expressed that I would like to but the distance was too great for me to travel. Not mentioning Pieri, this mega giant of business told me about his longtime relationship with Joe DiCarlo. After thanking him for the opportunity and leaving his office, Gus Regis led me to the office of Marv Rader, another corporate bigwig. Marv showed me the other bids received and told me to underbid the lowest by five hundred dollars. In addition, I was to send a list of the equipment I had available for snow removal.

After the Ohio meetings, I returned to my normal schedule and my weekdays were filled with Local 210 activity. My Saturdays and Sundays, however, were put aside so I could work on my equipment, even though I didn't know the first thing about machinery and engines. I would clumsily assist the two hired mechanics I had. Interested in my welfare, my father would come by to see how things were going.

The Mob Takes Over My Plowing Business

ONE SATURDAY, I NOTICED MY FATHER walking over to where I was working and I could see his eyes were cast toward the ground. I knew something was up. "Ronnie, I want you to take a walk with me, I have something to tell you." He went on to say, "I was summoned to a meeting at Sammy Frangiamore's house and the Borgata want you to give half of your snow plow business to Nick DiMaggio." I asked my father how much money Nick was going to pay for his 50%. It was clear from his expression and voice that he was not able to protect his son from the mob's tenacity. Putting the blame on me for allowing the mob to assist me in the first place, he told me DiMaggio was not coming up with anything and that he would be given 50% and I would have to keep all the bills and loans in my name to shelter DiMaggio from all documented activity.

I explained, "Maybe, I could sell my contracts to somebody else."

"No, you can't do that! You have to see it through."

From that night on, depression was the norm and my emotional changes were not unseen. I thought about everything from leaving Buffalo to turning and fighting back.

Knowing the mob, my limitations and what I could do, made me feel paralyzed. I took my anger out on the FBI and law enforcement agencies for allowing this to happen by not doing more to stem this type of activity in the first place. I turned back to Al Hartel for advice. This old OSS (Office of Strategic Services), CIA officer remained my sounding board, and even though he was my friend and confidant, as well as a sympathetic listener, his feeling that they would screw up and get buried, didn't console my feeling of helplessness.

With Nick DiMaggio in tow, I soon accepted that the only way out of this paradox was through it. I hoped that the contracts that I had would generate enough money to meet the debt service and pay off my unwanted partner. Besides the Eastern Hills Mall, I still had the plowing operations at local apartment complexes.

November of 1976, was the beginning of a disaster for Western New York, with record cold temperatures and snowfall including nearly three feet by the end of the month that carried into December. It wore out my drivers and broken equipment was standard. It became necessary for us to call in subcontractors. The previously hardworking DiMaggio brothers had changed and instead of helping they now slept in their warm beds, while I ran around without sleep attempting to keep the constant customer complaints for not removing the snow faster at arm's length. It was a miracle that I was able to keep functioning and get the job done. Even the population of Western New York had had enough. These resilient citizens, as used to snow as they were, could not cope with the constant below-freezing temperatures and the everyday snow fall.

Most years Lake Erie freezes over and for Buffalo and the areas south of the city, this usually brings a reprieve from the lake-effect snowfall. This season, though, was different. By December the lake was mostly frozen over but the snow kept coming. One night late in January 1977, worn out and frazzled, lying in bed with my eyes closed and seeing only white, I somehow fell asleep. The ever-present sound of the heavy equipment flowing through every nerve in my brain would intermittently rouse me and made it difficult to resume the rest I desperately needed. The loud fury of wind, whipping the house as if it were made of straw, also woke me up and after trying to look out the completely caked-with-snow window, I went downstairs opened the door and was almost knocked off my feet by the storm's rage. It was then that I fully realized the extent of the blizzard and the disaster befalling the Western New York area.

Fortunately, the phones were still working and I checked out the size and extent of the storm. It was widespread and had paralyzed the area. I made arrangements to have those operators and drivers closest to the equipment and trucks get to our projects as soon as possible. Because Nick DiMaggio wanted his own pickup truck to drive, I previously let him have the one I used. I tried to make arrangements for someone to pick me up and drive me to the Eastern Hills Mall, but because of the whiteout conditions and the blocked roads no one could take a chance and drive to my home. Snowmobiles were the only transportation I could think of that might make it through with cars and trucks blocking the streets. I called my brother Patrick and asked him to pick me with his and take me to the work area.

Three hours passed and I wondered what had happened

to him. He finally called and said it was impossible to get to me, let alone travel the 10 mile distance to the Eastern Hills Mall. Drivers started calling in; they couldn't make it either and only those that could walk to the equipment were able to arrive at the work sites. Our two-way radios echoed just how bad the situation had deteriorated. Stranded people caught in the fury were aimlessly wandering around and looking for refuge. I called the manager of the Eastern Hills Mall and arranged to have the mall opened up for stranded travelers. The television and radio stations poured out disaster warnings and told stories of courage and horror.

That day, with the storm in full swing, I received a call from an Army officer who was assigned to the Army Corps of Engineers. He told me what I already knew, even though I had not really ventured out into the elements for a first hand appraisal. He wanted to know if I could mobilize my equipment for emergency relief and disaster response. I explained that we were having a tough time making it to our equipment, but of course we would assist as soon as we could.

The next morning my brother was able to reach me. The ride from my house to the mall revealed just how disastrous the situation really was. On a normal day, the trek would take less than 30 minutes. Along the way we pulled out a number of marooned travelers from their vehicles; helping the half-dead travelers who had unexpectedly ventured out in this storm of the century to find shelter.

For a brief moment my mind drifted back to my childhood and the story *To Build a Fire* by Jack London. The errant traveler filled my brain with visions of how peaceful his death from freezing had been. Here I was, basically dealing with that emotion as we carried and walked confused people to the nearest home. The good people whose doors we pounded on were more than happy to be of help and no one ever refused to shelter anyone that was in need.

Five hours later we arrived at the mall. I was astonished to find the corridors of the mall packed with travelers who were leaning against the walls and the steel store grates that would normally be open and congested with happy shoppers. Even though the mall was warm, many of the weather-worn shelter seekers were suffering from frostbite and were quite uncomfortable. I contacted the manager of Sears and after he called some corporate superior, I was given permission to enter the store and take whatever I needed. Without disrupting the shopping complex we procured blankets, pillows, some air mattresses and made the stay for the stranded a little more comfortable.

Even though the blizzard was at full throttle, a brief interlude of its wrath allowed me the opportunity to inspect the mall's parking lot. Surprisingly, most of the snow had blown across the clean parking lot harmlessly into the fields and with the exception of the 100 or so stranded automobiles, which were the catalyst for drifting and creating a couple of 15-foot-high snow walls against the corners of the mall, the area was basically free of snow. I would only need a front-end loader for the cleanup. Before that, I had to free the remainder of the fleet which consisted of three other front-end loaders and seven dump trucks equipped with snow plows.

I contacted the Army Corps and made arrangements for moving the machines into the city. Having to dig our way through the car and truck-blocked streets, the journey took us over eight hours. After arriving at the City Barns, where the City of Buffalo Department of Streets and Sanitation kept its equipment, we had the drivers and operators of our equipment join the ranks of the city workers who were appreciating the warm coffee that was available. I went up to the snow command area and talked to a couple of friends of mine who were responsible for the city's cleanup. They complained about their broken equipment and its inability to handle the 30-foot snowdrifts that covered even tractor trailers. Their attitude spoke volumes about the inadequate trucks and plows purchased more for political reasons and the payback to some political supporter rather than the type of equipment needed for city street plowing.

I met with the Army Corps of Engineering representatives who were still drafting a removal plan. More equipment was needed, much more. Arrangements were being made to have C-5s, the largest aircraft available to the United States Air Force, to fly in front-end loaders and troops from Army bases. They assigned me an area that started at the City Barns and went due east to the city line, and due south to the city line. I would be allowed to hire whatever additional equipment was needed.

One of the areas that our crew was responsible for was in the inner city (which had become run down and a bastion of street violence). The hard storm had subsided and we tried to tow and move hundreds, if not more, of the stranded vehicles that blocked every street. Street gangs were darting in and out of buildings with the catch of the day in their hands and the abandoned autos and trucks suffered the same fate.

One of the problems we encountered was in assisting some of those still huddled in their vehicles and refusing to leave them. Our plow drivers were threatened by some of the gang members and told to move on or pay them for being in their area. While aiding the crew of a fire truck, which was half buried in a snow bank, gunshots were fired at our crews from the windows of a nearby housing complex. The Army responded by supplying us with an armed escort and the gangs scurried to other parts of the city.

After a while Nick DiMaggio showed up with a request that we had to dig out the cars and driveways of Victor and Dan Sansanese. I thought to myself, *Here we are in the middle of an emergency and we have to go and cater to the whims of the Sansanese brothers, that I was sure never once in their life ever held a shovel in their hands.* I remarked, "Okay, send a pickup over there." Nick snapped back, "A pickup can't handle it, they need a front-end loader." I argued that there was just no way that we could spare the equipment that was with us or the equipment assigned to the mall and our other operations. I futilely called around to try and find a contractor in the area of the Sansanese brothers' home. Everyone was making use of their equipment for the cleanup. The mall was too far away and DiMaggio then demanded that I send a front-end loader and he did not care whether the Army Corps liked it or not. I knew that the Corps inspector assigned to our crew would not relish the idea of our having to send a needed machine for a private operation; especially when we were still digging out people trapped and possibly dying. I told DiMaggio, "I will not split our crew. Tell them that we would be more than happy to send them one of our machines that would be finishing up at the Eastern Hills Mall in a couple of hours." DiMaggio angrily yelled that the business was half his and because of the stature of the

Sansaneses, he was not about to ignore their request.

He proceeded to order the operator of a front loader to get out; then he jumped into the machine, leaving his pick-up truck running and the door wide open and drove off. He left me to fabricate a story to the perplexed looking inspector that we were having a mechanical problem with the loader and it needed immediate attention. For two damn days the machine was used by the wiseguys and their cronies. DiMaggio and his brothers cleaned over 50 driveways and businesses until they really did break one of the pistons that lifted the bucket. Afterward, DiMaggio told me I owed *him* one (!) since he didn't mention that I refused to allow the machine to answer the beckoning call of the Mafia.

The loss of the machine caused us many problems. Besides the $3,000 it cost to fix it, we also lost over $22,000 in revenue because of its unavailability and the loss of the use of five dump trucks that it previously loaded. Every day of my life was a learning experience. I decided if this is my future, I didn't want to learn anymore; I didn't like the lesson I was being taught. My only hope lay with the FBI and that they do their job and place these bastards where they belong.

After the cleanup was accomplished, the City of Buffalo and the Army Corps of Engineers handed out awards and thanks for assistance. Sears and its organization were never even mentioned. I regretted not revealing what the Eastern Hills Mall and Sears generously did. Their care brought warmth and comfort to many.

After two weeks of snow removal, the city was in pretty good shape so the Army Corps of Engineers and the city ended the outside assistance operations. In that short time, our company had been involved in the rescue of more than 30 people. I was proud of that. I was also proud of the way most of our operators worked long hours and withstood the desire to be home with their loved ones during the snow removal operation. Our employees rate of pay was the highest enjoyed by any of those working on snow removal. The City of Buffalo employees were amazed when they found out what our operators and drivers were paid. We had performed over $500,000 in business for the Army Corps alone; it bothered me that we were making all this money, but at what cost, with so many people suffering and dying as a result of the storm.

Little did I realize that with over $100,000 profit after taxes that I would not benefit from my labors. Moving quickly, DiMaggio wanted his cut, in cash, and he wanted it immediately. Even though we had not finished paying off the subcontractors and our damaged equipment was in need of repair, I turned over $20,000 and the books to DiMaggio, not taking any for myself.

After an article in the local newspaper showing that we received more than $500,000 in payments from the Army Corps of Engineers I received a call from Sammy Pieri, who had read the article. Thinking that it was all profit and not taking into consideration taxes, wages, subcontractors, fuel and repairs, he expected 10% of the Eastern Hills Mall proceeds for assisting me in getting the contract and an additional $50,000 from the blizzard cleanup that he felt he deserved. In his ranting and raving he went on to say that DeBartolo was sending an additional $23,000 to me and that money was to be turned over to him and to send $10,000 through his friend Poochie (Frank Cimento) immediately. What could I do? He wanted his pound of flesh. Pieri and DiMaggio were a heavy burden and even a major contractor would be strapped when having a grab-it-while-you-can fate such as I had.

After receiving the money from the Army Corps and DeBartolo and paying the bills, the company had around $68,000 in profit. Giving Nicky DiMaggio $20,000 as well the $10,000 to Poochie Cimento and the additional $23,000 from the Eastern Hills Mall proceeds to Sam Pieri, who wanted even more, but agreed to wait, there was not enough left to fix the broken equipment.

I know this sounds like I am a glutton for punishment but for those that do know the ins and outs of the mob are aware there is just no place to run or hide. I put myself in this position! If it wasn't for committing the worst sin of all, greed, and I lived on what I was receiving, none of this would have happened. If I only avoided asking them for help in the first place, maybe, just maybe, I could have pulled it off. Putting forth my best foot, I tried to develop plans with ideas that I could use to put aside this insurmountable burden.

The bills were paid and Pieri and DiMaggio were not to be seen, probably enjoying sunny warm vacations in Florida or somewhere with the money I paid them. I then set out to see if somehow I could find the finances to get my equipment repaired.

After I got the books back from DiMaggio and with the union taking up most of my time, I tried to spend as little time as possible on my misfortune with Sno-Go Plowing.

1978 Providence, Rhode Island and the Mob

I should have been happy, I should have felt successful, but I didn't. Sno-Go Plowing's reputation was growing and even Nick DiMaggio was relishing the expansion and the additional equipment that would make our plowing and rapid response easier to accomplish. Sammy Pieri was burdened with legal problems and, fortunately, kept his presence to a minimum. After the calamity of 1977, the business community and the city did not want to get caught with its pants down again; reaching early agreements with snow removal companies for rapid response assistance, they were ready for the next year's onslaught.

DiMaggio, with his "Mob comes first" mentality, decided that we would be better served by joining forces with other contractors and peddling our wares as a massive combine. I voiced little objection to this concept, since, by this time, I lost quite a lot of interest in the plowing business and knowing that even if I did mention an objection, it would be overruled.

Contractors Combine was formed with mob associate and close friend of DiMaggio, Thomas Barillari as its chief spokesman and leader. Barillari, the nephew of Anthony and Joe Fago, was a longtime mob and politically-connected developer. The Combine consisted of 12 local contractors who possessed the necessary equipment needed for most any emergency. Three of those contractors were mobbed-up and not by chance controlled the board of directors and officiating positions created in the combined merger. The snowfall in Western New York in 1978, was not as bad as the prior season but was above normal and we did achieve a few hours of response work from the City of Buffalo.

The Atlantic seaboard states and especially New England, however, was the recipient's of this year's blast. Many municipalities were hindered in their efforts to cope with the record snowfall. In what I thought would be a useless effort, I called the Army Corps of Engineers and made arrangements with the officers who would be responsible for the removal operations in New England. I was surprised by the positive responses I received, especially because I knew that New England had plenty of heavy equipment available for snow removal operations and really did not need our assistance. I could only surmise that I was able to sell our services because of our involvement in the 1977, Buffalo blizzard.

One of the problems facing me was that I could not be there and had to depend on others. I had to be at the winter meeting of the AFL-CIO in Bal Harbor, Florida and attend a multi-trade session over new, in-plant national agreements. Even though our agreement with Contractors Combine only covered snow removal operations in Western New York, DiMaggio and his uncle Roy Carlisi wanted us to perform all removal operations under the blanket of the Contractors Combine. Tom Barillari moved the snow command into the offices of Rhode Island Governor J. Joseph Garrahy. While in Florida attending the labor union sessions, I tried to take my mind off the Rhode Island project, even though I was somewhat bothered why DiMaggio was not calling me.

Arthur E. Coia, Laborers' International Union General Secretary-Treasurer was grooming me for a future and major role with the union. He informed me that Rhode Island Governor Garrahy was a personal friend and ally that he could rely on. Calling him without my knowledge he notified the Governor about me and my snow removal capabilities and made sure that Garrahy took care of us. I could only presuppose that Coia made this call just to show me how powerful he was.

One afternoon, after I had finished with a Building Trades meeting, I tried to reach Nick DiMaggio, but the telephone number I had did not work. I dialed information for the state office building and asked the operator for the Governor's office, and to my surprise instead of Garrahy or his secretary answering the Rhode Island Governor's phone, I was connected to Joe Barillari, Tom's brother and owner of Northern Demolition, a Combine company involved in the snow removal project.

While waiting for him to find DiMaggio I overheard someone in the background say, "Is that fucking Wilkinson again?" Keith Wilkinson was one of the legitimate contractors who joined the combine and was pretty much frozen out by the mob companies and only allowed to utilize two of his machines for the snow removal. After a few minutes Barillari replied that he checked and that he hadn't been seen DiMaggio for a couple of days. I also learned that my equipment was assigned to splinter operations and our operators were scattered throughout Rhode Island and the State of Massachusetts. After a few more phone calls I learned that Sno-Go Plowing was in trouble, and the equipment was down part of the time. The operators were more concerned with their meals and finding the right hotels rather than with the job before them.

I knew I had to leave Florida and the convention and get my ass to Rhode Island. I arranged to have my father pick me up at the Buffalo airport, take me to my house for winter clothes, and then drive me back to the airport so I could grab a flight to Providence. Upon arriving there I could see that the situation was bad, but it was nothing like what Buffalo and Western New York had endured. Based on the blocked streets it was evident that Rhode Island and Massachusetts were not aware of how to proceed with removing the snow and where to dump it.

Walking into the state office building and the Governor's office, I found Joe Barillari in an office adjacent to the Garrahy's, who was not present. It seemed that the whole floor was taken over by Barillari and mob-connected contractors. DiMaggio was nowhere to be found and I became quite upset after learning that my company was only acting in a support role to the mob-associated companies. Not one of the legitimate companies that were in Contractors Combine had any say in the operation. I also discovered that the mobbed-up companies had numerous subcontractors working for them directly and that the money they made would be hidden from the Combine's share and benefit. Joe Barillari informed me that the unconnected companies should not benefit from their lack of presence, even though they had placed their trust in the Combine and those of us responsible for their operations and equipment.

After checking into the nearby Marriott Hotel DiMaggio finally called and I arranged to meet him at Camille's Restaurant, a local hangout and frequented by the Patriarca Family and the Coias. DiMaggio introduced me to a couple of local mobsters and in concert they told me not to cause a problem over the Combine structure, everything had been approved by both the Buffalo and Patriarca Crime Families. DiMaggio told me not to worry about the limited effort by our equipment, "we were getting our fair share." I continued to argue about the legitimate contractors and their lack of participation, but to no avail. He told me that if I wanted to bring that up, that I knew the only forum available. Without mentioning a family sit-down, I felt that I should make it known that it was not only wrong, it would alienate the legitimate contractors and possibly bring about a lawsuit for a breach of contract. I was also told to stay out of it and voice no opinion about the removal operation.

After five days of not having any say-so and wandering around the Governor's office, I went back to Buffalo and my family. I called my father who had very little knowledge about the snow removal arrangement. I decided it was time to have a sit-down with the family. Joseph Pieri had since gained in prominence and had probably merited his position as family consigliere. My father told me Pieri knew the rules and was an expert on the Cosa Nostra infrastructure.

Joe Pieri never reflected his wealth by extravagant spending and dress and his home was quite modest. The remainder of the leadership was also present and included family boss Salvatore Frangiamore, his nephew and personal adviser Joseph Todaro Sr., Roy Carlisi, Sammy Pieri and my father.

Before discussing the matter before us, Joe Pieri asked my Father if he took the necessary precautions against being followed. My father answered in the affirmative. The sit-down started differently than I had expected. Roy Carlisi started yelling at me for interfering with his nephew and the directive he was given. Even though I humbly argued back, I was told that I was *allowed* to have this company and I should be thankful for that and that I was the business manager of Local 210. It was quite apparent that there was animosity with the Pieris on one side and Joe Todaro Sr., and Roy Carlisi on the other, with Sammy Frangiamore humbly acting as more of a mediator than a boss of a family.

My father, whose power was gone, was but a mere spectator to this whole pecking order scenario and the rending of the proceeds from his son and his business. Roy Carlisi and Joe Pieri yelled at Sammy Pieri about his constant meetings with me. They told him to stop it. They did not want the fed connecting him to Local 210. Carlisi, in his anger, asserted he wanted his nephew Nicky bought out and away from me. Taking the typical Mafia approach by not taking into consideration any expenses I had, he insisted that I give DiMaggio $150,000, saying that the three mobbed-up Contractor's Combine companies were going to pay $30,000 each and they were also going to give Sno-Go Plowing an additional $145,000 for its use of its equipment. Besides that amount, which he wanted to be turned over to DiMaggio, Carlisi additionally wanted $50,000 in cash now and $40,000 the next year. I explained that I didn't have that kind of money and that his nephew knew that the company couldn't afford it. I offered to let him look at the books. Sammy Pieri, interrupted, looking for his share of the money and reducing the Carlisi demand. An agreement was reached without my input that DiMaggio would receive two $30,000 payments as well as $20,000 a year for the next four years. I was also told not to bother the mobbed-up companies about what they rightfully owed the legitimate contractors. I fathomed that our share was probably much larger than what we were being paid and I also believed that DiMaggio could not be that short-sighted and made a lot more off the New England contract than I was aware of.

It was also concluded that from now on I was to answer to Sam Pieri via his nephew Joe Pieri Jr. and that Sammy Pieri would not only take over DiMaggio's 50% of Sno-Go, but I would be required to talk to my father or Joe Pieri Jr. before I acted on any union issues. Joe Pieri Sr. told me not to get involved or talk about in any way the illegal activity taking place at the union. Carlisi and Joe Pieri again yelled at Sammy Pieri, "We want him clean (referring to me); we do not want him in any way used to promote or implement any of the plans you told us about earlier." *What plans?* I thought to myself. What the hell were they talking about? Nothing was solved and again I was compelled to hide my anger and frustration.

The ride home was a bitter one; my hatred for these bastards was so intense and filled with visions of not only killing them, but taking pleasure in the act. At the same time, I felt so sorry for my father, disheveled and agitated over this broken shell of a man, who in his heyday probably would not have let this happen.

I was aware that there was no way out and wise to the fact that there was just no way I just could afford the loss of the New England snow-plowing receipts, let alone the $20,000 a year payment that would probably have to be made in cash. With no place to run, I again resigned myself to taking it on the chin. I was really glad that I was assisting the FBI in their effort to eradicate this cancer that had not only hurt me, but so many people. Looking back to that time, I, like most Americans, believed that the FBI always got their man and for these no-good bad actors, it was just a matter of time. Envisioning that cries for help would be answered and the sight of the cavalry coming over the hill to the rescue would be more than just a dream, I soldiered on.

I received a call from Jack Porstel, who wanted to meet. We arranged to meet at the home of the Buffalo Bills, Rich Stadium in suburban Orchard Park. I drove to the rear of the stadium and there was only one car parked in the middle of this vast lot. I parked alongside the vehicle and entered the back seat where Porstel introduced me to Agent Gregg McCrary. Porstel let me know that he was being transferred to Pittsburg, Pennsylvania and McCrary would now be my contact. McCrary seemed affable but was rather new to the Buffalo organized crime game. Later in his career Gregg McCrary would become quite famous as a profiler based out of Quantico, Virginia.

Normally an FBI agent is sent to any one of the field offices located throughout the United States after completing training and becoming a *Special Agent* (SA). This assignment will last for a couple of years and is considered a learning-the-ropes period. After the agent has completed his first office, as it was referred to by the bureau, unless they have certain specialized skills, the agents are then placed in one of the then big 12 field offices in the major urban areas such as New York City. This tour would last around 10 years. When that duty is completed, the agent can put in for an *Office of Preference* (OP), which is not always granted, and there the agent would normally complete his career. After McCrary gave me his home number and expressed his pleasure over working with me, I left and thought about my father and my circuitous predicament.

My father knew Al Hartel and he knew of my relationship with the CIA. He not only respected Al, he viewed him as a Hollywood-type of character. In reality it is often a very difficult life for those that do venture into the world of shadows. The FBI was a horse of a different color. Even though my father admired many of the agents and had provided information in the past, he was now disillusioned about them. He would tell me in our moments of leisure how the FBI under J. Edgar Hoover turned its back on Cosa Nostra activity. Some sort of strange allegiance existed (stay off of our turf and we'll stay off of yours). But this was not the 1950s, it was 1978, and the bureau was not the same. Al Hartel believed that this change was brought about by the John F. Kennedy assassination and the political and public pressure to go after the mob.

The November 1957, meeting in Apalachin, New York, at the home of a Magaddino Family member, was uncovered by the New York State Police. This revelation revitalized enforcement efforts and by the FBI. In addition, highly publicized mob informant Joseph Valachi, who in reality was a mere soldier, but still one of the biggest wiseguys to violate his oath and fealty to the Mafia, also raised the question about what, if anything, was being done. The disease that was the Mafia was resilient and foxy enough to use the laws of this country to protect itself. Armed with all this knowledge and clamoring, Hoover had to have known about the secret society, but, for whatever reason, refused to use the FBI to go after them. I am aware of the fact that Hoover perceived the real threat to be communism and its goal of world domination and FBI agents were compelled to make the "Red Threat" their main priority.

The John F. Kennedy killing caused the FBI nightmares and even though, at least in my opinion, the mob was probably not involved in the shooting on that fateful day, the Kennedy assassination did have a positive effect for the Cosa Nostra; it aided in curtailing the power and constant pursuit of them by Attorney General Bobby Kennedy, at least temporarily. Bobby Kennedy was aware of Operation Mongoose (the Mafia involvement to cause mischief and if possible eradicate Fidel Castro). He aided those federal agencies that were involved in the cover-up. Robert Kennedy felt that if the public started looking at the Mafia, they would uncover his and his brother's escapades with Mafia molls.

With the Watergate debacle out of the way, this was a different FBI, with diverse objectives. The mob and its influence on business and labor became a major target. The problem of having the Organized Crime Strike Force still heading the investigations with its big-brother attitude toward the FBI caused the bureau to adjust to what was considered a subservient role. Little did I know at the time about the problem and the animosity that existed between the two organizations and how I would eventually be placed in the middle of a tug of war.

Onyx Construction Chicago Snow Removal 1979

SAM PIERI WASTED LITTLE TIME IN his role as my Buffalo Mafia helmsman and ignoring the orders that he was to communicate with me through his nephew, he introduced me to his bodyguard and close associate, Tom Giammaresi, a Buffalo Police detective who provided him with sensitive information about ongoing investigations. As we sat in the kitchen of the Pieri home (owned by Giammaresi), Sammy told me that he wanted office space for a business that was envisioned by the elder Mafioso and his obedient police officer. The plan was for Giammaresi to form a minority company to take advantage of the current laws that required all state and federal projects to award a percentage to minority-owned contractors and businesses. Enjoying the assistance of the family-controlled Local 210, they decided to take advantage of the proposed multi-million dollar light rail rapid transit project that was a focal point of Buffalo's future and viability. Their idea was to start an equipment leasing company that would make machinery available for the general and subcontractors that would be awarded the massive amount of work.

Giammaresi and Pieri contemplated the use of three different minorities before they settled on a guy that was a member of Local 210. William Sterling was previously a member of a local street gang and was befriended by Giammaresi after he was arrested for some crime. They also decided to enjoin the services of Carl Mastykarcz, a local bank manager for Manufacturers and Traders Trust Company, who first entered prominence by assisting Joey Pizza in his pursuit of loans without collateral.

The Onyx Construction Company Inc. became a reality by utilizing Frank LoTempio, a local attorney and nephew of Pieri, who structured the company with Bill Sterling owning 51%, Giammaresi, Mastykarcz and a local Catholic priest shared the other forty-nine percent. Even though I was sure that Sterling's 51% was somehow going to be shared with Pieri and possibly others, I was never told how this would be accomplished.

My offices were located at a railroad depot located 30 miles east of Buffalo, and I made the necessary arrangements for Onyx's operations and needed office space. I allowed them to take over our train depot itself and we moved the snow operations to the main building, which I wanted to lease out. The Giammaresi idea was to purchase dump trucks for the rapid transit project, but Pieri objected because Nick DiMaggio and his uncle Roy Carlisi had already purchased trucks and this might have led to a family conflict. Shifting gears, Giammaresi then decided to purchase bulldozers and other heavy equipment and broker any additional equipment that might be needed. I was asked about purchasing equipment because I was heading to Louisville, Kentucky for an annual auction to look for a new front loader.

Traveling with me was Doug Ackerman, my equipment expert, and Tom Giammaresi. Giammaresi decided to wander around the auction and told us that he would meet us at the end of the day. We were shocked to learn that he went nuts and purchased a bulldozer, a crawler loader, and two front-end high-lifts without checking them out mechanically or even knowing their value.

After we learned that he paid much too much for the equipment, and not taking into consideration the problems and cost of getting the machines to Buffalo, Giammaresi then floored me by saying that he didn't have enough money and wanted to know if I could lend him some. I told him that I'd like to help but I needed the money that I had on me for another auction because I couldn't find the bargain front-end loader I was looking for.

That night Giammaresi told me that Sam Pieri wanted to talk to me. I called Pieri at his home and he told me to assist Giammaresi in his plight by loaning him the money that he needed and not to worry, because as soon as I got back I would be reimbursed. I was not only suspicious but I knew I was opening a Pandora's Box with this loan. I really could not take it anymore, it seemed the more I tried to get away, the deeper I got. I only wished I could just sell everything and walk away. Even if they did let me, which I do not believe they would, I knew that the money that I owed was more than the company's assets and I would lose my home and everything that I pledged to the bank. The next morning before leaving I went with Giammaresi and not only loaned him $12,000, I also had to arrange for equipment haulers to have the machines transported back to Buffalo. As usual, I knew I was fucked again with no way out.

Back in Buffalo I attempted to explain to Sam Pieri that the money I loaned to Giammaresi was borrowed from the bank and that it was needed for our snow plow business. I also informed him that the equipment that Giammaresi had purchased was a pile of garbage, and that it would cost a small fortune to repair. He curtly responded and told me that the snow plow business was half his and I still owed him a lot of money. He said he knew what he was doing and that Giammaresi would soon return the money.

Sammy was pissed at me and I knew I went too far with my attitude towards him and Giammaresi's schemes. He then responded that I was to use his share of the money that was owed to him and have my mechanics fix the damn equipment. He violently said, "You had better listen to me and my request or face the consequences of having no one in the family to protect you." He boisterously ranted that my father had no one to turn to either and that I better listen to him. He tried to reassure me and said I should try and be more positive, that success was just around the corner.

In order to accomplish this impossible task, I hired two more mechanics to assist Doug Ackerman. These mechanics turned out to be the only bright light in the whole damned mess. Robert Ellis and Jerry Herling were members of the Operating Engineers Union and they quickly became aware that I was not the boss but a front for the rarely seen Sam Pieri. They wondered why I allowed Pieri's nephews and Giammaresi's kids to cut the locks on the fuel pumps and steal gas, even charging auto parts for their personal cars and signing my name to the credit vouchers. It was a bloody nightmare for me. The repair on Sno-Go's equipment stood idle while we had to concentrate on the Onyx equipment.

Giammaresi and Mastykarcz decided to shift Onyx's direction. Thinking that they could play a bigger role than just supplying heavy equipment, they decided they would attempt to join forces with a major contractor bidding on the rapid transit project. One of those contractors was Fruin-Colnon Corp. At the time I had no knowledge about this except a leaked word or two every now and then. When I was finally informed of their new approach I questioned this method to myself, because there was a good chance that they could lose the bid to another company.

In the second phase of the project, after being unsuccessful on the first, they hit pay dirt. The joint venture of Fruin-Colnon, Traylor Brothers and Onyx became triumphant on the $30 million phase of the rapid transit project. Sam Pieri and all involved were overjoyed. I too was happy, thinking maybe I could get some of my money returned and Sammy Pieri off my back.

My half brother Rocky Fumerelle was working for me at Sno-Go Plowing services and one day he told me that Giammaresi wanted him to work for them instead. Being loyal, Rocky asked me if it was okay. I really did not need him at Sno-Go so I told him that it was all right.

I didn't see much of Giammaresi and his cohorts after they were awarded this major project. I was too busy with my normal responsibilities at the Union Hall, and they were spending most of their time in meetings with their new-found partners. The winter season was now upon us and in watching the news I realized just how bad the situation was in the Midwest with record snowfall and their inability to handle it.

I had Bob Ellis, who was now involved with my operation, call the Chicago mayor's office to find out if they needed any assistance. Thomas Howe, an assistant director of purchasing, not only requested assistance, he needed it immediately. He wanted us to mobilize our machinery and trucks. The City sent us a purchase order guaranteeing us a minimum of two weeks work. We quickly made arrangements for operators and drivers as well as transportation for our machines to move out in 24 hours. After making the necessary arrangements with the states of New York, Pennsylvania, Ohio and Indiana for state police escorts of the massive convoy, I flew to Indianapolis, Indiana, due to the fact that Chicago's airports were snowed in.

After renting a car I drove to Chicago City Hall where I was greeted as a savior. Tom Howe introduced me to Peter Schivarelli, an assistant commissioner. I knew the importance of having a snow command center and a proper survey of the roadways in Chicago and the surrounding areas. I also informed Howe and Schivarelli that hotel arrangements would be needed for our operators and I would need a source of fuel and equipment supplies.

The next morning I visited the site where my machines, trucks and operators were parked and awaiting orders. I let Bob Ellis know that he would be responsible for field operations and informed him where the equipment could be parked and where the hotels were located. I then told him to check into the hotels and await my instructions; I was still meeting with city officials and going over our plan of attack.

After I completed a helicopter tour and realized the dire straits that the city was in, I attended a meeting with Tom Donovan (the protégé of deceased Mayor Richard Daily

Sr.) Even though Mayor Anthony Bilandic wasn't present, I soon realized that he was not the real power, it was but Tom Donovan. He ushered me into a meeting with the heads of the police, streets, sanitation and fire departments. I told them just how bad the situation was. Their driving the giant powder blue garbage trucks up and down the streets was only making matters worse. I lectured the audience about our previous snow removal operations; how we assisted the Army Corp of Engineers and having them involved is a major priority. After a couple of hours I was asked to wait in the hallway while they reviewed what I had told to the Chicago officials.

More than three hours had passed when Tom Donovan reported to me that they wanted me to help them; I would have the full cooperation of the City and I would be allowed to set up a command post in City Hall. Disregarding my advice, they felt that they could handle the operation and did not want to have the Army Corps or any federal assistance. I couldn't believe what I was hearing, knowing what they knew and after my report, they wanted to control the cleanup alone.

It was decided that the state would have the cleanup responsibility for the expressways and our crew and operations would remain with the City. I requested that city inspectors and police be assigned to our operations to avoid problems with gangs and to keep track of our equipment and hours of work. I stayed and even slept at City Hall and rarely had an opportunity to visit my crews. I handled logistics as well as supervised many of the Chicago employees and tried as I could to bring them up to speed on removal operations. Explaining that maps and progress reports would be necessary, as well as snowmobiles to assist those trapped in their homes and in need of medical assistance.

I instructed on the need for control and communication. I pointed out employee wage rate requirements and the need to monitor each and every snow removal contractor. I assigned my equipment to two main arteries and pointed the convoys in the direction of the center of the City from the city line. I used the mayor's two vans to shuttle my employees (who were divided into two groups that worked 12-hour shifts) back and forth between their four hotels located in the Oak Lawn area and their equipment. This way there was no need to shut down the snow removal machinery and temporarily stop working. To avoid down time (with the exception of major repair) the mechanics would fix and service the equipment in their assigned areas of work. Food and coffee would be brought to the workers; bathroom facilities would be designated by the crew supervisor. It soon became apparent to the City of Chicago streets and sanitation employees, and anyone else who had an opportunity to watch our operations, that we knew how to remove snow.

The press started asking the city employees why they did not have a procedure similar to the one our crews implemented, prior to the storm. The praise and platitudes for our snow-plowing ability came pouring in. The media called me the "Red Adair" of snow removal (in reference to the renowned oil-well firefighter). I was called the expert who saved not only Buffalo and New England from disaster but also bailed out Montreal, Quebec (a town that I had only visited a couple of times and never assisted with snow removal). Calls were coming in from all over the Midwest asking if we could help them with their plight. As we basked and relished all the fanfare, Mayor Bilandic asked me if I would go on national television with him and explain how the Chicago disaster compared to the problems we encountered in Buffalo and New England. I didn't like being away from snow command, but I knew that the Mayor wanted to point out just how badly widespread the damage was. The local NBC affiliate was the first to interview me; I addressed the problems that the removal crews, as well as the public, would encounter. I reiterated that hotlines were open and that most hospitals would be the first to be cleared.

I noticed that one of the contractors involved in the cleanup was employing dump trucks and listing them as dump trailers, which received a higher hourly rate. I brought this to the attention of Pete Schivarelli, who, after hearing this, requested that I take a ride with him and visit the site. During the ride he asked me if I was Ron Fino, the labor leader and if my father was Joseph Fino. After saying yes, he went on to tell me that we had mutual friends and that it would not serve those friends' interest by my pointing out that the contractor in question was cheating. He further voiced, "Some of our mutual friends are benefiting from this and I am sure you understand." Schivarelli clued me in that this was a major consideration for not having the Army Corps involved with the cleanup.

I knew the power of the mob in the Windy City. Making waves, especially after being warned, would lead to retaliation against me. I let him know that I would, of course, back off. (At a later date I passed this information on to SA Gregg McCrary.) Schivarelli continued on about his role as the manager of the famous band Chicago and his closeness with Ara Parseghian, the former coach of the Notre Dame Football team.

Onyx Makes Headlines

BACK IN BUFFALO I ALSO WAS making headlines, though these were not of praise; but of me being involved with the minority contractor, Onyx. The front page of the *Buffalo Evening News* carried a story that a local labor leader is tied to a minority contractor that had become a successful bidder on the rapid transit project. I was, of course, bothered by the articles but felt that I had nothing to worry about. The FBI and Al Hartel were aware of who really owned the company.

Soon the Chicago newspapers and television stations were not only linking me to Onyx, but also linking me to organized crime. Mike Royko, the famous nationally-syndicated columnist, wrote in his column: "IMPORTED MUSCLE" and went on to state that I was a top east coast enforcer for the mob, and I had enough connections to make a federal agent's nose quiver. As funny and as false as the article was, it hurt me and my ego. All the local television stations were carrying the story and mayoral candidate Jane Byrne started calling for an investigation into my presence in Chicago, as well as organized crime's ties to the Bilandic administration.

The Buffalo newspapers and television stations acquainted the public with my Chicago involvement with the snow removal and that I had become an issue in the Chicago mayoral race. In concert with the daily reporting about my so-called Onyx involvement, it wasn't long before I was the talk of the town.

Bilandic and his political advisers felt that the situation would be best served by my departure and that I should immediately suspend all snow removal operations. Transportation was arranged for the majority of my workers as well as my equipment. I was able to subcontract out some of the machinery but overall our involvement came to an abrupt halt.

I realized all too well that no matter what I did in life, no matter how I scrubbed and tried to excise the image of the Mafia, I would have to carry on with that sinister icon ingrained in the public's mind. It was as if someone had tattooed "Mafia - Stay Away" on my forehead.

The Onyx headlines were causing me headaches and it soon became apparent that an investigation into Onyx and its relationship with me was going to commence.

Martin Steinberg, who headed up the Miami, Florida Strike Force, had recently been transferred to head the Strike Force in Buffalo. While in Miami, the forceful U.S. attorney stepped on many an FBI agent's toes and their dislike for him was widespread. Countless law enforcement officers in the Justice Department and the FBI considered Steinberg to be the U.S. attorney later depicted in the Paul Newman-Sally Field movie Absence of Malice.

I found out from McCrary that Steinberg was leading an investigation with me as the main target. The agent inferred that he didn't think I had anything to worry about. Still, the headlines continued and I felt that I should contact Al

Hartel. In visiting Hartel at his home in Akron, New York, it was evident that he was not just ill from cancer, which I had already known, but he was now close to death. The intravenous bottle and its contents entering his frail body together with the agony that this friend was suffering made me question why I was there. I felt awful and didn't enjoy having to ask this buddy who was living his last moments to make a phone call to the Strike Force and let them know the truth. But survival is a strong instinct and my continued existence was paramount. Even though I was concerned about my mentor, I asked him to look into the matter of my investigation. Through his spasms of pain, he listened; he told me that he would take care of it and not to worry. A phone call to Steinberg's assistant Richard Endler would suffice. I thanked him and then kissed Al's loving wife Francis goodbye. "Al had always talked about you so fondly, as a dear friend," she said and thanked me for taking the time to visit with him. I felt so damn guilty about soliciting him for a favor at this time. Within days he was dead and yet I wondered, was he able to make the call to Dick Endler?

As the investigation continued my rashness and direct approach led me to have the FBI contact Marty Steinberg and to arrange a meeting for me. The Amherst Manor, a hotel on the north side of Buffalo and frequent location for FBI debriefings, was chosen. I was told to arrive at 1:00 p.m.; Martin Steinberg and Dick Endler, together with two other Strike Force attorneys, were already present. Don Hartnett, the supervisor of the FBI Organized Crime squad and agents Charlie Mauer and Gregg McCrary accompanied me.

At that time I was not aware of the acrimony that existed between the FBI and Strike Force but I was soon to learn and join in with those FBI agents who voiced their disapproval of its bulldog stratagem. Steinberg's first words were, "We are not interested in you Ronald, we know the truth, we are however interested in what you know." He told me that the Onyx problem would be put on the back burner and that he wanted me to tell him everything I knew about Angelo Fosco, the general president of the Laborers' and Arthur E. Coia (or as I referred to him, Arthur Sr.), the general secretary-treasurer.

Steinberg went on to say that he knew that Pieri was behind Onyx and asked me if I had any information about Giammaresi and his relationship with foreign businesses. "What is Giammaresi's involvement with former FBI agent James LaLime?" Not knowing that the FBI did not reveal my undercover activity with them, I wrongly assumed that Steinberg had been already in possession of all my FBI conversations and the information that I had provided throughout the years. I tried to think of things that I may have left out and answered his inquiries with this in mind and limiting what I told him. I said, "All my information about Fosco and Coia is with the FBI" and he would have to obtain that from them. "Regarding Giammaresi and Jim LaLime, I do not know about any overseas involvement." I hit a nerve and it was a bad one. Clearly Steinberg was upset over my "see the FBI" response and I could perceive that a fight was about to begin. Abruptly, irate and with fire in his eyes, Marty Steinberg and entourage left the hotel room. Immediately I grasped that he was not a crusader, cleansing and incarcerating the mob, but a promoter, looking to build his reputation and image.

After the get-together was completed, I left with Don

Hartnett. I was shocked when this senior agent called me a fucking idiot and said that Steinberg wanted my scalp. Hartnett uttered, "The FBI is reluctant to turn over its information to these types of people because they are here today and either running for office or representing the other side tomorrow." I told him that I always thought the FBI and Strike Force were one big happy family, a sentiment I believed was shared by the public as a whole. He replied that the FBI would absolutely not be involved in any investigation of me and everyone in the bureau office considered me as part of the family of agents. Still, I was big news and Steinberg wanted headlines. Hartnett went on, "Don't be surprised if he attempts to gain and further those headlines by trying to put your scalp on his belt." I responded by telling him, "You know I am innocent; the FBI knows and Al Hartel told me prior to his death that he would straighten out the problem."

He then remarked, "Steinberg isn't interested in Onyx; he only wants it to make you go public and testify in other important areas."

"I could never do that! It would mean the end of everything that I hold dear, as well as living my life." I was reassured that "the FBI would never compromise you or your other identities, and that's a promise."

"This is not the FBI, Ronnie," referring to the Strike Force, "this is an organization that we have no control of and can only ask for special condition consideration."

The answer came Easter of 1979, as a grand jury was impaneled to investigate my involvement with Onyx and all my business activities. It seemed that a Sunday didn't go by without my name plastered in bold letters across the front page of the newspaper. It was so unnerving for me to wake up on a Sunday morning and venture out to the mail box and sneak up on the newspaper in the hope that this Sunday would be different.

I received a phone call from Gregg McCrary and from the way he was talking I could tell that something was wrong. We decided to meet at an Orchard Park restaurant not far from my home and convenient for the FBI agent.

The meetings I had with McCrary had been more open and visible to the public than those I had with other bureau agents, except for the Porstel incident. It wasn't that we were less concerned about discovery; it was that both of us knew Gregg was still an unknown and his presence sitting next me really posed no problems. Agent McCrary was glum with an expression of despair that I greeted that day in January of 1979.

After he sat down he informed me that he would no longer be working with me and that I was going to be working with a then-unknown other agent. I asked him why the change and for what reason? I sensed that he knew the answer and that he was not allowed to tell me the rationale behind the move. He whispered softly that he didn't know and he believed that he was going to be moved out of the organized crime squad. He wished me well and after a brief chat about a previous skiing arrangement that we planned, he departed. Later on I was apprised from other agents that McCrary was threatened with dismissal for his insistence and strong stand that I was a victim and that the FBI should oppose the Strike Force. I was also enlightened by a number of agents that the *Special Agent in Charge* (SAC) of the

Buffalo office rolled over and could have done more, but was afraid of Steinberg and the problems that could befall him. One agent put it, "Gone are the Richard D. Rogge's and Neil Welsh's." (In reference to previous Buffalo SAC's.)

After having caved in to the Strike Force, SAC Walter Weiner was transferred and Richard Bretzing was named the new SAC of the Buffalo office. It was too late to change anything, the damage was already done.

Still hoping that "a better head and an eventual understanding would prevail," I went about my Union business and started to receive the funds from Chicago. While I was in Chicago, I was paid $540,000 for a portion of the plowing services. I used this money to pay our subcontractors and operators who needed cash for their families back in Western New York. All in all we grossed over $1,500,000 in the three weeks we were there and, according to my calculations, over $300,000 were profit before taxes and equipment repairs.

The first person to greet me on my return was my nemesis, Sam Pieri. I met him at his house and he informed me that he had read the papers and wanted to know when we were going to cut up the $1.5 million. After telling him that there were expenses and that "I am under investigation, Sammy," a subject he didn't want to hear or seemed to care about, he furiously said to list Onyx as a subcontractor and pay them $150,000 and to pay some other front company, that I cannot remember the name of, another fifty thousand dollars.

"Holy God, Sam! How the fuck is the company going to survive?" I was loud and angry, Pieri and this Onyx idea had become a living nightmare for me and I let him know that. I rebuked, "I also have to consider the legal cost, Sammy, and you're not thinking of me."

I knew I had gone too far with my angry tone and attitude, but I had no choice but to stand strong. Pushing his finger into my chest, he told me, "Pay up or face the consequences." I loudly said, "That's *it*" and abruptly left and sped away from the Pieri home.

I contacted SA Gregg McCrary about his threat and he told me that FBI agents Charles Mauer and Steve Naum were the agents that I would be working with from now on. A meeting was arranged at the East Aurora Country Club, where I was a member. My addiction to golf and the club being located not that far from my home led me to this club and many a new-found friend.

Charles Mauer, Steve Naum and Steve's brother Dean, who was also an agent, sat down with me. Dean did most of the talking and told me that the bureau could not protect me from the Strike Force; orders had come down from FBI headquarters that all offices and agents must comply with Organized Crime Strike Force requests and for agents to stop their contact with me. Dean Naum went on to say, "There is not much we can do for you except hold your hand and support you in any legal way we can. The easy way to kill this case is to go public, but that will lead to your being compromised and kill your ability to obtain additional information that is badly needed."

Charlie Mauer interrupted Naum and said, "Ronnie, you are one of the best sources the FBI has ever had, unlike everyone else, you are clean. You came to us not to make a deal but to help. Everyone in our office is pulling for you. The best thing is to get this matter out of the way and let's go from there."

About a week had gone by when I was asked by my father to go and see Sammy Frangiamore at his home. I had told my father about the Pieri problem and that I thought that was what the "Farmer" wanted to discuss. Upon arriving at his home, he warmly greeted me and ushered me into the kitchen. "Ronnie, you have a cousin, Paul Fino, that is working for a Local 210 contractor (who's name I cannot remember) and we want him off of there and out of the union."

"Why Sammy, what has he done?" I asked. "This is a bad kid Ronnie, who talks to everyone about things he should not discuss, the family, killings, you name it. The other laborers on the job are calling him 'motor mouth.' We want him out, period." "Sammy, I'll remove him, but please let me talk to him and when another job is available to send him there. I am sure that he will listen to me and keep his mouth shut in the future, Please Sam, this guy has no other place to go." "All right, but you are to take responsibility for him." "Okay, I will." I then asked him if he heard about the Sammy Pieri incident, to which he answered yes but didn't say more. That night I grabbed my cousin Paul, growled at him that he has to keep his big mouth shut from now on or he will find himself out in the cold.

Reluctantly, I had to pay Pieri, but not the amount he wanted. Trying to carry on as if my life was normal was a challenge and hard to deal with. Because of all the publicity, Onyx moved out of my facility and relocated into the offices of a Giammaresi-Pieri associate, Dr. Joseph DeAngelo.

The publicity was intense and banks started calling in my notes as well as canceling my checking accounts. With Pieri siphoning off all the profits as well as with the company's inability to meet its debts, I was left with little choice by the spring of 1980, but to sell the snow-plowing business and the contracts. After the last piece of equipment was auctioned off, I had less than $2,000 left. All the work and effort I put into this company and snow plowing was for naught. I did, however, avoid having to lose my home and filing bankruptcy. I felt a big sense of relief. I would have no partners, I wouldn't have to worry about the IRS, or get up in the middle of the night anymore. The Pieri control didn't go away, though, as there was still the union and all the problems associated with the mob and its ever-present demands.

Ivan the Terrible

THE PRESS AND ITS OUTCRY CAUSED the lead company's of the joint venture, Fruin-Colnon and Traylor Brothers, to buy Onyx's share of the contract and discard the thorn in their side. I never found out what the purchase price was, but I am sure the mobsters made a lot.

The sale of the contract didn't stop Giammaresi and Pieri from conniving, it was in their blood. At least to me, Tom Giammaresi was always a strange sort of fellow. I had previously noticed that when he and his Onyx cohorts were based on my property he would make phone calls all over the country as well as to the Middle East and Western Europe. One time when I was meddling around with my lead representative Bob Ellis, we came upon Giammaresi's phone bills. I marked down many of the numbers that were regularly called. When we attempted to call one of the numbers we discovered that in order to complete the call you had to enter a code. If you didn't have the code and tried random numbers, the call would automatically be canceled. Giammaresi's phone bill reflected that the calls were going to and from Columbia, Maryland. As I said, Giammaresi was very strange and in my chats with him he would mention that he was involved with our intelligence agencies. I tried to confirm this with the CIA but was told that it was not true and his name did not appear anywhere. Even so, I still felt his story just may have some validity.

The reason I say this is that just too many incidences popped up for him not to have some connections. He mentioned his relationship with the National Security Agency and someone named Dr. O'Connor, whom he would refer to as his contact. I, of course, passed this information on to the agency and the bureau, who expressed just a passing interest. Even though the bureau was supposed to stay away from me, their avoidance never really took place and we remained in constant contact.

Giammaresi teamed up with Dr. D'Angelo, Carl Mastykarcz, former FBI agent James LaLime and a man from Cleveland by the name of John Demjanjuk. They were in possession of millions of dollars of, probably worthless, German bonds that were issued to Nazi Germany by the American bank, J.P. Morgan back in the 1930s. Giammaresi claimed he had some notable works of art as well. I obtained one of the J.P. Morgan bonds which I turned over to the FBI. At that time I did not know where they came from or what purpose they would serve. I also was not aware of Demjanjuk but later learned he was believed to be "Ivan the Terrible" and alleged to have been at the Treblinka concentration camp in Poland during World War II. According to victims, he would go around with a whip and sword, taking swipes at the naked Jewish captives as they ran from the train box cars. As a result of these atrocities, Demjanjuk was extradited to Israel in 1986, and went on trial for war crimes. He was convicted but the conviction was overturned by an appellate court and he then returned to the States. He stayed here until May 11, 2009, when he was sent to Germany to stand trial. On May 12, 2011, he was convicted as an accessory to the murder of 27,000 Jews.

What is strange and deserves further study is what his relationship was with Tom Giammaresi and the person named Dr. O'Connor. According to Giammaresi, Dr. O'Connor's son Mark is a Buffalo-based attorney who somehow ended up on the Demjanjuk legal team. Later, in trying to put 2 and 2 together, I looked at Mark O'Connor's background and from what I gleaned, he was not a criminal attorney; so how did he get, or who picked him, to represent Demjanjuk?

I didn't get to see Giammaresi that much anymore and the only times we did meet related to the Onyx trial preparation discussions. Giammaresi and his team formed a company called American Hydrocarbon Inc., which was established to take advantage of the fuel shortage and the world problem of soaring oil prices. Their new place of business was now somewhere in Indiana and they had an oil-from-shale procedure which was considered quite novel at that time. Eventually their company had investors from all over the world who poured their savings into the company and its extraction formula. The FBI asked me if I had any information about this company or Giammaresi and Mastykarcz frequent trips to Germany and Switzerland where they would meet with representatives from Iraq and the United Arab Emirates. I told them of the limited knowledge I had but my suspicions told me they were up to no good.

Sitting Down with Jack Kemp and Federal Judge John Elfvin

EVEN THOUGH I WAS ASSURED BY the FBI that I would not surface, I knew I was on uneasy ground and it wouldn't take much to publicly let slip my role with the FBI. I called Congressman Jack Kemp and asked him if he could meet me to discuss something important. He was in the process of campaigning for the upcoming congressional race and agreed to see me at the Prior Aviation terminal at the airport. I knew I was taking a chance by letting him know of my involvement with the FBI and CIA. It was a gamble that I hoped would not get back to the mob and Jack Kemp's close fundraiser and associate, hotel magnate Jim Cosentino, who was close to Buffalo mobster Joe Todaro Sr. I felt I had no choice but to reach out for help. I knew a little about the law and that it required that all statements made by me to federal agents and officials that related to the innocence or guilt of all parties subject to prosecution, be made available to them prior to trial. This, of course, included my statements about Giammaresi, Pieri and Mastykarcz.

Spinning and reeling from this Onyx debacle caused me

to start taking chances and if successful, at the very least, maybe I could narrow down my exposure.

I first became involved with Jack Kemp in 1974, during his run for Congress and we knew each other quite well. When we met at the airport he started by saying, "Ronnie I don't have much time, so let's sit over here." I explained my government cooperation and the dire straits I was in. He answered, "If you were dropped from this investigation, would that stop the problem?" "Hell, no," I answered, "it would make it worse. If I were dropped from this case then red flags would go up on why, especially after I received so much media attention."

I stated that the only way out of it was through it. After telling me that he would look into it, he asked me if Jimmy Cosentino was mobbed-up. I answered him by saying, "Just be very careful, Jack." I did not tell him about his assistant Russell Gugino and his connections to the mob (why, I do not know). After exchanging thanks and an introduction to a tall, attractive female assistant, his commuter flight was ready for departure. He departed reiterating that he was going to look into the problem.

The FBI arranged for an ex-agent who was a practicing attorney to help represent me, because I could not tell Paul Cambria, the attorney that was representing my interest and defense over the Onyx problem, of my cooperation without risking exposure. Tom Shea was not only congenial; he expressed sympathy over my dilemma and becoming a victim in the power struggle. He expressed, "The FBI wants to help you but is powerless because of a new cooperation policy with the Strike Force."

As my future in Buffalo became doubtful, the FBI was

still doing everything they possibly could. They then arranged for me to sit down with the Federal Judge that was presiding over the Onyx case, John Elfvin. I had met Judge Elfvin in the past, I helped him with his golf swing on a couple of occasions, and I had a lot of respect for him. After entering his private chambers, he took his court frock off and asked me to sit down next to him as he lit his pipe. I told him of my situation. Half laughing he told me that the Strike Force and FBI wanted Local 210 for years. His expression turned serious and I sensed that he felt compassion for me when he told me that he would see what he could do.

Lyndon LaRouche

IN THE LATE FALL OF 1979, at a meeting with CIA officer William Long that took place in the parking lot of the University at Buffalo, he voiced concern about the Onyx investigation. I could tell from his attitude that he was quite concerned and wanted to keep the Agency free and clear from fallout. I told him I had been contacted by Arnie Stanton again, the former spokesman for the SDS who now wanted to introduce me to the Lyndon LaRouche movement.

He listened intently. After I had finished, he asked me, "To follow up on Stanton's request and see what you can discover about his involvement in Columbia and South America." I surmised that they suspected LaRouche and his followers might be involved with drug traffickers. At that time LaRouchites were reaching out to the Mafia-controlled unions in this country as well as possibly using LaRouche anti-drug coalition for illegal activities.

Long told me not to contact him anymore. If I wanted to meet with him I was to lean a rake or a broom against a tree in front of my house. After a couple days he would call me and let me know when and where to meet. He didn't like to mention the location over the phone so he would leave me a note in my mail box. After reminiscing over the late Al Hartel, we departed.

Lyndon LaRouche was making a swing through Western New York in preparation for the 1980, presidential race. In following up on the Agency's request I set out on attempting to get close to him or his followers. After contacting one of his Buffalo, New York followers I listened to the story of LaRouche and his methods, experiencing what many travelers encountered at airport terminals. The LaRouchites were very persistent and their persona was that of being brainwashed and quite robotic.

Eventually I was introduced to Lyn (as his close associates referred LaRouche) and quite surprised to find that he was equally interested in me. He was keenly aware of my past and my current catch-22 with Onyx and the Strike Force. It was quite obvious that his preparation for the meeting went beyond what was in the newspapers, but not far enough to suspect my contacts with the FBI and CIA.

The hotel room was quaint and as I listened to this man whose political views ran the gamut from communism to his current position, which was more in line with the teachings of *Mein Kampf* and the tyrannical Adolf Hitler, I could not accept his concept that the Jewish race was responsible for the world's problems and that they were behind developing a new world order. I explained to LaRouche my own personal views, that each and every one of us that inhabit this planet was, at least in part, to blame and as long as we covet our neighbor's possessions and territory, mankind will eventually destroy itself, as well as this orb that we call home. I went on to say, "There is no question about our country and its immediate future. It currently exists under the oligarchic rule and true power and the control of the working man's fate rests with big business and multinationals."

In my ramblings of capitalistic control of Western Europe, North America, and elsewhere I elaborated, "The eventual horrific cleansing that eventually takes place via war is intertwined throughout the history of mankind." I obviously touched him because this tall, rather sober being listened intently to my questioning of his views and those of my own. He asked some of his followers to listen to what I had to say and as if drawn by some magnetic force, they huddled closer. I talked about how labor unions had lost their identity by becoming big business and forgetting the workers they were supposed to represent. "They bring a select few up to good standards of living and forget the majority's quest for better wages and conditions." I sensed that he did not believe that the Jewish race was the catalyst for disaster but had accepted this falsehood to placate his wife Helga and her input into the theories that he was spewing. I had to be careful not to offend him too much. My big mouth could shut the door and end the meeting with an abrupt, "Goodbye."

Instead, just the opposite took place. LaRouche wanted to get closer to me to discuss the incorporation of some of my views and ideas with his own and those of his wife. Not wanting to push too hard and attempt to discover the questions posed to me by the Agency, I left this area of inquiry for a later encounter. I couldn't help but wonder as I drove away, why this attack on Israel and the Jewish race as a whole? His answer to Zionism and their status in the Holy Land was one thing, but to blame a people for each and every act with hate and uncaring was so far-fetched and without a scintilla of evidence. It created an air of personal hatred for this person and his followers. How was he going to campaign for president and expect to further his cause? Perplexed by this approach, I not only questioned his mental state of being but pondered what his future would have been like had he enjoined the rights of people of all religions.

Lyndon LaRouche reached out and wanted me to fly to Michigan and have dinner with him and his wife Helga at their home in a suburb of Detroit. I was picked up at the airport by some of his supporters and driven to Grosse Pointe, Michigan where LaRouche was to speak to a group of potential benefactors. The topic was balanced with subjects ranging from alternative energy sources to bringing back the gold standard. After traveling to his home LaRouche pointed to a sitting room that was clustered with maps and reports and asked me to sit in one chair while he lounged in another. It was quite obvious that our previous meeting had an effect on him because he tried to purge the view of being an anti-Semitic that I had perceived. "Ronald, I am not anti-Jewish, in fact, we have many supporters who are Jewish. What we are opposed to is the discarding of the Muslim peoples and their being relegated to a subservient status in their own homeland."

I let him finish his fifteen minute speech clarification of my original perception and then voiced my personal convictions. "I concur in part with what you just said. I totally agree that the Muslim people of the world are our equals and deserve their rightful place in the world, but trying to achieve their goals through terrorist acts is not the answer. I'm not saying all of them do this, of course not. Most Muslims are peaceful and should be viewed as our brothers and sisters. However, the Jewish people also have those same rights and the location of the county of Israel where they migrated to thousands of years ago." I then told him that if the Muslims stopped reacting with violence and stopped considering Judaism as a flawed religion which is now ingrained into every Islamic student in the madrassas located throughout the world, then we would have a chance at togetherness. I went on that if what he was telling me was his view, he should then correct that misnomer and project himself and his political organization as a man and a politician that stood for brotherhood and rationalization versus the negative opinions that many Americans had of him.

LaRouche elaborated about the problems of being misquoted by the press and the misinformation being stoked by his numerous antagonists. I questioned him about his multinational associates and followers and inquisitively looked for an answer to what the Agency wanted to know. He always skirted the issue and his response was, "In order to solve the problems of a diverse nation that does not limit trade and idealism to its borders, one must address the needs of the international community as a whole. We cannot turn our backs on the Third World and its poverty which are the very creation of a capitalist order that advantageously reaps the harvest of the ignorant and poor."

I thought to myself; *these were not the words of an anarchist, nor the ideas of an uncaring lost soul!* Still, I felt skeptical, and even though I wanted to believe, I knew that so many prior political figures voiced the same concerns and once in power were quickly corrupted by their authority and invincibility.

After listening to me, he calmly said that he would like to join forces with me and have me as his Vice Presidential candidate. I responded by letting him know, again, that I was under federal investigation and that it would be a hindrance to him and his candidacy. "Jesus and Thomas A. Becket also suffered from investigations and persecutions, Ron. The history of mankind is drenched in the sorrow of wrongful misuse of investigative authority." I thanked him for the honor that he had bestowed on me and his personal view of my problem, even though Jesus and Thomas A. Becket were poor correlations for my plight to be compared to. I told him I would like to have a week or two to think about his offer.

The flight home was smooth but the emotions and self questioning I felt was troubling. I told myself that if this man really was misquoted in his being anti-Semitic and about some of his views, then he is innocent and should not be condemned by the rest of us. If this was an act of trying to convince me of his brotherly approach just to win me over, then he is the guiltiest of the guilty. As a note: I later found out that LaRouche lied to me and is really anti-Semitic. This is unfortunate, how can anybody be so hateful?

After placing my rake against the tree and meeting with the Agency I was notified that because of the federal investigation against Onyx that they could not have any further contact with me and that once it was over, we could renew our relationship. My snarling lips spewed words of not assisting me when they knew the truth, and that if Al Hartel was alive I would not have been left high and dry to fend for myself.

Angry and upset, I thought, *I never took one penny from the Agency or the FBI. I followed my conscience and here I am—a victim of my attempts to correct injustice. Boy what a fool I have been, what a fucking, fucking fool. I must be the dumbest person alive.* Here I was, not only deceiving my loved ones, but I was misleading myself. My belief is a panacea, but a figment of a wild imagination that has no place in the real world. My thoughts were of despair; any hope was left to my daily prayers.

Despair

I DECIDED TO SEVER ALL TIES WITH the feds and even though I would never align myself with the despised Mafia, I now started questioning whether evil is ingrained in all of us and if there is a way of escaping its madness.

I have always queried my motives; ever since I became a source, I believed that I acted with my feelings for the less fortunate and the emotional sadness that I feel when confronted by social injustice.

Still, I knew I had a shadow side. I didn't like it, but it was there and it desired revenge and I got down on my knees and prayed for a violent death and punishment for the Mafiosi and their league of vicious men. What bothered me the most was that I wanted it to happen, I wanted them out of the way and that they were made to suffer for their sins. But who am I, a judge and jury? Those decisions should be left to God, his wisdom and the general public. My hatred had now lowered me to their standard and I became ashamed of my feelings and what I had become. I started to think the only way out of this dreaded emotion was to focus my attention elsewhere, but I couldn't leave the union. I remained tied to a paycheck as well as my fight with the Cosa Nostra.

I turned to a close friend of mine, the Reverend Herb Reid, a black Baptist minister who preached at a small rundown church, and my closest friend, James "Tex" Smith. Our conversations were laced with my despair and even though I never let them know of my cooperation with the feds, I did inform them of the many crises I faced and hoped that I could maintain my strength to see this ordeal through.

I started attending Gethsemane Baptist Church gatherings (in my old Fruit-Belt neighborhood) and continued my previous assistance with fund raising and whatever else I could offer to the parishioners. I have always tried to assist the needy and I'm proud that something inside of me and my feelings for them was ever-present. Unfortunately, however, I knew that in my life I had achieved gains at the expense of others and I hated myself for doing that. I never lost sight that my life has also been fastened with self gratitude, getting more, even when I didn't need it. This bothered me and it bothered me a lot. Just because I organized relief support for earthquake victims, helped feed the poor and assisted with many charities, this was not good enough. It just wasn't enough and I would re-enter my world of darkness. Feeling exposed with the reality of a probable calamity, I tried to get hold of my emotions and tried to focus on the positives; my family was healthy and well fed and I was still here. Wanting to use the union to aid the needy as I tried to do in the past, would be greeted by the mob and its "How can we financially benefit from this" type of attitude.

On September 28, 1983, together with Tom Giammaresi, Carl Mastykarcz and William Sterling, we went to trial on the Onyx matter. It ended in a mistrial because of some prosecutorial misconduct. Our second trial ended on March 27, 1985, with a hung jury. What was very strange, and maybe miraculous, about the case was on the very first day of court my wife and I, while walking towards the courthouse, spotted a woman crying and confused. It was quite cold outside and I walked up to her and asked her if she was all right. She responded that she was cold and was looking for the federal building. I took off my coat, wrapped it around her shoulders and escorted her to the building. When we were selecting a jury, I noticed that the woman was one of the potential jurors. I told Paul Cambria to keep her just in case she remembered me. After the hung jury was announced I learned that she was one of the jurors that found us not guilty. I felt then, and still do, that fate and God's hands brought about this chance encounter and its possible assistance in the outcome.

The government did not want to go through the expense of having a third trial, nor did we. It was arranged that we plead guilty to a misdemeanor and get on with our lives. What a relief this was to me and the hell I was going through. The FBI, it turned out, felt the same way and let me know.

Buffalo – Rochester War

I BECAME MORE ACTIVE AGAIN WITH THE bureau which really did its best to stand by me and I was proud to be involved with such a bunch of great people. Marty Steinberg was now out of the Strike Force and a welcome relief for me and many others.

By 1980, the Magaddino realm was torn by a war with the forces of Frangiamore-Todaro on one side and a breakaway faction led by Rene Piccarreto of Rochester, New York on the other. Back in 1969, when my father was given the reins of the empire, he, for whatever reason, decided that the Capos under him should be given more power and the power of the boss become more of an overseer with less authority. This gave Dan Sansanese Sr. and Roy Carlisi more power than my father had.

He allowed Toronto, Ontario (which had been under Magaddino control since the 1950s) and Paul Volpe to exercise its own authority and not have to pay any tribute. The same held true in Rochester under Frank Valenti. When he was ousted in 1972, Rochester did not relinquish what had been given to them. Animosity broke out and even the Commission rulings could not bring Rochester back into the fold. Shooting started and soon both factions were subjected to disloyalty.

It was long suspected that Billy Sciolino had made a deal with the Rochester faction of the family and this led to his being watched and monitored by the Frangiamore-led forces. Somehow they learned that he was also an informant who was flipped by the bureau after being jammed up on a couple of felonies. It was said, but I do not know if it is true, that while working as a union steward on the rapid transit project, Sciolino was discovered talking and leaking information to an FBI agent. I personally think it was his joining Piccarreto and turning his back on his Borgata that brought him the lead-filled fate that soon would befall him.

The die was cast and on March 7, 1980, Sciolino was gunned down by at least two shooters with well aimed bullets to his midsection and to his head while he relaxed in a construction trailer on Main Street in Buffalo. There was nothing new in this, killing was a way of life to the mob, and every now and then it would send a message or cleanse itself of informants and disloyal servants.

I was at the Union Hall when the shooting took place and was in the middle of a grievance hearing with the Construction Industry Employers Association and was quite surprised to see the two Pieri brothers, Danny Sansanese Jr. and Joey "Pizza" Todaro decide to sit in and be part of the grievance procedure. This was the first and *only* time that they ever sat in on a grievance hearing. At the time I thought—Finally, they are taking an interest in the affairs of the union. That feeling soon departed after I learned that it was merely a ruse to have eyewitnesses for their whereabouts during the time of the shooting.

In 1985, I quietly established a new snow-plowing company named Timoney Technology Inc. and placed my brother Patrick as the owner. I wanted to take every precaution to avoid what had happened to me with Sno-Go Plowing Service and the mob. This time it was different. I had the assurances of the family boss that the new company was not going to be victimized by the mob and its leaching.

Unlike my father, my relationship with Joe Todaro Sr. was good and I sensed he liked me. Deep inside I knew this powerful Mafiosi would keep his word and while he was the boss, he always did. In 1986, while my brother wanted to plow driveways, I told him to hold off and I talked to Buffalo Mayor Jimmy Griffin and the New York State Department of Transportation. After reaching an agreement with the state, I called my brother and told him to get the equipment ready for a major project in the city. This time I made more than $270,000 in profit and in a very short time. I suggested that my brother use the money to repair the equipment and after taxes, to save the profits.

Bringing Back Vic Randaccio

Danny Sansanese was totally out of control. He removed the custodian, Oliver Wright ("Snowflakes" or as Danny Sansanese would say, "Old Black Joe"), whom I placed in his position after my election and who was only receiving a pittance of a pension and needed the extra money. Sansanese didn't care and gave the job, as well as all purchasing of office supplies, to his brother-in-law Frank Fragale's company.

With the exception of the needed Jennie DeAngelo, the secretaries were replaced with Dan Sansanese's daughter Roseanne, and Vincenza "Vinny" Frangiamore, the Farmer's daughter.

I had to somehow neutralize this maniac, but how? I devised a plan that the mob could not refuse; bring back Victor Randaccio! In my mind it had to work. His brother, the powerful Freddy, would be getting out of jail soon and I felt sure that The Boys wanted him to come back to a clean house.

The first thing I did was to arrange a secret meeting with Victor and Freddy's nephew Joey "Blue-eyes" LoTempio, the ousted Union Benefit Fund administrator. LoTempio was very affable and I told him of my plan. He liked the idea and assured me so would Vic. After telling my father to arrange a meeting with the Farmer and after a couple of postponements, it was arranged for the Farmer to meet me at the Howard Johnson's restaurant located in the Buffalo suburb of Athol Springs. At first, the Farmer didn't like my proposal, but after listening to me tell him of its advantages, he seemed to change his mind.

The very next week I was commanded to attend a sit-down with the Buffalo Family hierarchy at a restaurant on Military Road. Besides the Farmer, Joe Pieri Sr., Joe Todaro Sr., Roy Carlisi, Mob Capo Charlie Cassaro (who took over the Cammilleri Family) and my father were present.

My father was asked to go into the other room as we spoke. I reiterated what I told the Farmer about bringing back Vic Randaccio. They asked me why I wanted to do this. I explained, without telling them my ulterior motive, that Vic needed a couple more years to obtain his pension and it would be a good move. It would unite the still-separated members. I was then excused and told to join my father in the other room. Within 15 minutes they asked me back and wanted to know what would happen to the Mutt, referring to Danny Sansanese Jr., who currently held the secretary-treasurer's job. I told them that I could create a new business agent position for him. The Farmer then said, "Ronnie, I speak for all of us, you go ahead and arrange it. Tomorrow when the Mutt comes into the Union Hall, tell him secretly that you have been told by your father to bring him to a meeting. Then come here at 1:00 p.m." I told them that Danny didn't always come into the Union Hall office and rarely that early. "If that happens, tell your father and we will rearrange it."

One never really knew when this creep would bequeath his presence upon us, but on this day he arrived at the Union Hall around 11:00 a.m. Whispering, I told him I wanted to talk with him and he told me to go into the walk-in-safe, normally left open during business hours. I told him that we had a meeting at 1:00 p.m. with the Farmer and that I did not know what it was about.

We arrived at the same restaurant where we had the meeting the day before. Joe Todaro Sr. asked the bewildered Sansanese to take a seat next to him. The Farmer said, "Danny, I am speaking for all, we want you to give up the secretary-treasurer position. Victor Randaccio will replace you. Ronnie is to create a new business agent position for you in the union." Sansanese said in Italian, "Se il mio padre fosse qui questo non stava accadendo; a chi dai il dito si prende anche il braccio." (If my father was here (referring to his deceased father) this would not be happening; give them a finger and they'll take an arm.)

Anger spewed from the table and Joe Todaro Sr. stood up as did the elder Pieri and both in a rage scolded the Mutt. "You are to apologize to this table immediately and don't ever talk to us like that again." Sansanese immediately apologized to the hierarchy and humbly begged their forgiveness. "Ronnie," the Farmer said, "implement the changes and do it in a way that does not bring any unneeded publicity." After regaining a little composure, the still-shaking Sansanese asked if he could be the one that speaks at the meeting and announces that Vic Randaccio would be the new secretary-treasurer. "Okay," said the Farmer, "but just make sure everything goes smooth."

The ride back to the Union Hall was not the most pleasant ride I ever took. The Mutt continued his tirade about what just took place and blamed it on Todaro Sr. little knowing that it was really me.

With Vic back in the union, everything quickly changed. After being belittled in an election against me, he was a different person. Soon the animosity that we previously had for each other disappeared and we became extremely close. We both enjoyed each other's company and talking about the union and the way it was. Danny Sansanese wanted to keep his office, which Randaccio agreed with and really didn't want anyway. Randaccio also wanted to get rid of the soda pop and cigarette machines that the Mutt put in the area where the unemployed workers would meet. Sansanese fought tooth and nail to keep the machines and eventually the family agreed to let them stay. The attitude in the office was much better, but Sansanese still tried to maintain his authoritative rule that we all ignored.

Mobbed-up Unions

As a result of the *National Labor Relations Act* of 1935, (NLRA) union growth in America blossomed. By 1950, many major U.S. ports and municipalities had already fallen victim to the rapidly growing list of mob-controlled unions. The mob hierarchy was not what you would call school smart, but they knew enough to surround themselves with attorneys and consultants who were.

Knowing that if a segment of the construction industry and dockworkers were controlled this could springboard their input into the indirect control of the other unions active in these areas. The mob's influence could now mutate to numerous employee unions and utilize them not only for financial gain, but more importantly for political power. In cities such as New York, the control was deep and under the tutelage of John "Dio" Dioguardi, a member of the Lucchese crime family, control of unions spread. Dioguardi, ventured to many American cities and explained to the various criminal Borgatas how to wrest control from the honest union officials and replace them with the mob's chosen representatives. By the late 1950s many Western New York unions were deeply influenced by the mob. Buffalo Teamsters Local 449 with Anthony Sorrentino, his brother Paul and future head Vic DiFlavio were under control. In concert with Laborers' Local 210, the mob could control many jobs and deliveries to construction projects.

Hospital Council and Local 4 of the Hotel & Restaurant Workers under Frank Ervolino, the nephew of Sam Cariola, would provide kickbacks to the mob as well as protect mob-connected hotels and restaurants such as the Executive Inn owned by Patrick Cosentino, and after his death by his two sons James and Patrick Jr. To a lesser degree, but still controlled, the Buffalo Firefighters Union, the Police Benevolent Association and the Buffalo blue collar city workers were influenced.

The International Longshoremen's Association was highly controlled via the Gambino and Genovese families and the Chicago Outfit. International Union officers such as John Bowers, Thomas W. "Teddy" Gleason, Gambino mobster Anthony Scotto and Robert E. Gleason all answered to the syndicate. The Tile, Marble, Terrazzo, Finishers & Shopmen International Union merged with the Bricklayers International Union under Pascal "Patsy" Di James (formerly of Buffalo). The Building and Construction Trades Council of the AFL-CIO was under Robert Georgine.

The Buffalo Family did not have any control, at least, to the best of my knowledge, of the Longshoremen. Pat Sullivan, who headed up some of their Buffalo operations, was a close friend and confidant and I know that he was not mobbed-up. He had a personal dislike for the mob and on a number of occasions he spoke about his bitter hatred of their control and what they had done to his beloved union.

Union expert Johnny Dioguardi appeared in a series of 33 articles in the 1949, *New York Sun.* Reporter Malcolm

Johnson wrote about organized crime's control of the New York City and northern New Jersey docks. The mob and its lackeys were taken aback by the stories and in 1954, when the movie, *On the Waterfront,* starring Marlon Brando came out; they were dumbfounded and bitterly angry. Mostly because this noted actor would take such a role after the mob helped him with some requests. *On the Waterfront* was supposedly based on corrupt union official John Bowers and mobster Albert "Mad-Hatter" Anastasia, who was boss of what is now called the Gambino Family.

It was the highly regarded Johnny Dio and the Philadelphia-born Sam Cariola (whose expertise dealt with hotels and restaurants), who together did more than anyone else in bringing the workers of that industry into the mob's fold. After Cariola moved to Buffalo (at the request of Magaddino) he was attending but not caught at the now-famous 1957, Apalachin meeting that took place at the home of Joseph Barbara Sr. Vito Genovese, besides being the boss of the largest family in the United States, remained quite close to Stefano Magaddino and Russell Bufalino (who later became the so-called Boss of Northeastern Pennsylvania and answered to the Buffalo Family and later directly to the Genovese Borgata). I met with Russell Bufalino on a number of occasions and he was always affable.

Under the tutelage of Magaddino and his son in-law, Capo Jimmy LaDuca, Cariola took control of Local 66 of the Hotel and Restaurant Employees Union located in Buffalo. Cariola was all over the map and overall was a prominent figure with the International Union headed up by Edward Hanley and controlled by the Chicago Outfit. Joseph Todaro Sr. and Cariola would refer to each other as cousins, but I do not know if this was true. Because of his ability to travel to many cities under the pretext of union work, Cariola became a messenger, not only for Buffalo, but many of the syndicate families. Contrary to public opinion, Sam was never a made man. His trips to New Orleans and his meetings with Carlos Marcello and company or Santo Trafficante Jr. of Florida may have involved conversations related to the killing of President Kennedy, but I do not believe Cariola was involved. The mob does not operate that way. If they really were involved in the killing of President Kennedy, only highly trusted wiseguys would have been included. Eventually Cariola headed up the large Western New York Maritime Trades Department of the AFL-CIO. Over the years Cariola and I were together on hundreds of occasions and our conversations always pertained to mob activity. It was Cariola who arranged for a couple of International Unions to loan the Diplomat Hotel (located in Hollywood, Florida) needed money. Eventually the hotel was purchased by the Plumbers and Pipe Fitters Union for $800 million.

Joe Todaro Sr., Sam Cariola and numerous mobsters would have their evening meal at the plush beach-located hotel in a secret vaulted room which was built to hold clandestine conversations. Cariola and his legal cohort, David Knoll, also arranged for the Todaro Family to purchase the Golden Strand Hotel in Florida. After the Todaros and Nicholas "Sonny" Mauro took ownership, we, as well as a number of other union representatives, were required to stay there while in Florida. The rooms were not great and the food not that good but the hotel soon became a mob hangout. We were told not to discuss business in the rooms but to put on a bathing suit or a "Members Only" shorts and jacket (mobsters always wore them with gold jewelry hanging around their necks) and discuss our business while swimming in the ocean. In Buffalo the Cosentino's Executive Inn was designated as the hotel we had to use for all functions and for any guests we brought to Buffalo.

In early 1983, while flying back to Buffalo from a Washington, D.C. meeting, I was spotted by Jack Kemp who was also flying coach. He changed seats and sat in the empty seat next to me. After exchanging pleasantries, he said, "You have all this money in the union pension fund, why don't you and the other unions invest it in new construction projects?" After telling him of the problems that the Teamsters Union had with kickbacks, he said, "You can do it Ronnie."

Some time after that, Kemp followed up with a phone call and informed me of a new downtown hotel that the legit businessman Paul Snyder wanted to build. I agreed to meet with Snyder and Ross Kenzie who was then the president of the Buffalo Savings Bank. I contacted Bob Logan, who headed up the employer trustees of the Buffalo Laborer's Pension Fund, and Michael Fitzpatrick, business manager for the Ironworkers Local 6 Union. (Mike later became general secretary-treasurer of the Ironworkers International Union and a member of the Erie County legislature). We met in Kenzie's posh office at the bank and learned that a proposed Hyatt Hotel was in need of an additional $7 million. After about a month of wrangling, I, together with Fitzpatrick, informed Paul Snyder and Ross Kenzie that we thought we could get the money if approved by the other pension fund(s) trustees.

In Hot Water Again

AFTER LEARNING OF MY INVOLVEMENT IN the Snyder project, Joe Todaro Sr. told me not to get involved; I should not have even started the talks with Snyder and company. I wrongly put the blame on Bob Logan, but I think the smart elder Todaro (who had become the boss of the family in 1981) knew the truth. I did not rush back and inform Snyder that we would were not able to get trustee approval. Soon, however, I had to see the Buffalo Mafia boss again. This time, Todaro agreed to have the benefit fund finance the project, but pointed out that he never wanted me to finance another project or use the benefit fund assets without family approval.

In late 1983, the Western New York Building Trades formed a foundation to invest in area construction projects with me as its chairman. I knew that the mob would take full advantage of it, but I also felt that here was an opportunity for the bureau to finally catch The Boys and help put an end to their revolting reign.

Soon after the construction of the Hyatt Hotel began I learned that Philip Schwab's Cuyahoga Wrecking (also the owner of North American Demolition, Daniela Corporation, Iroquois Wrecking, Phoenix Wrecking, Irondequoit Corporation, Berlin Wrecking, Rapid Demolition and many other companies) was going to perform cleanup and interior demolition. Schwab was a throwback to the old way of doing things. Born in Buffalo, Schwab became connected to the local Jewish Mafia as well as the Cosa Nostra. His ability to kickback and bribe public officials led him to national distinction and a favored partner status.

At one time Schwab controlled a large amount of the Hilton Head, South Carolina resort where he laundered a vast amount of the resorts proceeds. He also was involved in and controlled seven banks in the United States. Through his connections he also gained control of a racetrack in the state of Washington. The affable Schwab (who was of Irish and German descent) was reaping millions, as were many of the mob dynasties. Schwab companies gutted the old Yankee Stadium and demolished the original Madison Square Garden.

I knew, as did many law enforcement officials, that Schwab would tell his supervisors to destroy any and all records that they had in their possession in an effort to thwart any current or planned investigations.

No sooner did Cuyahoga Wrecking start demolition for the new Hyatt Hotel that I ascertained that Schwab was using non-union employees. Pieri-connected workers were taking the marble flooring from the old building. I informed Dan Domino about this and told him that this was really embarrassing. Our loan agreement contained language that all work being performed at the Hotel must be union. He eventually corrected the non-union problem but did not stop the Pieris from pillaging the decorative walnut, mahogany wood, and polished stone from the former furniture store.

Dresser-Rand Scandal

In 1986, I was made aware that the vast Dresser-Rand plant, a former compressor manufacturing and railway parts facility, was turned over to the *Erie County Industrial Development Agency* (ECIDA) and was going to be put up for sale very cheap, with a caveat that jobs must be created at the facility. I contacted the Building Trades to see if there was any interest in purchasing the large facility. Most every trade was interested in the site and it would be perfect to set up as a Building Trades training facility. I also got in touch with the head of the Buffalo AFL-CIO, George Wessel, who had a seat on the ECIDA. He liked the idea and also had a couple of major companies, like Canadian-based Bombardier, interested in developing an American-based facility in the Buffalo area. At that time they were refurbishing and making metro and railway cars and the Dresser plant facility would be perfect for them. Wessel then made arrangements for me to visit the Dresser plant. I was totally in awe of what I saw. Everything was left by Dresser including very valuable equipment, a train locomotive, millions of dollars of machinery, as well as numerous offices and outer space.

Ironworker Union leader Mike Fitzpatrick was also an official with the ECIDA. He contacted me to let me know that a James H. "Harry" Williams-connected businessman, William Irr, who ran a small plumbing outfit called Irr Plumbing, also wanted the Dresser property. There was some hazardous waste at the site that needed to be cleaned up but it was not much and the Laborers' and other trades could easily clean it.

I was staggered to learn that it would only take $1.00 to purchase this large plant and all its equity. I contacted local businessman Leonard Greenfield who agreed to pay $250,000 for the scrap steel that was on the site and then contacted Buffalo attorney Richard Wyssling to represent the Building Trades. We drafted a proposal for the property which included: we would not sell any of the equipment or any of the property, an offer to the county of $250,000 plus a guarantee to bring in new businesses and a timetable to create more than 1,000 jobs. We felt that this was a deal that they had to accept. The ECIDA head, Richard Swist, asked me if I could meet with him over our proposal. I went to his office with the knowledge that William Irr could never match our bid or the ability to create the number of jobs we projected.

Swist advised me that the deal with Irr was already complete and it was too late for us and our proposal. I checked with George Wessel and Mike Fitzpatrick who emphatically stated that it needed the whole board's approval and was not complete. I called Swist back and told him that he had lied to me and I would pursue the matter legally. Within a few days Erie County Executive Edward "Eddie" Rutkowski telephoned me and asked if I could meet with him.

We met at ECIDA headquarters and Rutkowski beseeched me to see if I would take a smaller portion of the facility because they already had Irr on board and he wanted to take over the larger portion of the plant. I asked him just what smaller portion he had in mind and he said that it was only an office building that did not really serve our training needs. I enlightened Rutkowski that this was a scam and I would bring the matter to court. I immediately had attorney Wyssling start preparing for a lawsuit when Roger Bennett, the brother-in-law of James "Harry" Williams called me and asked if I could meet Harry at the Cosentino-owned Executive Inn. At the meeting Harry asked me if I could back off, that William Irr was a close friend and partner. I stated loudly, "No way, Harry!" I told him we would fight this transfer in court. I then abruptly left.

Within days Joe Pizza Todaro grabbed me and demanded that I back off. Telling me that there was more to this than I knew; I was to back off totally and stop any lawsuit proceedings. It was Danny Domino who then clued me in on who was behind it. He said that the Todaros, and Danny and Victor Sansanese had taken over what were previously Sammy Pieri connections to the Williams brothers. I expressed my total dissatisfaction; I now had to go back and tell the Building Trades, Leonard Greenfield, and Wyssling, that we had to back off.

With little fanfare the facility was transferred to William Irr and after secretly selling and transferring quite a large amount of the equipment and machinery, he auctioned off what remained. Dan Domino later let me know that the Sansaneses were given $400,000 in cash of which $150,000 was kicked-back to Joe Pizza and his father. Only a handful of jobs were created and the bust out of the site was completed. I was really surprised and disappointed that the media or a watch group did not pick up on this.

I had had it with these rape artists—how corrupt political officials and business leaders could do this kind of bunkum. Hell, I needed money too, but my conscience seemed to kick in every time my desires took over and I thought about going along with their illegal activity. There were a number of times that I almost went along and took a kickback, but something inside of me took over and stopped me. I am a very open person especially when it comes to my many faults. I am sure I would not have been able to live with myself knowing that I took money from the poor and the people that I represented. I still, to this day, cannot fathom how these people can enjoy the acquisitions made off the backs of innocent workers.

My last hopes to see a change with the union were dying fast and I wanted out. The bureau kept telling me to "hang in there, please, Ronnie."

Here it had been almost 15 years and any chance of success was passing into a memory. I hung in there, but I knew I could not take much more of Joe Todaro Jr. and the Sansaneses' slop. To add insult to injury, I was now being required to bring Joe Pizza's brother-in-law Peter Gerace in as a business agent.

Laborers' International Union – Death of Peter Fosco

BACK IN 1975, PETER FOSCO DIED and I attended the wake together with Genovese-controlled New York City Mason Tenders District Council President and power Gaspar Lupo. While at the wake it was learned that the general secretary-treasurer of the LIUNA, Terence O'Sullivan, wanted to take the vacated president's position. He was previously appointed to his position with the mob's blessing in 1968. Lupo informed Vice President Mike Lorello and me that they would not allow O'Sullivan to have the president position. I was approached by Vince Solano, a powerful Chicago Capo who I knew quite well and previously visited us at our home, and asked to go outside with him for a minute.

We proceeded to a parked car that was a block away and driven by Tony Accardo's son-in-law, Ernest Kumerow. In the passenger front seat was Tony Accardo, who said he could not go inside because the feds were most likely watching. Accardo voiced, "Say hello to your father and Roy Carlisi for me." He went on about how fond he was of them and softly demanded that I not get involved in the campaigning taking place inside the funeral home. He said the general president position was going to go to Fosco's son Angelo and that Vernie Reed would replace O'Sullivan, who would be required to retire from the union, or else. I assured him that I would never get involved and that I was already made aware by Gaspar Lupo and Vinny Solano.

This was my first meeting with the Laborers' Union's real power and he apprised me that if I ever needed help, he would always be there for me, I just needed to contact Vinny (Solano) and he would get a message to him. I leaned over to kiss him on the cheek but he told me, "Not here, we may be being watched." After that he departed and Vince and I walked back to the wake. I chatted with Vernie Reed (who was from the state of Washington) and whom I first met when I was in Washington, D.C. Unlike the mob-controlled officials, Reed was smart and knew the union business. I liked him quite a lot but deep down inside I fathomed that he had to be aware of the real control of this International Union; he was only a loyal front man. Solano then grabbed me and introduced me to the Chicago Outfits-controlled union officials. One by one they greeted me with respect and dignity. Many said they knew my father and all knew Roy Carlisi.

Within a few days Angelo Fosco's appointment to president and Vernie Reed's to the general secretary-treasurer of LIUNA was made public. O'Sullivan was out and even though he remained close to Arthur E. Coia and his son Arthur A. Coia, (or Jr.), Chicago and New York wanted nothing to do with him.

In 1979, Vernie Reed died and the New York City-based Commission, together with the Patriarca Family, appointed Coia Sr. to the vacant position.

Mike Lorello would point out that it was he and Gaspar Lupo who had lobbied and got the approval for their good friend Coia. I knew this to be true. Arthur E. Coia was liked by most of the Eastern U.S. crime families. When control of the Laborers' International Union was established, it was agreed by all that Chicago would have responsibility for the president's position. The general secretary's position was open and could go to anyone, provided they were controlled. Most of the vice president and regional managers were open positions with the exception of the New England, New York and Illinois regional areas.

Like the general secretary-treasurer position, the people appointed to this echelon must be under control. To maintain an air of legitimacy, Robert Powell, who was black, rose to the rank of vice president. Both Coia and Fosco considered Powell a threat and wanted him and his supporters out of the union. I liked Bob Powell and considered him a decent and hardworking union official but I was ordered by Lorello and Coia to stay away from him. According to Powell, Angelo Fosco threatened him with death, which he took very seriously. One of Powell's supporters, Philadelphia Local 332 official Benny Medina, who I knew, was openly campaigning against the International Union's hierarchy; he was shot and killed in 1982. I do not know if this was a Powell-related incident or because Medina announced his candidacy to run for the Local Unions Business Manager position; but soon after the killing Bob Powell resigned.

Terence O'Sullivan was a born insurance fraud schemer who was indicted in 1981, with Anthony Accardo, Santo Trafficante, Angelo Fosco, Alfred Pilotto, James Corporale, Paul Fosco, Johnny Giardiello, Sal Tricario, George Wuagneux and Bernie Rubin. (Fashion designer Albert Nipon's brother Edward and his wife Sylvia were killed at the bequest of Rubin in 1987). The scheme involved selling and administering fringe benefit programs for union members and also served as conduits for kickback monies from consultants and administrators as well as the companies Sage Corporation and an associated entity known as Drake Towers Joint Venture, both located in Florida. Joe Hauser, who ended up in the witness protection program, claimed in his testimony that he set up the scam and that ten cents out of every dollar of the membership contributions would be kicked-back to the mobsters and corrupt union officials.

Santo Trafficante was excused from the trial because of illness. On June 18, 1982, Anthony Accardo, Angelo Fosco and Terence O'Sullivan were acquitted. The remainder were convicted. I knew that Jimmy "Caps" Corporale, "Big" Sal Tricario and Johnny Giardiello agreed to take the rap to protect Accardo, Angelo Fosco and Terry O'Sullivan. The Chicago Family was supposed to take care of the convicted fall guys, but only took care of Corporale. In February 1984, while in Florida, Tricaro and Giardiello, who were awaiting their appeal, complained to me that Fosco and Accardo had fucked them.

They also griped to Coia Sr., who was sitting with us at the table in the Fountain Bleu Hotel, who secretly agreed to help them financially. At future Florida meetings with Coia Sr. he surreptitiously slipped a stuffed envelope to the two labor leaders who were out on appeal. Coia would point out to me that it was he, not Fosco, who was providing the needed financial assistance. By this time Coia Sr. hated Angelo Fosco and wanted him out of the union.

Joseph Hauser was the main witness in the Fosco-Accardo case. He got his start as an insurance dealer and a swindler via his relationship with Irving Davidson, who previously used his lobby services to assist Jimmy Hoffa and the Teamsters International Union. Davidson had ties to many Unions, including Laborers' International. Davidson, had a strong relationship to the New Orleans-based Marcello Family and later on with Ralph Sorrentino, a Buffalo wise-guy and friend of my father.

In the early fifties Sorrentino moved to Florida and aligned himself with the Trafficante's. Financially strapped, Hauser familiarized Carlos Marcello and other mobsters on how to make millions through labor racketeering benefit fund connivances. Marcello reached out and had a couple of International unions invest some of their benefit fund money with his new so-called money making-machine, namely Joe Hauser.

By 1978, Hauser had to turn over almost all the proceeds that were coming in illegally and the mob stripped him bare. The Securities and Exchange Commission and FBI conducted an investigation into the now broke Hauser and his companies. He was indicted and pleaded guilty. But Hauser wanted no part of being confined to jail and quickly made a deal with the FBI. Hauser helped the bureau with Operation BRILAB which resulted in only two convictions out of the 70 who were indicted.

Irv Davidson was not only a lobbyist; he had strong connections in Central America as well as with the CIA. He previously worked for the oil baron Murchison family of Dallas and allegedly developed close ties to President Lyndon Johnson's friend Bobby Baker. He was a mover in the "shadow world" and the "Industry" as many a CIA officer would call it.

Even though my father never met him personally, in a conversation about him he said, "Sorrentino referred to him as a door opener and Davidson had previously performed superbly for The Boys." My father then questioned why I was asking him all this dung. I countered that Davidson's name kept popping up and Mike Lorello (who at that time started talking about everything) kept telling me that this guy (Davidson) was smart and Lorello was constantly cursing union attorney Robert Connerton and blaming Angelo Fosco for bringing Hauser into the fold. My father then said Hauser was a paid liar and even though some of what he said was true, the guy liked to exaggerate and build on more than what was really there. On oh-so-many occasions, Sal Tricario (who was killed on September 20, 2011, after he lost control of his car and crashed into a concrete pole) said that Hauser told him that Marcello said he was involved in the assassination of President Kennedy and that Davidson had played a part in the killing. I told him I didn't believe that garbage. He knew as well as I did that if Marcello was involved in the planning and killing of a president, he was not going to let some swindler like Hauser know about it. I expressed to him all I knew about Davidson was that he was a person who makes things happen and was probably too smart to be involved in something like that.

I eventually did meet Joe Hauser, I think sometime in 1991. I was invited to speak at a *Department of Labor* (DOL) gathering that was taking place at the Hilton Hotel in downtown Seattle, Washington. One of the criminal investigators introduced me to Joe Hauser. I was very cool to him, but still

I shook his hand. He said, "I respect you, Ronald, for what you are doing." I thanked him for his remarks and rejoined the others. To me he was like most of the informants used by the bureau; in my opinion Hauser was just a criminal looking to stay out of jail. Many of them tend to exaggerate the truth in the hope that they got a better deal from the Justice Department. In my opinion, Hauser was no different.

In September of 1981, Arthur E. Coia and son Arthur A. Coia, together with Raymond Patriarca Sr., boss of the New England Family, Albert J. LePore, the law partner of Arthur A. Coia., and Joseph J. Vacarro were indicted and had to stand trial in the Southern District of Florida. The government alleged that they had conspired to engage in labor racketeering. The indictment also alleged that the five defendants conspired to use their influence over the Laborers' International Union of North America and its subordinate bodies and affiliated employee benefit plans. According to the federal charges, the conspirators funneled the union's insurance and service business into insurance and service companies they had set up, and then charged the union members for the most expensive form of insurance. The conspirators thereafter looted the insurance premiums through the use of kickbacks, payoffs, unearned salaries and fees and improper personal expenses.

The charges that the government brought were true and Coia Sr. told me this on a number of occasions. Unfortunately, the solid case that the feds built was dismissed by the Florida District Court. The court concluded that as a matter of law the indictment failed to satisfy the statute of limitations and should be dismissed. Coia Sr. apprised me of the fact that he helped arrange for more than $300,000 to be secretly sent and used as bribe funds. Allegedly, the federal judge involved in the case was one of those bribed and it was allegedly arranged by Florida Congressman Alcee Hastings. Coia was not afraid to talk about his mob relationships and illegal activity. He always said he looked up to Patriarca and would do whatever the New England Boss wanted. In addition, he said that one of the witnesses in the case was killed in an automobile crash made to look like an accident. I never did find out who he meant but later on I asked Federal Prosecutor Ken Lowrie to look into it. He told me that it really was an accident and that Coia was probably just bragging.

Coia Sr. wanted me close to him and appointed me as a Trustee with the Laborers' International Training Fund. My visits and trips to see Coia, allowed me to see how he was prepping his son to take over. The law offices of Coia and LePore were located in the same Providence, Rhode Island building as the LIUNA office. Coia would arrange for me to stay at the Marriott Hotel located downtown and Armand "Mondo" Sabitoni, whom Coia Jr. traveled with quite frequently, would pick me up and take me to where I would meet the elder Coia.

Mondo was extremely close to Coia and Mondo's son, who had the same name, is a lawyer in the Coia Jr. law firm. Arthur Sr., at one of our many get-togethers, informed me that together with his son Arthur Jr., had set up the New England Defense Fund to pay the court costs for the victims of the wrath placed upon them by the FBI and Justice Department. Arthur and his son were wealthy; "The Kid," as Coia Jr. was referred to by many mob wiseguys, drove around in expensive Ferrari's. Like their respective fathers, the Kid and Raymond Patriarca Jr. were involved in many illegal activities and took kickbacks from their illegal operations. The one legal interest that both had is dog breeding. The Kid raised Rottweiler's and I never learned what type of dogs Patriarca Jr. raised.

We would visit Camille's Restaurant and have a plate of pasta with sauce name after the elder Coia. Mobsters, mobsters everywhere! The restaurant was a major mob hangout and serious business would take place in the kitchen. At one of the Camille meetings I was introduced to Steve Saccoccia who was a friend of Coia Jr. Later on Saccoccia was charged with laundering over $100 million in drug money.

Anthony Triani, a close friend and associate of the Coias, was asked to find Saccoccia a good attorney. The attorney he chose was Robert Luskin, who would later become somewhat famous as the Laborers' general executive board lawyer, directly responsible for the cleanup of the mob-controlled labor union. How or why they chose Luskin (a former Special Counsel to the Organized Crime and Racketeering Section of the U.S. Department of Justice) I do not know. Saccoccia paid Luskin more than $500,000 in gold bars obtained as a result of his illicit drug deals as well as more than $160,000 that was wire transferred to him from a secret Swiss account. Luskin claimed he never knew the booty was obtained from illegal activities. After reaching an agreement with the feds, Luskin forfeited $245,000 of his proceeds of the drug money. Eventually Luskin was chosen to represent President George W. Bush's advisor and Deputy Chief of Staff Karl Rove regarding the CIA leak scandal involving Valerie Plame Wilson and the revelation that she was a covert intelligence operative.

Toronto, Ontario - Infighting

By 1981, the Todaros were in complete control of the Buffalo mob. My relationship with Arthur E. Coia grew and he was constantly calling me at home and asking if I could travel with him to Toronto or elsewhere to solve a problem.

John Stefanini rose from the rank of being a laborer to becoming the business manager and secretary-treasurer of the Toronto-based Laborers Local 183, the single largest Local under the Laborers International Union umbrella having more than 13,000 members. Stefanini was not liked by Michael Gargaro, the business manager for Laborers Local 506. Gargaro blamed the more powerful Stefanini for interfering in his election and his union affairs. Coia did not like Stefanini either and privately told me that Gargaro was under his protection and he was going to stop the Stefanini interference one way or another.

Gargaro was defeated in an election and to prevent him losing his job and control, Coia Sr. placed the local union under trusteeship. My good friend Ugo Rossini, who was a LIUNA vice president at that time, accompanied us when the trusteeship took place. Compelled by Coia, Ugo Rossini had to secure the trusteeship and take any action necessary to complete the trusteeship. He pleaded with the elder Coia and humbly begged him not to make him do it. Rossini knew that the Canadian Laborers as a whole disliked the International and Coia; they considered the International Union as an enemy and not a good parent organization. I met with Coia, Stefanini (who I liked), Gargaro, Bob Connerton (lead attorney for the LIUNA) and Rossini on at least 15 occasions in Toronto. Stefanini made it quite clear with his initial coolness towards me (probably as a result of my being with Coia) and assuming I must be the enemy also.

Being on the border with Canada we Buffalonians have developed a better understanding about our neighbors to the north and their feelings about us. I knew that these fine people felt that some Americans would, for whatever reason, talk down to them or at least appear to do so. I mentioned this to Coia and advised him to be careful or we could have a revolution with the Canadian workers. Coia kept telling me that he would not desert Gargaro who by now became one of our regular travel companions.

Once when visiting and dedicating a newly completed training facility located in Albuquerque, New Mexico, Dominick Lopreato (the business manager of the Connecticut Laborers' District Council and Hartford-based Local 230) accompanied us and was constantly asked by Coia Sr. to "Sing for me, Dominic." Lopreato discussed his dislike for former Hartford-based mobster William "The Wild Guy" Grasso, the underboss to Patriarca who was killed in 1989, by rival Gaetano J. Milano. He would constantly talk about his freedom to act and how Coia Sr. kept the local hoods off of his back. Also joining us at the dinner table was James Merloni Jr., the head of all training operations in New England and Dominick DiGregorio, who ran one of the Boston locals. While Merloni Jr. drove us back to our hotel, Coia Sr. and I listened as Mike Gargaro, who was in the back seat with me, openly said that he wanted Stefanini killed. "I am willing to pay whatever it costs. I am not kidding; I want the son of a bitch out of my life."

None of us said a word and sat silently. Gargaro again repeated his requests a couple of times. With no response from us, Gargaro loudly and in a huff said, "If you guys don't want to listen, I will find someone who will." Even though he sounded as if he meant it, I tried to pass it off as only anger but I did not want to take a chance and when I returned to Buffalo let the bureau know about the threat.

In 1981, the bureau believed that they had a case against the Local 210 business agents and officers who every winter would use union funds to travel to Florida for a vacation; implementing a deception of visiting the Sunshine State to attend the annual AFL-CIO winter session meetings. The case was based in part on the information I provided. I was there for a meeting with Leo Nazdin, who headed up the International Union's Jurisdiction Department and was a very close friend. The union agents never attended one of the meetings and they were supposedly monitored by the Local FBI SPIT Team (I never learned what SPIT stood for). Vic Randaccio, Joe "Pizza" Todaro, Daniel Domino, Salvatore Caci, Leonard Falzone, John and Joe Pieri and Danny Sansanese were indicted by a federal grand jury in Buffalo for embezzling union funds. I was the only one not included and that obviously bothered me quite a lot. When asked why, I answered, "I probably was not included because I was really performing union work and spent at the minimum 8 hours a day in meetings"

The Local 210 agents needed a cover story cloak and Leonard Falzone asked me if Leo Nazdin and Arthur Coia Sr. would assist. I replied that Coia would but I had my doubts about Nazdin. After a phone call request, Arthur Coia Sr. immediately came to Buffalo and the following day we picked up his lawyer Anthony Triani at the airport. We proceeded to meet with the union lawyers at the Lipsitz, Green firm and later that day with attorney Harold Boreanaz. I did not, nor did the bureau, want me to be involved in the cover story and when I did meet with Nazdin, while in Buffalo, he let me know that he was going to limit his testimony to the truth and that he conducted Local 210 business with only me.

A shifty strategy was augmented whereby I was conducting the union's business but could not make any decision without my assistants and the other officers present. This was all a bunch of crap. I was there regarding jurisdictional problems with other building trades and my being there would not involve decision making. At first, I was to be called as a defense witness, who would have created a real quandary for me but the lawyers decided that Union General President Angelo Fosco and Arthur E. Coia were all the witnesses they needed.

The case was a mess from the start. The SPIT team had all the defendants mixed up and they identified pictures as Leonard Falzone, when, in fact, it was someone else. I personally know that surveillance of someone is much more difficult than what is perceived by the public. Long boring hours in waiting then losing the suspect at a red light happens quite a lot. All the defendants were acquitted and the bureau and DOJ were left to start all over again. After the trial, the defense attorneys told us all to keep a very low profile and that the feds would not give up.

Death of Joseph Fino

On his birthday in March of 1984, my father died from a heart attack. I was in Rochester, New York at the time assisting Loren Piccarreto (son of Rochester Mafia consigliere Rene Piccarreto) regarding the restructuring of Teamsters Local 118. The local Wegmans grocery chain planned to expand into Erie County and Loren wanted me to assist them with organizing. While in Rochester I also met with Robert Brown, the new business manager of Rochester Laborers' Local 435. I liked Bobby mostly because of the mob's and International Unions' dislike for him and his desire to help the workers. Todaro Jr. and Victor Sansanese repeatedly warned me to avoid him because he was black as well as uncontrolled. Like I said earlier, overall, many mobsters did not like black people! Why, I don't know. My father, Joe Occhino, Vito Domiano and Dan Domino always spoke highly of them and they were definitely not racist.

Regardless of my orders I met with Bob Brown anyway. By this time I started getting a little bolder but still leery. During our discussion I immediately sensed that Bobby Brown had guts and wanted to help correct the mob's control of the Local. I did not let him know of my feelings for his plight because I feared that it might get back. I indirectly tried to support him and later on when I was directed to establish a New York State Training Fund, I told him secretly to be careful. Today Bobby is somewhat of a hero in Rochester for helping to curtail the evil that for so many years controlled the Rochester construction industry and his local union.

I quickly departed from Rochester and did the 100 miles back to my home. I called Lombardo's Funeral Home located near my father's residence and made arrangements for the funeral of my beloved, dear father. My wife Donna and I went to my mother's house and were greeted by a very somber family. At the wake my good friends, Buffalo Mayor Jimmy Griffin, as well as Erie County Executive Edward Rutkowski, paid their respects, as did Jack Kemp and a number of political figures. Quite a few of the mobsters made an appearance, even though it was a shunned practice in part due to the unwanted publicity it would bring. By this time Joe Todaro Sr. and I were pretty close and he mentioned, "Ronnie, your father's death changes nothing and I want you to know that you are needed at Local 210 and you have my total support." I believed him and after my father's departure nothing changed except a rapid growing dislike for the Pieris by the Todaros and the remainder of the family.

Pieri / Todaro Friction

THERE WAS BAD BLOOD BETWEEN THE Pieris and the Todaros. It started over the placement of union stewards on key moneymaking projects. Joey "Pizza" Todaro, together with Leonard Falzone, were upset that they were not getting enough of the good steward positions; they felt that Dan Domino, who I still relied on to do the work, was giving the premium steward positions to the Pieris. The Union Hall was split! The Pieris rarely ventured out of their back offices and visited job sites. Vic Randaccio was with me and we tried our best to stay out of it.

Unlike my father, I got along pretty well with Joe Todaro Sr. He was probably the smartest of all the family bosses, which, in my opinion, included bosses from all over the country. We would talk union business in the walk-in-safe located at the La Nova Pizzeria that he owned. He wanted me to assist him with the internal union fight. I told him Danny Domino may be a thorn in his side but he was needed. He was the only one I had who would visit the jobs. Todaro did not object and said, "I want you to develop a plan that would keep this problem from boiling over."

The geographical area controlled by Laborers' Local 210 included Erie County, part of Cattaraugus County and part of North Tonawanda located in Niagara County. I decided to establish boundaries for each and every business agent. The southern tier would go to the Pieris, Cheektowaga from the Buffalo airport to West Seneca went to Danny Sansanese, the north side, which included the Tonawandas, Williamsville and Amherst, were given to the Falzone and Todaro faction. Danny Domino would have the downtown Buffalo area, but all stewards and plush positions would be split between the Pieris and Todaros. Victor Randaccio and I had none. Though I had members of my family in the union, they, together with my friends, were rarely placed in steward positions. It's not that I wanted to see them receive less than other members; I really did not want them open to the criminal activity that quite a few of the union stewards were involved in. I recollect that only my father and cousin Mike Burke ever received a steward position from me.

The new procedure helped but it did not end the bickering. The Pieris even went against me, though Danny Domino remained close. One time I told the Pieris not to appoint one of their cronies on a project located in Gowanda, New York, in the area of the Seneca Nation of Indians. I explained to them that all workers for those projects are usually filled by American Indian members who lived nearby. I was always close to the Indians and they really turned out for me when I ran against Vic Randaccio.

The Pieris, of course, refused to listen to me. Later that week I received a phone call from my friend Calvin Lay, who was the president of the Seneca Nation of Indians. He bellowed his displeasure about what the Pieris did. I told him I would meet him in Gowanda to discuss a remedy.

The ride to the Gowanda area was not short but enjoyable and for me a few moments away from the in-union trouble. After kissing and hugging Calvin Lay I confided in him the truth about what had happened. I informed him that I did not have the power to change it, but he did. I said, "Send Paul Twoguns (another close friend) and a couple other members to the Union Hall and confront the Pieris. And send a strong letter to me complaining about what they did and that you will make this violation of a long-standing agreement public by notifying the media and preparing a legal action."

The next day a truck and three cars emptied out at the Union Hall and more than 20 Americans Indians demanded to see the business agents responsible for keeping them off of the job. Jennie DeAngelo went to the back office and told John and Joe Pieri that the Indians were here to see them. They both refused to leave their office. The Indians confronted Jennie telling her that other laborers told them that they were in and they would wait until the Pieris came out. I later learned that both Pieris were so scared that they spent the night in the Union Hall. At the Pieris' request the very next day Danny Domino went to Gowanda and replaced the cronies with the people that rightfully belonged on the job.

I thought the incident was over but later on when I was in Florida and going to dinner with Joe Todaro Sr. and his close associate, New York City Mason Tenders Union Local 23 Business Manager Louie Giardiana, the elder Todaro requested that I go outside of the restaurant with him. He inquired if I had sicced the Indians on the Pieris. I said, "Yeah I did Joe, do I have a problem." The Mafia boss replied, "Do you know what you did? This matter was brought before the Commission by Tony Salerno and I have to meet with them over this. Don't worry; I will take care of it."

Todaro also discussed with me the needs of his good friend Shelly Leventhal, who owned the Emerald Hills Golf Club located in Hollywood, Florida. Leventhal needed financial help and the elder Todaro wanted to know if I could use the union pension funds to loan him the needed money. In return, 10% of the loan monies would be kicked-back. I told him that the fund was not set up for projects outside of the Local union's jurisdiction, but the Coias had access to funding programs such as the one he was presenting to me. I explained that Arthur E. Coia told me that he, together with his son and Santo Trafficante, owned a strip plaza somewhere on the west coast of Florida and he arranged financing for a few projects there. Further, I told Todaro, "When I have a chance to meet the Coias I will talk to them."

Later that night, I bumped into Arthur A. Coia and told him about the Leventhal proposal. He seemed quite interested and wanted to personally see the golf club and meet with Leventhal. I again met with Todaro Sr. and told him the younger Coia was willing to talk with Leventhal. After arranging the meeting, I traveled to the golf club with Arthur A. Coia, his son, Arthur Coia III and Danny Costello (the son-in-law of Mike Lorello who made a few bucks singing at labor union conventions). We were also joined by Coia cronies and underlings Armand Sabitoni Jr. who was Coia's law partner, a Laborers' and International Union representative and his close friend, and the ever-present Dominic Lopreato, who was later convicted of receiving $345,000 in bribes from the Connecticut-based Colonial Realty Company.

After completing our round of golf, Arthur A. Coia and Sabitoni sat down with Leventhal to discuss his needs. When we were leaving Coia informed me that he could help Leventhal, as long as all the contracts were in order. I never did learn if the deal came to fruition. Besides talking about his rapport with Raymond Patriarca Sr., the elder Coia would repeatedly discuss his affection for Santo Trafficante who, besides being a secret partner in the Florida strip mall project, benefited from fund kickbacks and a jointly owned offshore bank account.

Nicholas DiMaggio Trial

In 1985, my former business partner Nick DiMaggio was indicted for tax evasion. Part of the charges included the checks (not the cash) I gave him. Tony Bruce, the Buffalo federal prosecutor, was going to call me as a witness to authenticate the checks. I had just gotten over the Onyx matter and here I was risking exposure again. It was agreed that I would only have to testify to what were now public records. When I did testify it was limited to the transfer of some of my equipment and the fact that I had signed the checks; I was never asked what they were for.

The mob never questioned my fealty and understood that there was nothing else I could do. They had previously told me to respond that the checks were a re-payment for a loan, if it were asked. DiMaggio was found guilty and sentenced to probation. Within a short time he returned to Chicago with his brothers and the waiting arms of the new family boss, their Uncle Sam, Black Sam Carlisi.

Since becoming the business manager of Local 210, and as one of the trustees for the Laborers International Union Training Fund, I came to know many a mobster and union leader located in the Windy City. The Chicago mob possessed a widespread reach in the geographical area covering parts of California (open territory, any family could operate provided it was not stepping on the toes of another family), Nevada, Colorado, Texas, part of Canada and so on. The Laborers' Union, as well as the Teamsters, Painters, Hotel Employees and Restaurant Employees Union, and Maritime Trades Department of the AFL-CIO, were the Unions that were almost totally mob dominated.

By 1985, the Foscos and Coias hated each other. Coia informed me that Angelo Fosco's son Peter (or as he would call him, "Bean-Belly"), was one sick puppy and together with his friend Indiana-based Laborers International representative Jerry Lee, used union and Training Funds monies to set up their respective girlfriends in a dress shop. After learning of this, Coia revealed to the Chicago Family this revelation and together with his son Arthur A. Coia, covered it up. "I got the bastard," Coia Sr. said, "and I am going to make sure that Bean-Belly is removed from the International Training Fund," which the Coias did temporarily accomplish.

After Bob Powell was pressured to resign from the Laborers' International in 1985, change was in the air that would bring controlled minorities into the union's chain of command. In order to make the transaction smooth, Angelo Fosco and Coia Sr. were ordered by their respective organized crime families to each pick a person of color to replace Powell and a newly created vice president position. Fosco opted for Louis Bravo, a man from California. The Coias opted for Vere O. Haynes, who, before becoming involved with the Laborers', worked in the health care industry. I knew Haynes quite well and no matter what I questioned him about he would respond by saying talk to Arthur E. Coia Sr. or Jr. about it. Haynes was just another flunky who would go along with the Coia conspiracies and ventures whether it was legal or illegal.

By this time Coia and Lorello were constantly berating Fosco and Bob Connerton, the International lead attorney. Lorello would openly and loudly berate Terry O'Sullivan Sr. who was involved with World Wide Insurance located in D.C. and some plot involving *Union Labor Life Insurance Company* (ULLICO). O'Sullivan Sr. was now back in the fold and this time under the leadership of the Coias. Terry O' Sullivan's son (whose name is the same) was given a position with the West Virginia Laborers Training Program and when Coia Jr. took over the president's position he named the younger O'Sullivan as its chief of staff. Coia Jr. was quite fond of the younger O'Sullivan and very, very close to him. In 1987, and 1988, just before I left Local 210 and resigned as an International Trustee, the younger O'Sullivan would hang around the Coias and in our conversations he would avow his indebtedness to the Coias. I could easily see he was being groomed for a higher leadership role.

Arthur E. Coia Sr. desperately wanted the president's position and would tell me that all the families supported him, including Chicago, and joined him in their dislike of Angelo Fosco and that they made a mistake in placing him in the prestigious capacity as president. I conveyed my concern that I did not think that Chicago would ever give up the office holder.

"Ronnie, I have done quite a lot for the Chicago Outfit, and this drunken bastard (referring to Angelo Fosco), has done nothing. I already know that they support me as do the New York City families."

I was already made aware that he had the support of

New York, but I did not tell Coia that I was also briefed that Chicago was grooming Johnny Serpico as the next International Union president. John Serpico, an up and comer in the Chicago crime family, was under the control of Capo and Chicago Laborers' Union official Vincent Solano. Serpico had testified and perjured himself before Ronald Reagan's Presidential Organized Crime Commission. (Ronald Reagan truly did want to eradicate the mob and unknowingly made some appointments that were hand-picked by the mob). Serpico was a talker and he would constantly tell me hundreds of Chicago mob stories about the Outfit and about his role with Laborers Local 8. He was now an International Union vice president and his friendship with me was like my relationship with the rest of the Chicago Family, strong and very friendly. He also held a prominent position with the Illinois International Port District Board to which he was appointed by former Illinois Governor James Thompson.

We were once talking about Chicago Mayor Jane Byrne, who I knew was connected to Serpico. I asked him, "Why did she attack me when I was involved in the snow cleanup in 1979?"

"It was a mistake, Ronnie, she didn't know about you and was only doing it to attack Mayor Bilandic." Serpico was Vinnie Solano's boy and brought in millions of dollars from swindles taking place from his stint with the Laborers and the Illinois International Port District, of which he eventually became Chairman. In 1999, Serpico was indicted by a federal grand jury and in 2002, convicted for fraud.

I suggested that the elder Coia talk with Joe Todaro Sr. about his desire to become the International president, to which he agreed. I set up a meeting for April 24, 1985, at an unknown cozy restaurant not far from the Buffalo airport.

Coia Todaro Meeting

I PICKED UP ARTHUR E. COIA AT the Buffalo airport and we drove to the nearby restaurant. Todaro was waiting and I didn't have to make any introductions, they had met on a number of occasions and knew each other quite well. Listening in Coia explained to Todaro what he wanted. Todaro Sr. explained, "Arthur, you know we all love and respect you and all that you have done for all of us, but I am telling you, I just do not believe Chicago will give up the position." Coia slumped in his chair and still tried to convince Todaro that he believed he had the backing of Chicago.

"I do not know who is telling you that you have their support; even though they hold you in high regard; still I cannot see it happening." Coia still believed that the Chicago Family would support him.

Todaro then purported to Coia that he wanted Ugo Rossini (my friend) out of the union. Johnny "Pops" Papalia wanted him removed and they wanted Enrico Mancinelli to take his place at the International Union from Canada.

Ontario Takeover and Phil Schwab

After the lunch with Todaro ended, I drove the disheartened Coia to Toronto to impose the new directive and to try and quell the ongoing Stefanini crisis that was still taking place. Coia also wanted Ugo Rossini out and liked the choice of Enrico Mancinelli to take Rossini's place. Mancinelli, who was with the Hamilton, Ontario-based Laborers Local 837, was also the manager of the LIUNA Ontario District Council. Together with his younger son Joe, Enrico Mancinelli arranged for hotel suites costing an arm and a leg at a Toronto hotel. After we refreshed and changed our clothes we found the Mancinelli's waiting in the lobby preparing to drive us to see the new Laborers Training Fund site.

I walked around the white building, which was at that time called Club LIUNA and I told Coia this was not a training site, it was a restaurant. I could not find one wheel barrel or tool present. Soon the restaurant was filled with more than 100 people. At the dedication services Coia and I spoke.

Arthur E. Coia always had a prepared speech that his son, Jimmy Merloni or Armand Sabitoni would write. He was not a very good orator and when he veered from the script, his inability to publicly speak would rear its ugly head. He spoke first and went on to say Christopher Columbus had made a mistake, the United States and Canada should be one country and quite a few demeaning words that insulted Canada. Obviously his recollection of Columbus's history was inaccurate and I did not understand why he would make such a statement. It not only made him sound like an ass but it also reflected just how uneducated he really was. I could see that the Canadian labor leaders were totally confused by the remarks and somewhat offended. When I spoke I tried to put a positive spin on it and without insulting Coia I spoke about the Canadians distinguished role in helping the poor and needy and that we were truly a brotherhood of common men and women that were all equal or some words to that effect.

As bad a speaker as Arthur E. Coia was, Angelo Fosco was even worse. He was really that bad. He would constantly be told by the Chicago Family to leave the speaking to someone else. The same held true for Mike Lorello. Enrico died in 2006, and today Joseph Mancinelli is the International Vice President and Regional Manager for Central and Eastern Canada of the Laborers' International Union of North America.

Non-Union Movement

Laborers Local 210 was in trouble; the growing threats of non-union companies, who were taking work from the union, became a serious difficulty. I, together with my good friend Jack Wilkinson who was the regional manager for the Washington D.C., Virginia and West Virginia areas, worked together to come up with a concept to counter the growing non-union contractor threat.

In concert with non-Mafia-controlled construction unions, we looked to create what was called a market recovery program. It would remove some of costly work rules like show-up time (a worker would be paid for two hours if the project was rained out and four hours if he or she started to work and then it rained out). No 40-hour guarantee for those trades receiving it, more flexibility with work hours, and the removal of restrictive conditions. We introduced a lower apprenticeship wage rate as well as established training programs for those trades that did not have them. At the same time we wanted to bring legal action against those union employers that were starting up non-union, or alter-ego, companies to avoid their union contract obligations.

Numerous Buffalo and Western New York companies that had contracts with Local 210 have alter-ego companies. Our union did not have the necessary money to hire attorneys because the mob had pretty much drained all of its funds. I asked the reasonable Joe Todaro Sr. if I could use a small amount of what little we had available to hire a couple of law students to help me in this pursuit. He agreed and requested that I keep his son and Leonard Falzone abreast of what I was doing.

One of the employers I started with was Cuyahoga Wrecking Corp., the company owned and operated by Philip Schwab. I was kind of surprised that Todaro allowed me go after him since he was fully cognizant that Schwab had strong connections to just about every mob family in the country. One of the many alter-egos of Cuyahoga Wrecking Corp. was Jordan & Foster Scrap Corp. which was tearing down the old Donner Hanna Coke Company located near the Bethlehem Steel plant.

We decided to dumpster dive their garbage when it was placed outside the demolition area and close to the public streets. The trash proved to be very valuable and numerous documents reflected common insurance carriers, supervisors, equipment and so on that was used by both of the Schwab companies. We also became aware that Schwab was going to be tearing down an old theater building located near George Washington University Hospital located in Washington D.C. and that he would be illegally removing and dumping asbestos. I quickly telephoned Jack Wilkinson as well as the *Washington Post* and let them know what was going to take place. The *Post* took the lead in the investigation and soon reported that asbestos was everywhere and everyone in the vicinity of the theater and George Washington University Hospital were breathing in harmful asbestos fibers.

The Philip Schwab company's illegal asbestos activity was also taking place at the Stroh's Beer Brewery located in Detroit, at Kaiser Steel located in the Los Angeles, California, suburb of Fontana, Wisconsin Steel in Chicago, Ashland Oil located in Tonawanda, New York, four projects that Schwab had in New York City, Republic Steel located in Cleveland and the Ft. Lauderdale airport located in Florida. I could go on and on about this walking inhumane mob associate.

I had Chicago International representative Dan Dumo send me what he had on Schwab and the Laborers' Baltimore District Council sent over information on the Schwab project at the Sparrow's Point shipyard. I reached out to the employees of Jordan Foster and with the *Buffalo News* and local television stations present, we listened to horror story after horror story about how they were not only breathing in the flying asbestos but also the fumes from burning and highly toxic *Polychlorinated Biphenyls* (PCBs). Lake Erie and the surrounding area became the dumping ground for much of the waste along with creosote, benzenes and phenols. I notified the Coast Guard that Schwab was sending a ship laden with steel, PCBs, creosote and asbestos to South Korea as well. I contacted Howard Stecker, who was the Environmental Protection Agency's asbestos official in New York and New Jersey. Stecker said he would look into it, which he never did. Later that same week Joey "Pizza" Todaro said his father wanted to see me right away. I went over to La Nova Pizzeria and Todaro Sr. whisked me into the safe located in the sub-floor.

"Ronnie, what the fuck are you doing? I told you, you could go after Schwab, but that did not mean you use the

Navy, other Laborers' Unions or the media. I have to now answer for your actions. The only reason I allowed you to go after him was because he was not kicking back to me on the local jobs he is working on. Only the Pieris are getting a piece. You have the country up in arms and Schwab has visited a number of other families over this. Chester Liberatore from Cleveland has lodged a complaint. I want you to stop and stop now."

I told him okay, but that I had already started a court action against Schwab. "Well, just find a way to ease out of it."

About a week later I learned from one of my sources that Schwab was kicking back to the Department of Labor's Howard Stecker, who was later convicted for receiving kickbacks from a number of demolition contractors. I hated the fact that Schwab was getting away with murder and I had the tools to put a stop to him but could not. Like everything I did, I kept the FBI abreast of this and hoped that maybe there was something they could do. I found that every project that this criminal Schwab was involved in had asbestos, PCBs and other hazardous waste removed illegally. I could not believe it. Where are all the environmentalists? Where was the public outrage? Prior to Todaro telling me to stop, I went on television and called for press conferences to point out the illegal activity; but in the end no other group or enforcement agency really did much. A few fines and that was it.

Howard Stecker was finally arrested in 1986, for accepting $150,000 in bribes and became an informant, with 23 contractors caught offering bribes. Philip Schwab was one of the men in February 1986, and by November 1986, he was forced into bankruptcy, with outstanding loans of $400 million.

By now we had developed good alter-ego cases against around 20 western New York contractors and we were getting ready to file a legal suit against them. Joey Pizza and Leonard Falzone compelled me to drop the cases against Ciminelli Construction and Frank Ciminelli, who was connected, and the Mader Corporation run by Lawrence Reger (a Buffalo businessman indirectly controlled by the family) who made a fortune for the mob cleaning up the Love Canal hazardous waste. Falzone spoke in a nice manner, which was rare, "You know they are connected Ron and know that their construction companies are off limits."

I could see my efforts were unraveling, but I continued with the limited alter-ego contractors to see what I could do. I set my sites on bringing about the market recovery program. The Todaros were not opposed to it but the irascible Danny Sansanese spoke vehemently against it saying, "There is no way I will have any of my friends and relatives working as laborers or apprentices at a lower wage. We worked hard for our working conditions and I am not going to allow you to toss them away." I implored him to think about it and for him to tell me how we were going to save this union.

"Fuck the union, and for that matter, you might as well understand now that it is never going to happen so you might as well forget it."

By now Victor Sansanese was quite close to Joe Pizza, who stupidly relied upon him and joined in supporting Sansanese's brother. Falzone told me that I should drop the idea; the matter had been already settled. It seemed that no matter what I tried, my hands were tied and now that Victor was moving up the organized crime ladder, the future looked even dimmer than before and I knew I would not take much more. It was just too hard on me. I wanted to scream out loud about these no-good thieves and just get the hell away from them. Each and every time I told the FBI that I was going to quit, they always responded the same no matter what agent I was talking to. "Ron, you care for the plight of the innocents and you know that you're quitting will not in any way help the cause you are trying to achieve. You must stay and see it through."

During this time, I remained close to the minority community and would regularly meet with my close friend Dave Collins who was a Buffalo city councilman and Frank Messiah, a leader in the black community. Most of these meetings dealt with what we could do to help the high unemployment rate that minorities and others were suffering. I knew that I could only offer them vocal support knowing there was nothing I could do.

By this time, the senior editor of the widely read *Reader's Digest*, Gene Methvin, and I secretly discussed my activities and union corruption on quite a regular basis. We first met in Washington in the late 1970s and after our initial discussions we became very close friends. Methvin was a senior representative of President Ronald Reagan's Crime Commission investigation and hearings on labor-management racketeering, and knew of the problems faced by me and the bureau. I enjoyed our conversations and felt that in Methvin I had someone who hated the mob as much as I did. He knew that I wanted out and that the bureau wanted me to stay.

"Ron you have to stick it out for as long as you can. Later on if you decide to go public it will be of a tremendous value to everyone." I knew going public would cause me to lose my family and ability to remain in Western New York.

In 1987, Vic Randaccio told me he wanted out, even he did not want any part of the mess that the Sansaneses and Todaros were doing to the union. I asked him if he would let Todaro Sr. know.

"I have my pension, Ronnie, and it's time to get the hell out of here and you should too. Ronnie have you been told to remove Danny Boone Domino by anybody yet?"

"No, why do they want the Boone to go?" Randaccio said that Joe Todaro Sr. wanted him out immediately and that Domino had talked badly about Joe Todaro Sr.'s girlfriend, Terry Shanks. I did not believe it. That was not Danny Domino's way and he was too smart to say anything about Todaro, let alone say something bad her.

A couple days later Leonard Falzone asked me to go with him to a Denny's restaurant located on Delaware Avenue in Buffalo to see Todaro Sr. As I entered the restaurant Todaro Sr., Vic Sansanese and Todaro Jr. waved to me and Falzone to join them. Nearby was WKBW television reporter Irv Weinstein, whom I chatted with briefly. I introduced the Todaros, et al., to Weinstein, who seemed a little nervous when I mentioned their names.

After sitting in a nearby booth Todaro Sr. told me that the Boone had to go and he did not want me to help any of the Domino Family. He reiterated what was said about his girlfriend and said "Baldie," as he referred to Domino, "also has to retire from any family business." Once more I pleaded with Todaro to keep Domino. I would have no one to visit and watch over the construction sites, but his mind was made up that Danny Domino had to be removed.

Unlike many other Mafia members, Todaro Sr. would freely talk to me about the mob. One time in the basement of La Nova Pizzeria I spoke freely with him and told him, "Joe, you are a wealthy, successful businessman, I just cannot understand why you do not step down and only run your pizza and wings business."

"I would like to, but I can't; it would cause havoc and if someone like the Pieris took over, I would find that soon they would be running 'La Nova.'"

The very next day Domino resigned from the union. He called me and we met at a Denny's restaurant near his home across from the Eastern Hills Mall. Visibly upset, Domino told me the reason he was let go. He didn't have to speak; I already knew the real reason why he was forced into retirement. Without Domino, the Pieris would only be fixtures in the Union Hall. They rarely ever visited job sites and relied upon Danny Domino to do their work. Without him they would flounder.

◪ Leaving Local 210

A FEW MONTHS AFTER DAN DOMINO WAS fired, while I was waiting in the Union Hall for contractors to visit and answer a grievance we had with a local construction company, Dan Sansanese asked me to step into his office and in a demeaning manner asked me to take a chair. He was visibly upset and said, his company, MBN Park, was having a problem with the Ironworkers Union and wanted me to immediately drop what I was doing and go fix it. I explained to him that I had a meeting shortly and it would have to wait. I also apprised him that MBN Park was months behind in benefit fund contributions and I was sure the contractor trustees must know by now. Upset and perturbed, Sansanese snapped, “Frank 'Butchie' BiFulco (the benefit fund collections manager) is going to take care of it.”

“How is he going to take care of it, Dan? The debt is already public knowledge.”

“I do not give a good fuck about your meeting! Cancel it and go on the damn project now!”

“Fuck you, Sansanese, I have had it with you and this is the last straw, I quit. I am done. I just cannot take it anymore.”

Sansanese sat silently as I exited his office, still screaming that I had enough and I quit. He then followed me into my office and in a mild tone uttered, "You can't quit, you know it will never be allowed."

"Oh, yeah? You just watch me." In my anger I made sure that my remarks only related to him. If I mentioned the Todaros or his brother Victor, I knew that my name would be prominently displayed in an obituary column.

After the grievance meeting, Victor Sansanese came to the Union Hall and asked me to take a walk to a nearby restaurant where Joey Pizza was waiting. (He had received a phone call from Jennie DeAngelo.) Victor said, "You know, Ronnie, you should not let my brother upset you like this and what the hell is this shit that you are quitting?"

I told the two Mafioso that they knew as well as I did that MBN Park was in trouble and I just couldn't get involved in helping them and drop everything I was doing.

Pizza whispered, "You are needed here, how are we going to run the union if you quit?"

"Joey, Victor, I am really leaving, I really can't take it anymore."

"Ronnie, just wait until we talk to my father before you say anymore. At least you can wait until then."

"All right, Joey, I'll wait till then."

After two days Leonard Falzone asked me to take a ride with him to the Buffalo small boat harbor. Joe Todaro Sr. Pizza and Victor were already at the restaurant. Joe Sr. asked if my mind was made up and I answered him affirmatively.

"Okay, Ronnie, if that is the way you want it, okay, but you will still have to act as an adviser to the union as well as a trustee of the benefit funds for at least one year to help us in the transition. Have the Union Attorney Dick Lipsitz draw up an agreement whereby you will be paid for your services. Is that fair enough?"

"All right Joe, I will do that, but you know Joe, the union is broke! There is no money left." Todaro Sr. asked his son if that were true. He said it was, but Victor said I could be paid from the benefit funds.

I responded, "You can't do that, Victor, I can't represent the union and at the same time the funds."

"All right then, we will pay you from future funds as well as benefit fund contributions so your pension contributions and health and welfare benefits don't stop." I agreed and within a couple of days an agreement was reached.

On February 1, 1988, I left the union, at least in my position as business manager. The setup they arranged was terrible. I was still doing the same, if not more, work for the union and after a few months I had not been paid and did not have the ability to start afresh. I started to think that I would never get out of this mess. Even the FBI was pressing me to hang in a little longer.

My neighbor Judd Quimby, who previously worked in the health industry, wanted me to join him in establishing an elderly care nursing home facility. After a couple of months, my plans with Quimby were interrupted by another sit-down with The Boys. At the same waterfront restaurant as before, Victor Sansanese and his enforcer Sammy Cardinale, stipulated that they and the family wanted me to use my skills and start up a hazardous waste company. Actually getting nose to nose with me, The Priest said that I had no choice, the decision was made. Sansanese then remarked that I would be wealthy, but also that I would have to follow their implicit instructions. Trying to buy time I asked if I could think about it and both bellowed, "No! You are to meet with Joe (Sam's son) this evening and he will fill you in on the plan." I knew this was it. I immediately contacted bureau agents Steve Naum and Tommy McDonnell about the predicament and agreed to wear a wire and record all my meetings with the wiseguys.

I was already mindful that in 1985, Victor Sansanese, together with Joe Todaro Jr., Sam Cardinale and his son Joe Cardinale, had formed a hazardous waste cleanup company with the wives of Joe Cardinale and George Sembeida (a partner of Joe Cardinale in the insurance business) as fronts. The company had some success, but they did not know the construction business, let alone the toxic waste cleanup industry.

That night Joe Cardinale, who I really couldn't stand, said, "Ronnie, you know that you just can't walk away from us; the hazardous waste company is the very way for you to avoid any problems. You know what I mean! You will assist us. You should know our business is having growing problems and we feel that you would be perfect for straightening it out."

Puzzled about how I would benefit and leery about any business ties with the mob after my previous encounters, I asked him what percentage and authority would I have. His reply was that I would not have authority, but that I would make a good salary. George Sembeida was on the outs and I would be given his share. I obviously knew that this plan stunk to high heaven and hoped that the bureau would have a recording device for me soon. I told Cardinale that the little I knew about his company concerned me because of its lack of proper structure and key personnel.

"Ron, sit down with Dave Knoll and Jim Ryding because Pizza Todaro is going to have them involved."

David Knoll was a longtime mob attorney and had been used for some of the mob's illegitimate financial affairs. As previously mentioned, Knoll had been involved with the Todaros and the sale of their Florida hotel. Jim Ryding was a Canadian citizen and a longtime friend of the Todaros and Johnny "Pops" Papalia who handled some of their money laundering problems through his business and other operations run by him. I liked Ryding but I totally abhorred Dave Knoll and his involvement with the Todaros and their enterprises that led to bust outs and many financially destroyed victims. What more could I do than what I was doing? I knew wearing a wire and recording all this garbage should surely lead to their conviction. My time on the streets was almost up and my becoming public was a foregone conclusion. At the meeting Dave Knoll greeted me by saying, "I know you don't like me Ronnie, but I am no longer drinking and I will prove to be an asset."

His response left me befuddled, because he acted like I had a say in his selection or, for that matter, in any decision making. Ryding, on the other hand, was reserved, yet eager to get the business off the ground. After a few meetings, it was agreed that the Cardinale Company: (Environmental Abatement International Inc.) was not the way to go. It was understood that to work in the asbestos removal area that any link to Sembeida could prove to be a detriment in the future. Either we needed to form a new corporation or use an existing company with a proven track record. They agreed to make use of Knoll's office and continue to review the possibilities. The Cardinales did not like the idea and did not want to form a new corporation. As a counter they demanded that the existing company be purchased.

About a week later the Cardinales presented *Hazardous Waste Management Inc.* (HWM), a company owned by Phillip Badame (later a source of information for me) a former associate of Harry Williams and Norm Dobiesz who played a part in forming and operating the Envirosure Management Corporation, which turned out to be a good money maker for the mobsters involved. Envirosure and Norm Dobiesz ran into trouble in Kansas and James Harry Williams and Larry Reger thought it wise to cut Badame loose. On his own Badame started Hazardous Waste Management, but loose spending quickly erased the company's potential. Cardinale and Knoll felt that if we offered him a small piece of the pie and wrested control of the company from him that Badame would be a valuable asset. Another company, Wizard Systems from Niagara Falls, was involved in pumping non-toxic liquids out of storage containers and then disposing the toxins to a licensed operation. Wizard System's owner Garlan Stoneman previously informed Cardinale that he was interested in a takeover.

I knew the plan presented to me was just more of the same old crap. The only barometer that I had was the past and that was strewn with disaster and mayhem. Joey Pizza was not only elated about taking over Hazardous Waste Management, he also went on about Sembeida being out and eventually placing Environmental Abatement International Inc. as a wholly owned subsidiary of HWM, which would have over $60,000 in assets. He also articulated that Knoll could bring the company public and that with his connections he could guarantee over a minimum of half a million dollars from investors that included Jimmy Cosentino, Sam Santarosa (the owner of Buffalo Fuel), someone from the Bluebird Bus Company and numerous other sources. The biggest problem that a fledgling company normally had was the insurance requirements. Even established companies have a difficult time in procuring bid bonds and liability insurance.

I was aware of other company's difficulties and how Joe Cardinale was able to obtain insurance for them. Before one could bid on a project, this problem had to be overcome. An unfavorable and costly agreement was reached with Wizard Systems and Garland Stoneman made out like a bandit. The first target project was an asbestos removal operation at a State University of New York College, not far from Rochester, New York. After the numbers were plugged and the bid readied, Cardinale went to work and in less than two hours the insurance was acquired. Even though the project went to a lower bidder, Joey Cardinale proved that he really could handle the insurance problem. Equally important was the cost of insurance. Normally, a toxic waste contractor would pay 3% or higher of the project cost for the bid and performance bond and up to 15% for liability insurance. Cardinale smiled with cockiness as he bragged that the bid and performance bond was only 1.5% and the liability insurance was seven percent.

At a meeting I had with Bells Supermarket chain president Charles Barcelona (who was not mobbed-up) I explained that I was getting into the hazardous waste business. He voiced interest in joining with me in an environmental cleanup company. I knew Barcelona's involvement would never come to fruition, but made a big mistake by telling Ryding of my meeting with Barcelona. Victor Sansanese and Pizza were beside themselves; why would I discuss anything and even meet with this disliked guy, fully knowing of his friendship with the hated Paul Snyder? I was cognizant of the fact that Snyder and Barcelona were in the so-called uncontrolled area. As physically and mentally strong as I was, I still feared these mobsters and I knew that if I didn't follow their advice that I would be in hot water. I had gone quite far already in my attempt to ease out of the union. I responded that I only went to see him to see if he wanted to invest in our company.

The mob works on subtleties and a nod of the head is taken as an acceptance of whatever they are proposing. I assured them that I would negate what had taken place and I would not talk to Barcelona again.

My big mouth had got me in trouble again and felt like just like a piece of wood, to be used to build, or to burn. Victor Sansanese set up a meeting at Cosentino's hotel and he had Joey and Sammy Cardinale present me the finalized deal. Never having a chance to voice opposition, I accepted the position as a board of director. Jim Ryding would be president and Joey Cardinale would be the treasurer. The distribution of finances and check signing would be in the hands of Ryding and Cardinale. Forty-nine percent of the company would be offered to the public with the remaining 51% distributed among us. Joe Cardinale's shares would also include the silent ownership of the Todaros, Victor Sansanese and Sam Cardinale.

Unlike Sno-Go they said they would take care of the finances and that I would have nothing to worry about. It still did not make me feel any better. I knew that, like a leopard, they would never change their spots. They needed me to continue the union's work and with the friendship that Joe Todaro Sr. had shown me, maybe things would change for the startup company. After all, the Todaros were also businessmen and understood the problems of business, taxes and the cost of operating. I obviously remained skeptical and with the elder Todaro getting ready to retire, I knew matters could get only worse.

In April 1988, we moved into the old Westinghouse complex near the Buffalo airport. The property was owned by the disliked Paul Snyder and only with the promise of performing future asbestos removal at the mammoth complex were we given permission to utilize his facility. Joey Cardinale made arrangements with James Harry Williams to allow us to hire the knowledgeable Don Larder. I liked Don, and his expertise with insurance and finance was a necessity. I was constantly asking Larder about his past and his involvement in the toxic waste industry. I learned that he started working for James Harry Williams and Larry Reger during the Love Canal cleanup project and played an intricate part in the diversification of their holdings. He knew the ins and outs of the business.

Joe Cardinale liked the night life and on any given night you would always find him leaning against the bar at Jimmy Cosentino's hotel. He equally relished his notoriety and loved holding court in plain view and being recognized by all. Cosentino's hotel had worn many faces through the years and recently had ended a 10-year stint as a Playboy Club. One of the Playboy bunnies who previously worked there was Denise Erb, who, while a student at the State University of New York toiling for her master's degree, led her to the Playboy Club. She became the girlfriend of Bill Dellamore, a senior advisor to Cosentino. Dellamore was a childhood friend of Joe Cardinale and had a reputation as a person to be reckoned with. He was also Cosentino's personal bodyguard. The hotel and club had become a hangout for the Buffalo mob and Cosentino would always make rooms and amenities available to out-of-town hoodlums. Jimmy and his brother Patrick had taken over the hotel upon the death of their father, Pat. The elder Cosentino built the hotel with mob assistance and for years catered to the Buffalo Family. The hotel also saw to the needs of many celebrities and politicians and rooms were made available for a hop in the sack with some of the waitresses or bunnies.

The Buffalo Cosa Nostra allegedly took advantage of this and arranged for certain suites to have hidden cameras installed. I never learned if the Cosentino's were aware of this but I do not believe so. One time when talking with mob associate Frank "Chicky Botts" Grisanti he stated that they were secretly installed during reconstruction periods that the hotel undertook.

Exploited victims supposedly included noted politicians, celebrities and sports figures. Joe Todaro Jr. loved to talk about the videotapes of the escapades of Andy Williams in the sack with Evel Knievel's sister; Rick James; O. J. Simpson taking on three girls at a time and so on. Back in 1976, when Henry "Scoop" Jackson was touring the area for votes in the presidential primary, without explanation I told him to occupy a regular room and not a suite. It was commonly known by the Buffalo mob and its cohorts that this practice was ongoing and I always wondered why with so many people knowing, it was never more public. My father used to talk about the practice with disgust and that it led to many compromises and to many a granted favor.

The FBI was also monitoring the activities of mobsters Joe Todaro Sr. and his girlfriend Terry Shanks, but if they were aware of the recordings and videos being made by the mob, they never told me.

Joe Cardinale was going to hire Denise Erb, not because of any expertise, but because she was Bill Dellamore's girlfriend. Even though she had studied Hydrogeology and had held a master's degree, she knew very little about the demolition and hazardous waste cleanup industry. Cardinale uttered, "She does Ron, and you should sit down with her."

I cautiously mentioned that our needs were in the asbestos removal area and that we didn't have the money or the immediate need for her services. Cardinale then remarked that his father and Victor Sansanese wanted to see me again. After agreeing to a meeting, we sat down at the Cosentino hotel.

At the breakfast meeting they informed me that they were making arrangements for Hazardous Waste Management to receive an influx of more than three hundred thousand dollars. Once Knoll brought the company public, I would have to hire Ron Cardinale at $50,000 a year salary, advising me that he is an expert on government contracts and to sit down with Denise Erb and find a place for her. "Don't worry about the cost, Ron; we have made all the necessary arrangements for the company's needed cash."

Of course I had no say-so in these decisions, so why were they even asking me? I didn't believe them and I started to doubt that they even wanted to see the company become a success. I interviewed Denise Erb and found her quite knowledgeable and willing to learn about the asbestos abatement program. She was slim and quite chesty but hid it well when she was professionally dressed. She was not the girl I pictured.

After the conclusion of our agreement to purchase Wizard Systems, to celebrate Garlan Stoneman brought his huge house boat from its Niagara Falls location to Buffalo. Over 20 of us went on board and joined in the festivities. By the trip's end Denise was quite drunk and could not drive. Her girlfriend who accompanied her asked me if I could drop them off.

After I dropped off her girlfriend, I drove Denise to her home and helped her into the house. With her arm propped over my shoulder I struggled to her apartment. In the process of searching for the key she kissed me, but because of her stupor I placed her on the couch and left. I passed it off as a brief moment of her drunken state, but the seed was planted. The following Friday she asked me if I wanted to go for a cocktail with her after work. I agreed. By the third drink we were holding hands and cuddling. I told Denise that I had to leave and that I would see her on Monday. She said that she didn't want me to leave and wondered if I could meet her later at another local night spot. I told her that I would try.

After I started my car, confusion set in. Lustfully, I wanted her. I did have a prior affair with a girl that I have known since high school, but the love of my wife and children at that time caused me to curtail that relationship. This time, however, was different. I had been separated from my wife for about six months and living in my own apartment. Within a couple of hours I was back in Denise's arms and subjecting myself to the siren's lure. She asked me to take a ride with her. Her car was small and the attempted sex was confined to the passenger seat and quite trying. I was surprised how big her breasts were but the heavy consumption of booze and the confined space caused me not to enjoy the act as much as I should have. After we kissed each other good night we knew that we would be back together after the weekend.

One afternoon Don Larder asked me to travel to Niagara Falls with him to look at the Envirosure operation. Harry Williams and Norm Dobiesz had a subsidiary that performed toxic waste laboratory analysis and was also working on conceptual neutralizing techniques on toxins. Larder introduced me to Dr. Ian Webber, who seemed more interested in our fledgling company than his current status. He asked me if he could talk to me privately to see if our company would have any interest in joining him on a procedure to remove PCBs from transformers without removing or destroying the transformer. I was interested but lacked the knowledge to understand what he was talking about. I agreed to meet with him.

The following Saturday we sat down and discussed his concept as well as his position with Envirosure. Webber informed me that his PCB removal procedure was not only possible but further studies could be a catalyst for grant funds from various universities and government agencies. He talked about his dissatisfaction with Envirosure and that he possessed proprietary rights for the removal concept.

After telling him to supply me with all his documentation and proof of his ownership of the procedure, I called friends of mine at the State University of New York and at the New York State Department of Environmental Engineering to look into the need for Webber's extraction procedure and available grant funds.

Don Larder informed me that Norm Dobiesz had reached an agreement with Union Carbide to share in the concept without Dr. Webber's knowledge. After talking to Jim Ryding about this we both asked Dave Knoll to look at the proprietary rights agreements that Webber had to verify if they were legal and could be utilized in a possible lawsuit against Envirosure and Union Carbide. Ryding and Knoll felt that we could generate needed funds by bringing Webber and his project on board. After concurring with them, we arranged to have Webber sign an agreement that included sharing his proprietary rights with Hazardous Waste Management.

Immediately after his signature and that of Ryding was on the dotted line it was agreed that a lawsuit be instituted against Envirosure and Union Carbide. After receiving notice of our intent to bring a civil action against them, an irate Joe Cardinale voiced his dissatisfaction with the hiring and lack of consultation. I told him that Jimmy Ryding approved it and I thought he would be happy about this coup and the financial potential. Cardinale responded, "Harry Williams and Joe Todaro Jr. are quite upset about your stealing Webber and Ryding has already been reprimanded! This fucking lawsuit is going to stop and stop now! Joe Todaro wants you to call Harold Boreanaz and set up a meeting with him and Dobiesz." I was beside myself; this could solve our cash needs and I immediately questioned their loyalty to Hazardous Waste Management, their own company.

Boreanaz loved to peer over his glasses and talk down to me. He declared that not only is he representing Dobiesz but also that the Todaros were part owners of Envirosure and the legal action I sought was quite disturbing. Dobiesz and Joe Cardinale, who were also present, sat quietly as Boreanaz offered suggestions on how to solve the problem. He recommended that Hazardous Waste Management make available 50% of the finances necessary to complete the prototype and in return would receive 25% of the proceeds of any money made. In total disagreement with this arrangement, I told them that I would talk to Joe Todaro Jr. and argue my case there.

At the meeting with Pizza, who by now was the acting boss of the Borgata and accompanied by Victor Sansanese, he demanded that I stop the lawsuit immediately and not only agree to the Boreanaz arrangement but that Hazardous Waste Management was going to enter into an agreement with Envirosure to bring it in as subsidiary and it would continue to perform cleanup work under HWM.

The federal investigation of Envirosure and the reluctance of communities and other businesses to use their services made it necessary. They laid out the proposal, which included more than 20 Envirosure employees being transferred to our payroll.

I said, "Joe you know HWM can't afford it, how the fuck can we help them when we can't even help ourselves?"

"Ron, HWM is going to receive 50% of their current receivables and they have established connections and clients."

For the first time in my life I defied them and told them that I was opposed to it. Victor Sansanese responded by telling me, "Your opposition to it doesn't matter. Jim Ryding, David Knoll and Joe Cardinale are going to make sure that you do not interfere." Again, I knew I was in trouble, but by now I didn't care.

After Envirosure moved into our facilities, everything went to hell. James Ladue was named as president of our company and the bust out began. The Cardinales, Dave Knoll and Ladue secretly transferred our company's assets, as well as having our personnel who were still on our payroll, work for Environmental Abatement International, Inc.

The only satisfaction I could take from it all was in knowing that I was secretly recording the meetings with these rape artists. The only place that the FBI did not allow me to make recordings was in lawyer's offices.

John Riggi

Joe Todaro Sr.

Leonard Falzone

Herbie Blitzstein

Tony Accardo

John Gotti

Tommy Eboli

Boris Berezovsky

Yuri Schefler

Robert Barr

Fadi Darwish

Jack Tocco

Joe Wilson

Gennady Vasilenko

General Gennady Troshev

Joe Colombo

William Delmont

Ambassador Valery Tsepkalo

General President Angelo Fosco (left front) and General Secretary-Treasurer Arthur E. Coia (right front) head the LIUNA delegation at the AFL-CIO Convention held in Florida in October.

Laborers' International Union general executive board. Ronald Fino - fifth from the left.

Marshall Miles and Joe Lewis

Mayor Jimmy Griffin with Burt Reynolds

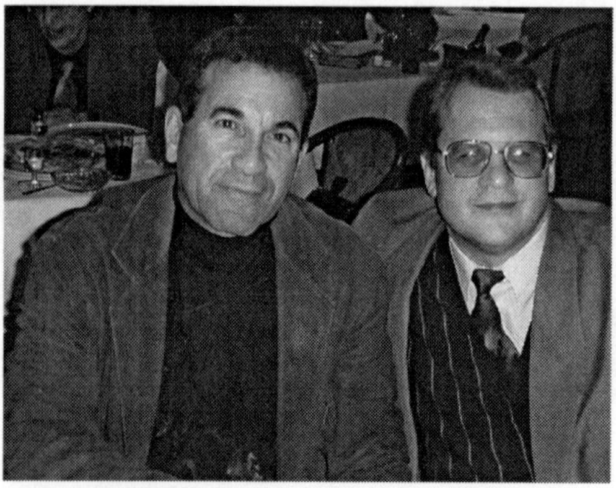

Ronald Fino with Anatoli Massiuk

Vladimir Peftiev

Wesley Michalczyk and associate

With the Ukraine ambassador

LIUNA Training Center, CA. Jack Wilkinson, Ron Fino, Felix Conti

Daniel Sansanese Jr., Ronald Fino, Laborers Training Center, California

Joseph and Arlene Fino - my parents

Joseph Fino - a mug shot of my father at age 16

Ronald and Alla Fino

Joe Fino

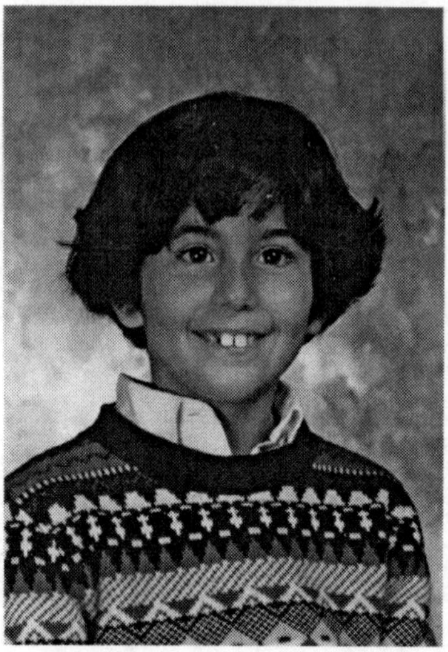

Danielle Fino

Alla and Daniil Fino

With my two grandsons

August 23, 2012

The Love Canal Disaster and Its Profiteers

DURING THE LATE 1890S, A NEIGHBORHOOD eventually called the Love Canal, located in the City of Niagara Falls, New York, was wishfully destined to become a marvelous location for development and to bring industry, cheap power, transportation and residential housing for the neighborhood. William T. Love, for whom the site was named, eventually and with remorse, discarded his dreams and hopes for the area.

In 1925, Niagara Falls started using the area as a municipal refuse dumping area. By the 1940s the U.S. Army, the nearby Hooker Chemical Plant and others, joined in the utilization of the site for dumping its by-product waste, including highly toxic chemicals and carcinogens, with little regard for the eyesore they were creating. In 1953, the canal was covered, vegetation grew over it and Hooker Chemical sold the land to the Niagara Falls School Board for one dollar. Subsequently two schools and low-income housing was built in the area.

In 1976, as a result of discovering that the sub-surface of the ground that the housing and children's play areas of the Love Canal was built on contained toxic chemicals, the residents of the area loudly demanded that the federal government act and act immediately. The residents wanted them to address their dire situation and take the necessary steps of investigating and removing the hazardous chemicals after they helped move the residents out of the site. By 1980, the United States Congress established the Superfund Program, a concept for locating and cleaning up hazardous waste sites nationwide.

At that time I knew very little about toxic waste outside of what I read in the news or watched on the television. I did know that it would take workers who had to be educated and equipped to safely remove them. Quickly I incorporated this sector of work into our union agreements with our employers. For years as laborers working in the steel mills and other industrial plants, we were quite used to handling and breathing in these chemicals. We of course didn't know they were harmful, we weren't scientists, no one told us. When someone came down with cancer or other diseases, we thought of it as only a natural incident. Tearing asbestos off of the pipes, removing PCBs from transformers was just an occupation and most laborers, including me, worked on these jobs on a daily basis.

I wasn't alone in looking at the amount of work this novel industry would create. Innovative entrepreneurs and their companies quickly created spin-offs to benefit from the millions of dollars the federal government was going to spend.

In October 1978, not waiting for the federal government, New York State commenced a $9 million Love Canal cleanup that would require a ditch be dug and a pipeline installed that would drain the toxins to a holding tank and eventually into the Niagara Falls sewage system facilities. A new company that no one ever heard of before, NEWCO Wastes Systems Inc. was awarded the contract. No one that I have ever talked to remembers this contract going out for bid.

The owners of NEWCO were none other than the Williams brothers who joined forces with mob-connected Lawrence Reger, president of a local drywall company. This was the start of a mega-conglomerate of corporations that still exists and is run by the same players. Sammy Pieri was in his glory. He and his cohorts found a new watering hole. Francis Williams had his office located at the Seneca Steel plant. I knew Francis quite well; he is the younger brother of James "Harry" Williams. During some of his strolls outside the building he would hand Sammy a bulging envelope. Pieri became a regular at the steel plant and always came back with his pockets loaded. I always wondered, *what the hell is Pieri doing with all his money?* I know he gambled, but the Williams kickbacks alone should have made him quite wealthy. I remember that it was sometime in the middle 1970s that the ownership of Seneca Steel, Beals McCarthy and Rogers Steel and a couple of other operations were transferred to the Williams brothers and Larry Reger's alleged secret partner, Kenneth Lipke.

The Love Canal was not in Local 210's jurisdiction and the laborers that performed the work on the project were members of Niagara Falls Laborers Local 91. The business manager for the local was Michael "Butch" Quarcini" who controlled his union with an iron fist. Quarcini allowed the use of non-union workers and made sure that the union laborers did not ruffle any feathers. Teamster's Local 449 business agent was Victor DiFlavio, a physically tough guy who took his orders directly from Joseph Todaro Sr. who equally went along with the concept. Chuck Lobish, a Harry Williams employee, handled the trucking which was mostly non-union and the drivers were paid wages lower than the federal and state prevailing rates.

It was always hard for me to figure out who Butch Quarcini answered to. I knew early on, when he first was elected, it was with the blessing of Magaddino's son-in-law Jimmy LaDuca and Benny Nicolletti Sr. But later on he was not well liked by Roy Carlisi nor by Joe Todaro Sr. They always spoke about him being a loose cannon and never said anything nice about him.

As a result of his father's relationship with Quarcini's brother Salvatore, Danny Sansanese Jr. became quite close to Butch and together they would play the finest golf courses in this country. Still, Danny Jr. was only a soldier with limited power and after his father died he had to answer to his younger brother Victor's orders. Victor Sansanese was well liked by Joey Pizza and climbed fast in the family hierarchy. Many of us considered him to be the new consigliere and not Leonard Falzone, as others have suspected. One time I asked Leonard about Butch and his reckless ways and he told me, "He answers, Ronnie, and is a good earner, but I cannot tell you more than that."

The construction at the Love Canal was a joke and everyone knew that the rings and clay containers were leaking even after they were inspected and approved. This was nothing new in the Western New York construction industry.

I remember one thing I was told that was considered a no-no and that was that NEWCO and their successor, CECOS

International Corp., were importing hazardous waste from other contaminated sites and landfills as far away as the New York City area. Surreptitiously they were carting and dumping the toxins into the Love Canal containment area. Many inspectors, employees and subcontractors supposedly became aware of this practice and nothing was being done about it. Roger Bennett, the brother-in-law of the Williams brothers, would travel with Sammy Pieri to New York City and be introduced to Angelo Ponte, Anthony Salerno and other members of the Genovese Family that controlled a large portion of the garbage industry in the greater New York area. Now capable of moving beyond the borders of their current Niagara Falls and Buffalo area of activity, the toxic waste barons started making contacts and spreading their influence in other states and municipalities.

The money was pouring in and overnight the Williams, Reger's and their legions were called geniuses. Politicians and community leaders praised them and in return they were rewarded with healthy contributions and well paying jobs after they completed their stint in the public service arena.

In 1983, CECOS and NEWCO were sold to *Browning-Ferris Industries* (BFI) for $83 million and millions of dollars in valuable BFI stock. It was a very bad deal for BFI; eventually they learned that the supposedly safe and well built containment structures and dump sites in Niagara Falls were in fact shabbily constructed and leaking. They also became aware that the dump sites they purchased in Williamsburg, Ohio and Baton Rouge, Louisiana, as well as others, were just as bad off. It was well known within the industry that they were poorly constructed and leaching toxins were ongoing, but with the mob covering it up the public and BFI were left uninformed.

The Williams boys and the Reger's were fully conscious they were violating numerous laws with potential harm to the public. They had to do something to protect them, so they put up firewall's that would shelter their involvement from the prying eyes of legitimate law enforcement officials. The establishment of front companies with fall guys to do the dirty work and take the rap, if they were caught, was now the path they would follow.

A non-compete clause with BFI prevented Larry Reger and James Harry Williams from re-entering the hazardous waste cleanup industry. However, during the sale the wheels were already in motion for them to remain in the industry and especially in the lucrative Western New York market area.

One of those front companies was the previously mentioned Envirosure Management Corp. operating under the guise of being owned by Norman Dobiesz. Envirosure had everything but money thus the Reger team in concert with the Williams boys involved the corporation known as Mader Capital, and supervised by Robert Richter a Reger brother-in-law, set up with separate books and money laundering operations. James Harry Williams invested more than a million dollars directly via an investment account that was in the name of his daughter and another $600,000 through stock purchases.

Around the same time, Dobiesz became chairman of another Williams-Reger owned company, Frontier Chemical Waste Process Inc. With Dobiesz's stature growing, James Harry Williams, using his Kansas City, Missouri connections, arranged for Dobiesz, together with the company's president, David T. Ryan, to meet with Jack E. Van Gundy, the chairman of PCB Treatment Inc., Environmental Resources Management Inc., of Nevada and Environmental International Electrical Services Inc. (EIES) of Kansas City. In 1986, with the help of the Chicago Mafia, and in particular Capo Vince Solano, who Van Gundy was paying tribute to, Envirosure Management Corp. purchased all the Jack Van Gundy environmental companies as well as a PCB storage facility (Rose Chemical) located in Kansas City. The storage facility had over 13.5 million pounds of abandoned PCBs.

The City of Holden, Missouri, its Mayor and the community were gaining national attention after numerous complaints by residents regarding the high level of toxins found in their water supply which was migrating to the community's neighborhoods from the storage site was exposed. By Christmas of 1986, Envirosure commenced a $6 million cleanup operation at the chemical site but soon the *Environmental Protection Agency* (EPA) discovered that they were not in compliance and new leaks were ascertained and flowing into the drinking water.

Dobiesz was in trouble and was caught illegally transporting the waste from the Rose Chemical storage site to places unknown. Back in Buffalo, he pleaded with James "Harry" Williams and Joe Cardinale to help get the EPA off his back. Congressman Jack Kemp's assistant Russell Gugino was asked, or probably told, by his close friend Joe Cardinale to help out Normy (whom Dobiesz was referred to by close friends) with the Kansas City problem. According to Gugino, who told me the story, he talked to Kansas

Senator Robert Dole, who did not help much, outside of giving him the name of someone in Missouri. All Gugino could accomplish was getting the EPA to slow down its investigation a little and buy some time. James "Harry" Williams was upset with Gugino's outcome and told him that he better do a better job or he would be off the payroll.

I have always been asked if I am aware of any connection Jack Kemp had to the mob and if he himself was mobbed-up. Did he have any connections? The answer, in my opinion, is: no! But for sure his influence indirectly helped the mob and its controlled employers. The reason I say this is I knew Jack Kemp quite well and I also knew that he gave a lot of latitude to his assistants. I cannot believe that he would allow his future goals be tarnished by some wayward activity. Russ Gugino had a lot of power in his own right and brought in a lot of money and support for quite a few people wanting to hold public office. It was the same with all of us who knew the mob! Many of us knew of the Kemp relationship with Jimmy Cosentino, James "Harry" Williams and Larry Reger, including many public citizens. What most didn't know was their connection to the mob and the widespread illegal activity they were involved in. Unfortunately, to get elected in this country it takes money and without it you have very little chance of gaining office. Kemp, like every political figure, knew this. Cosentino, the Williams and Reger's were some of the largest contributors in the Western New York community and they could make or break someone if they so desired. At the time, little did I know how in the near future their power would be used against me.

More mobsters wanted to make even more money in the lucrative hazardous waste business. Together with John "Pops" Papalia, Joe Todaro Sr. put together a team consisting of attorney David Knoll, Ted Gleave and Todaro associate James Ryding to assist a Canadian citizen by the name of Steven Crane who with others (whose names I cannot remember) secretly blended hazardous PCB laden oil with clean fuel (called cocktailing) and then sold it to customers in Canada and Western New York. David Knoll opened up an offshore account named Rhinestone Enterprises for Todaro and Papalia. Knoll was quite adept at establishing offshore accounts and previously set up an account for Todaro and Sonny Mauro when they sold their Hollywood, Florida Golden Strand Hotel.

Later on David Knoll, and confirmed by Jim Ryding, said more than $6 million in profit had been made from the illegal enterprise by the time they stopped in 1988. Unlike Ryding, Knoll complained that he was only given $200,000 and he should have gotten more for all the work he did.

In August of 1987, the EPA reached a consent agreement with Dobiesz whereby he would come into immediate compliance and all cleanup completed by the end of 1987. It also required that Envirosure stop shipping illegal PCBs by September of that year.

Eventually the EPA tossed Envirosure and Dobiesz off of the Rose Chemical Project. In 1990, they were charged with eight criminal counts of making false statements and one count of conspiracy.

Back in Western New York, regardless of the bad publicity Envirosure was receiving, they were awarded a $15 million cleanup of PCBs which were found in the popular summer resort of Wide Beach located in the resort town of Brant, New York. According to both Joe Cardinale and Russ Gugino, it was someone by the name of Vacco who helped in getting Dobiesz the contract.

After all the public clamor about Envirosure and its illegal charges, Williams and Dobiesz decided to back away from the Wide Beach project and let the sister company, Kimmins Thermal Corporation, which was being run by Harry's brother Francis, take over.

In 1988, Envirosure, Dobiesz, Reger and the Williams' were a focal point of a congressional investigation into their illegal hazardous waste removal practices. The FBI had raided the Envirosure offices located at Frontier Chemical Co. Inc. in Niagara Falls and Harry Williams and Larry Reger were quite concerned about the foray and hearings. They attempted to excise their names and any of the links that might compromise their hidden ownership of Envirosure.

A Saturday meeting was arranged for us to meet at the offices of Mader Capital. Larry Reger, Robert Richter and Norm Dobiesz were present when I arrived. Reger started by asking me to see if I could use the Laborers' benefit fund to finance and purchase the land that Frontier Chemical was located on for two million dollars. Fully cognizant that the land was contaminated and would probably cost ten times that amount to clean it up, I queried if the land was owned by Envirosure. Reger said he owned it with James "Harry" Williams. I said, "Before we go any further, Larry, I am no longer a trustee for the funds and that you would have to talk to Joey Todaro Jr." I asked Dobiesz how he was making out with the FBI investigation. Reger responded by telling me to talk to Dobiesz's attorney, Harold J. Boreanaz, who was also the attorney for the Buffalo Laborers' benefit funds as well, or Joey Todaro Jr., part owner of Envirosure.

After the meeting concluded Dobiesz asked to talk to me privately. Conversing in the Mader parking lot, he informed me, "The deal is already approved by Boreanaz and Todaro," and since I was still chairman of the Building Trades Investment Foundation I was to see if I could bring aboard other union funds in the purchase. I told him, "It would be impossible because it was in Niagara Falls and out of our jurisdiction. People are not stupid Norm, they know the site is contaminated and there is just no way anybody is going to invest in a toxic dump site." Later in the week I told this to Joey Todaro Jr., explaining that even if we invested in this project alone, we come under major federal and judicial scrutiny. Todaro, fearing FBI investigations, told me to hold off until he talked to Boreanaz.

In socially meeting Jimmy "Harry" Williams and Larry Reger, they seemed to be concerned about the Envirosure investigation but were confident that they could keep law enforcement agents from finding their involvement and the impossible task of perusing through the vast amount of corporations they possessed in getting at the truth.

Through people such as Joe Cardinale, they were capable of getting low cost insurance as well as with their own insurance company, Ardell Insurance. Ardell was an offshore company that was formed in the West Indies by Joe Cardinale, Roger Bennett, Donald Larder and James Harry Williams. The Williams-Reger team sometimes had more than five of their companies bidding on some projects.

Key municipality engineers, purchasing agents and politicians would have to be on board. The Williams-Reger-Mob team was the best at this! No other corporation could match their ability to devise schemes. Avoiding union problems? Because the mob controlled Teamsters and Laborers', the dominant trades involved in toxic waste, asbestos removal and the demolition industry were ready to turn their eyes! Only the operating engineers union still needed to be controlled but they really didn't seem to mind paying a couple of workers the right pay and maintaining their work rule conditions. Of all the Williams-Reger controlled companies only Kimmins Environmental and the Mader Corporation had signed union agreements, but it didn't matter because the union would not cause them a problem in allowing union employees to work alongside non-union workers.

In order to hurt and burden not-controlled companies, the mob-controlled unions would apply pressure on the competition, by enforcing agreements, notifying federal and state inspectors of safety violations, real and created, wage violations, sending unqualified workers and constant harassment. The very nature of hazardous waste work, even with the best efforts of the employer, is always some mishandling and spilling of asbestos and toxic waste. The unions and inspectors would make sure that the competitors were made to pay for their mistakes. When he was asked about his competition James "Harry" Williams would answer, "What competition? There is no competition."

When I was still at Local 210, Danny Sansanese and "Butch" Quarcini from Niagara Falls were spending a lot of time with Francis Williams in Tampa, Florida. While James Williams and Larry Reger were controlling operations from

Buffalo, Francis Williams brought Kimmins Construction (not subject to the BFI non-compete agreement) to Tampa, and changed the name to Kimmins Environmental Inc., making it a demolition and chemical cleanup company. Roger Bennett and a couple other employees temporarily left Envirosure to assist Francis.

The business grew quickly with the help of the mob. Dan Sansanese would meet the younger Williams and go over business strategy and how the mob would benefit. Among the plots would be the ability to benefit from insider trading when the fledgling company was listed on the over-the-counter stock market. During one of his numerous Tampa trips Danny purchased stock through one of his relatives and a small amount in his own name prior to informing the Todaros and the rest of the family. After a week had passed he passed the Kimmins revelation known to Joey Todaro Jr., but by now the stock had gone up a couple of dollars and the younger Todaro was enraged and asked me to take a walk with him. He told me what Sansanese had done and of the lame excuse of "forgetting" to tell Todaro. At that time Joey Todaro Jr. didn't like Danny, but tolerated him because he was a made guy and Victor's brother. Pizza said that he was going to invest through his children via a Canadian connection and for me to invest a portion of the Local 210 officer's retirement fund in Kimmins. I notified my contact at the FBI, SA Steve Naum, and told him what Todaro wanted me do and that the mob would be the recipient of insider trading information. Shortly thereafter the stock shot up and more than doubled. By this time Louie Giardina, a made member of the Gambino Family, and John Riggi, the acting boss of the New Jersey-based DeCavalcante Family, were among the many wiseguys who invested early on. The Chicago Family was also informed but I do not know if they reaped any proceeds from the insider info.

Russell Gugino and Joe Cardinale equally enjoyed doubling their money with stock purchases with the Kimmins Corp. Joe Cardinale was really not that smart and built his reputation and promoted his importance out of the fear that others had for his father, Sam. He did, however, know how to use, or maybe its better said, misuse, people and benefit from threats of violence, if he did not get his way with them.

He would spend his time on a golf course and when he did meet with people, he was always adorned in a suit and tie. He grew up in Lackawanna, New York, the town that reporter Walter Winchell once said he would rather be the Mayor of than the president of the United States, and almost totally controlled by his father Sam. Their connections went far beyond city hall and Bethlehem Steel, thus not too many decisions were made without mob approval. While attending Lackawanna High School he befriended a young Ron Jaworski, who would eventually become famous as the quarterback of the Philadelphia Eagles. Joe and Ron would hang around with Ron's brother Billy and Joe Cardinale's younger brother Ronnie. After Ron Jaworski joined the Eagles and started to receive accolades and the fame that went with it. The Cardinale brothers set out to use his prominence and apply it to a new money making notion.

One of these concepts included a charity that would raise funds for handicapped children and the sports figure was perfect as the focal point of this arrangement. Requesting contributions for such a worthy cause was easy and the brothers would then keep 25% of all cash proceeds as well as laundering 10% of check deposits. In order to conceal the siphoning of funds it would be necessary to show the exorbitant cost of the fund raising operation, including the cost of printing needs, (and unneeded) literature and advertisement.

William Delmont, the editor of the Lackawanna Newspaper and a leader in the Erie County Conservative Party knew that Sam Cardinale was someone to be feared. Reluctantly agreeing to print the ad book and charge more than it cost in order to kickback the difference to the Cardinales left Delmont in a quandary. They were not interested in the tax problems created by the cash payments and let Delmont know. Delmont took offense to their demands and soon word got back to the fearsome Cardinale father about Delmont's remarks and his reluctance to go along with the money laundering procedure. Sam Cardinale was no one to fool with, especially when it came to his kids and he responded by beating Delmont into submission and telling him that if he ever mentioned who beat him, they would be his last words. While recovering from his beating Delmont was questioned by the police and asked to describe his attackers. Knowing the elder Cardinale's reputation, he said that he didn't know.

Sam Cardinale was tough, and through the years he was an extremely violent mob enforcer. Nary a soul; including many of the Cosa Nostra members would ever offend The Priest, and they went out of their way to avoid him. He savored in his being a made man and he would carry out any mob order with zeal. Lackawanna and South Buffalo were under his domain and under the leadership of John Cammilleri and later the Sansanese's, Cardinale made certain that any problem that arose was quickly resolved.

One evening, a Lackawanna tough guy named Bob Aldrich was allegedly gunned down by Thomas Delmonte, a part-time associate of the Cardinales who acted on a request from The Priest since Aldrich had been critical of the Cardinales and their control. Even though the shooting was witnessed by many! No one would talk. Defiant to the end and as he lay dying, Aldrich answered the Lackawanna police inquiry of "who shot you" by saying, "it was John Wayne."

With the ever-present eavesdropping by the FBI and other law enforcement agencies, Sam Cardinale helped create a system by whereby the names of the mobsters and their associates were not uttered but gestured. A point to the lower front neck was an expression for Sam Cardinale, a finger pointed toward the eyes was for Joe LoTempio or "Blue-eyes," a nephew of Fred and Victor Randaccio; a brush of a beard would mean "whiskers" or the FBI. A hand to the sky was for Leonard Falzone (the tall guy), the cigar or a gesture to the mouth was Joe Todaro Sr., and a circular hand at the waist was for Pizza or Joe Todaro Jr., and so on. This made it complicated for the FBI, and even knowing what the gestures meant they knew making any case would be more difficult. Todaro Sr. created additional eavesdropping problems by telling the wiseguys to have their conversations in Canada, or go to an automobile dealership and enter a car being displayed on the showroom and talk there. They would go to extreme means to stem the flow of information being leaked or picked up by the big ears of the feds. Sammy Cardinale's kids were punks who lived in the shadow of their father's reputation and made a point of flaunting it every chance they had. Even Joe "Pizza" and Leonard Falzone did not like them and on a number of occasions mentioned this to me.

By this time new connected corporations were constantly popping up. A Houston, Texas-based company by the name of South Western Environmental and Demolition, operated by a Williams's relative, Jerry Williams, started bidding projects. Larry Reger had his nephews Herman Kellerer Jr. and James Biddle Jr., start up a non-union company, Innovative Insulation Inc., to take advantage of the "let them go" attitude of the mob. Joe Cardinale started up Environmental Asbestos Abatement Inc. with its offices located at the same address as another James Harry Williams company. He included as his secret partners, his father Salvatore, Brother Ronald, Victor Sansanese and Joey "Pizza" Todaro.

State and Federal Investigations of William Reger

As a result of the FBI information about the Love Canal, the mob and their involvement with the hazardous waste industry and bribery. In 1985, the FBI implemented Operation Plumline to investigate all the allegations. I was overjoyed. I felt it was about time and knew it would bring these uncaring bastards to justice. FBI agent Bernie Walsh really wanted to stop the mob and its connected employers. The information, as well as witnesses was being lined up for presentation to a grand jury and with it, numerous criminal indictments against the Williams-Reger-Mob operations.

◪ Corrupt Justice – Dennis Vacco

Where did he come from? How did he rise so fast and have the support to reach the high positions he held? Dennis Vacco was born on August 16, 1952, and grew up in the southern tier of Western New York. Prior to his senate confirmation as United States attorney in 1988, he served as an assistant district attorney in Erie County, New York for about 10 years. Vacco was hired by the no-nonsense crime fighting district attorney Edward Cosgrove immediately upon graduating from the University at Buffalo School of Law in 1978. It was alleged that Joseph P. McCarthy, the top assistant to Cosgrove and later a New York State Supreme Court justice, together with former Local 210 laborer and Family Court Judge Anthony LaRusso, prodded Cosgrove to give the green Vacco the prized position.

In the spring of 1988, I learned that New York Senator Alfonse D'Amato was going to have President Ronald Reagan nominate Dennis Vacco to the position of United States Attorney for Western New York. This revelation took place at a luncheon meeting I was having with former Congressman Jack Kemp's assistant Russell Gugino, Joseph

Cardinale and Victor Sansanese. They let me know about the pending appointment and were totally elated regarding it, exclaiming the benefits they could reap from having a *friend* in such a high position.

I answered them I didn't know much about him. Gugino retorted, "He is our guy and a great friend," and that Jimmy Cosentino, Tommy Reynolds (former member of the Erie County legislature and later chairman of the National Republican Congressional Committee), Lou Billittier (owner of Chef's Restaurant), Bob Gioia (Gioia Pasta), Louie Russo (Sorrento Cheese), Harry Williams, Larry Reger (and someone whose name I cannot remember) implored Senator D'Amato to present Vacco's name to the president for nominating. Gugino went on about Vacco and how he was extremely close to Vacco's father Carmen, the chairman of the town of Brant Republican Party. Additionally, some in the Democratic Party agreed to go along with the appointment and would not cause any problems for the Republican.

Sometime right after that Jimmy Cosentino and James "Harry" Williams sent word that they wanted to see me. When we met they asked me to gather up a group of people to attend an event they were holding for Senator D'Amato (I think the amount was $1,000 per person), that would be held at Cosentino's (James "Harry" Williams was a secret part owner) Executive Resort Hotel located near the Buffalo airport. Williams said, "Don't worry about the cost; the tickets are already paid for. Just bring bodies." He handed me around 20 tickets which I gave to some of the employees of Hazardous Waste Management.

At the event Jimmy Cosentino was walking around with the senator and introducing him to his friends and many of the other attendees. After guiding D'Amato to me, Cosentino did not know that we already knew each other and introduced me. D'Amato acknowledged that he already knew me and that we had met on a number of occasions. Then both D'Amato and Cosentino introduced me to Dennis Vacco and his father who were standing nearby. We shook hands and they greeted me in a very friendly way but no other words were uttered. While the senator was talking to Vacco, Cosentino pulled me aside and whispered in my ear that Vacco was going to be the new US Attorney. After apprising Cosentino that I already heard of the disclosure, he went on to say how he, together with New York City entrepreneur Phil Basile and Uncle Joe (referring to Joseph Todaro Sr.) helped make sure that the senator appointed Vacco. Cosentino and the senator continued making the rounds and after personally greeting some of the other guests I went over to sign the guest book. While looking over the names I noticed that Vacco signed in as the United States Attorney even though he did not hold that position.

His selection as the new US Attorney for the Western New York district was, to say the least; very disturbing news for me and immediately after the reception I let the FBI and SA Steven Naum know what I previously relayed to them was, in fact, true. This was a disaster just waiting to happen and in my opinion was going to cause serious consequences for me as well as the numerous ongoing investigations.

Naum still did not believe it and said, "The next Western New York US Attorney is going to be Roger Williams."

In a later conversation I had with Joe Cardinale he stated that it was Russ Gugino who brought Dennis Vacco into the fold. Sometime after that I went and talked to Conservative Party Chairman Bill Delmont, who was, for many years, a very dear and close friend, and I always liked him for keeping confidentiality. He confirmed that Vacco was indeed going to get the position and that he was concerned about my safety.

Then it happened, and on my birthday, June 1, 1988, United States Attorney General Edwin Meese named Dennis Vacco as the new United States Attorney. *Oh my God!* I thought to myself. *How does the FBI keep my role secret from a guy I know is the enemy?*

The FBI arranged for a secret conference to be held in Pittsburgh, Pennsylvania, well away from Western New York. Steve Naum was there as well as other agents and I was tipped off that they had no choice but to let Vacco know of my undercover activity, but did not have to go into specifics. "This is no damn good, Steve!" I said. "This man is going to know about my role and that alone is a significant danger." The four agents sat quietly and seemed bewildered about what the hell could be done. One of the agents said, "One way we could limit what Vacco knows is to put you on the FBI's payroll as a contract employee. This will help somewhat, but we still have to let him know that you are working as a non-official cover operative" (which was later called a NOC).

I knew I had no chance of success with Hazardous Waste Management, not even having a position as an officer with the fledgling company reflected just how little say-so I actually had. One of the agents, Tommy McDonnell, in addition to the already tragic news made it known that they had information that I was the victim of a bust out scheme and secretly many of our employees were working for the Cardinale-Sansanese-Todaro Company, Environmental Asbestos Abatement Inc.

On the ride back to Buffalo I was sick to my stomach over what I had just heard. Still, I was praying for hope that somehow the FBI could find a way to conceal my activity from Vacco or that he may turn his back on those that helped him get his powerful position. I still had Timoney Technology and I made a deal with Gene Amadori whereby I would have 30% ownership in his construction company.

Back in Buffalo, I learned from SA Tommy McDonnell that Dennis Vacco had been informed of my status. I repeated what I previously said, "This is nuts, this guy may blow me out of the water." My fears were soon realized. On September 30, 1988, I attended what I thought was a sit-down with the leaders of the Buffalo Family to discuss the Cardinale takeover of Hazardous Waste Management. Sammy Cardinale walked over to me and said, "Ronnie, I know you are expecting more people here but I can assure you that I speak for them." What was even worse and more serious was when he said, "I'm going to have to frisk you. You're not wearing a wire or something are you?" I thought to myself, *if he puts one finger on me I will break it off.* I immediately went on the offensive and angrily told him he should be ashamed of himself. He said, "Well, out of respect for your father, I'll let you go, I won't touch you." If Cardinale did frisk me he would have found the FBI recording device that I tried to conceal in a partially empty pack of cigarettes. I knew the jig was up and that my time in Buffalo was coming to an end.

During my conversation with the deranged killer and his kids Joey and Ronnie, Sammy showed his anger by grimacing and growling, "You have no more connections with the family, they are all gone. You have to answer to my kids." They were already on the payroll and stealing all the fucking money from my company, *these rotten rats,* I said to myself.

I went along with the elder Cardinale, knowing that the recorder in my pocket would soon bury them all. I even made sure I responded to his statement that I had no more connections by saying, "I still have political connections in the area." Joey Cardinale laughingly answered, "We're not talking about those kinds of connections."

Immediately after the meeting I met up with SA Steve Naum who had parked his car outside the Veterans Administration Hospital where the so-called sit-down took place and then drove to the designated place we were to meet at. Mad and stunned by what just happened I barked that I was fucked and that it was just a matter of time before I was completely exposed. I thought to myself that Vacco may have already mentioned to someone to be careful of me but did not come right out and say I was cooperating with the FBI. Just enough to question my trustworthiness, but not enough to make them totally shy away! The tape recording came out pretty good and captured their extortion of me which made Steve Naum quite happy.

My unease was further entrenched when on November 13, 1988, I arranged a follow-up chat with Victor Sansanese at the Cosentino-owned Executive Resort Hotel. He cautiously advised me that my credibility was in question and "it is not coming from us but from there" (referring to the government). Like other mob meetings I was now having, the recorder was capturing all.

Together with FBI agents Arthur Dave Webster, Steve Naum and Tommy McDonnell at a meeting that was held immediately after the Sansanese disclosure, I was assured by them that G. Robert Langford, Special Agent in Charge of the Buffalo office, "likes you Ronnie and the courageous act you are involved in. If you feel in anyway you are in imminent danger, immediately contact one of us and we'll get you into a secure location. The bureau will not let you down, you have many friends and you will have a future with us." I was somewhat relieved by their remarks but my thoughts were totally confused and I could not clear my clouded head.

The following day, November 14, 1988, I met with Danny "Boone" Domino at a Denny's restaurant located off Transit Road near the Eastern Hills Mall. I informed him that I was under suspicion by the family and asked if he could see what was going on and who was behind it. His reaction was not one of shock but rather somewhat subdued. "Ronnie, I will check and see if the Pieris have any knowledge about it." Domino said his brother in-law Joe Raco would meet me at 8:00 p.m. at a crowded downtown Buffalo restaurant and enlighten me as to what he found out. That night, Raco spotted me and rushed over and from the expression on his face I knew what his message would be. He came over and whispered, "The Boone told me to tell you to get out of town and that the mob knows you are cooperating with the FBI."

I immediately went home, grabbed a gun, packed a bag and with Denise Erb, who wanted to go with me and I left the city to get as far away as I could. I didn't even bother to call the FBI.

I really didn't know what to do. I was so confused and

still in shock as we drove in the direction of California. I really did not want this girl to be with me and I told her that she could potentially be in harm's way. She didn't care and refused to leave. I knew we would never last together and this was just a fling and would soon die. My hopes of ever returning to Buffalo were dashed and I knew what would happen if I did. I called my wife Donna and told her of my predicament. Saying, "If I go to the bureau, it would mean my having to testify in open court." She responded, "Just stay the fuck away from Buffalo, me and the kids and don't become a public spectacle." For all of the almost 20 years we were together, I never once let her know that I had been cooperating and of my role with the bureau or CIA, just like Al Hartel requested. I always kept this a total secret. I then asked her if she wanted to move out of Buffalo and join me. She stated, "Ronnie, if I had a gun I would blow your brains out!" I knew she did not mean it and was only saying that out of anger. I didn't blame her for her attitude. If she did go with me, I very likely could be endangering her and my children.

After a couple days of pondering and learning that my leaving and cooperation with the feds was making headlines, I called FBI agent Tom McDonnell at home one evening. He told me not to worry and that the FBI would take care of me. He also wanted me to talk to supervisor Ron Webb, who had been reaching out all over the place and attempting to contact me. The next day I contacted Webb, who reiterated what I was told the night before and he added, "Listen Ronnie, you have a good future with the bureau, Rob Langford likes you a hell of a lot and you have a good opportunity with the FBI." After telling him okay, what else could I do or say? He then said, "Send Denise Erb back by plane and have her start gathering all your belongings, drive back and go to the Batavia, New York area and call me when you arrive."

I sent Denise back to Buffalo by plane, then headed back east. After arriving in the Batavia area (about 30 minutes east of Buffalo) I called Webb and let him know I arrived. Soon SA's Dave Webster and Tommy McDonnell arrived. They arranged a room for me at a nearby Travelers Inn.

Ron Webb arrived about an hour later and the three of us sat down and discussed my future. We started discussing an agreement but we were miles apart on terms and I threatened to leave. Webb told me to be patient, but what I was requesting exceeded the power of Langford and would require FBI headquarters approval. I agreed to continue to bide my time for a while. I was looking for security and an agreement to protect my future. After around three hours of us going back and forth and getting nowhere, they departed for the night.

The next day I received an early call from Dave Webster who told me Vacco wanted to meet me and for me to be very careful with him, "He is not with us." Hell, I'm the one that told them that. I already knew where Vacco stood but agreed to meet him anyway. He arrived with Roger P. Williams (who was previously the acting US Attorney (and not related to the Williams brothers) until Vacco was appointed. It was agreed that we meet at the nearby Sheraton Hotel.

Vacco was very arrogant and I could tell from his lack of knowledge that the bureau did in fact keep him in the dark about my activities. For about an hour I listened as he ranted that he was hell-bent on not having me testify. He also said,

"The only way I will even listen to you is if you admit to something criminal," and if I didn't, "then there is no way I will have you enter a protection program." I responded, "Number one, Dennis, I haven't committed any crimes and the only reason you want me to admit to something like that is so I can be placed under your thumb. Number two, I am not looking to enter any protection program, nor will I! If that's the way you want it, I will leave." Vacco seemed satisfied with that answer, but the bureau wasn't. They were just as upset as I was over Vacco's remarks and Webster said, "Good for you Ronnie, good answer. He is a major thorn but we can find a way to get around him." That night I received a call from Rob Langford who warmly stated, "Just relax, we'll work out something."

That night Denise Erb arrived with some of my clothes. She told me that Ron Cardinale and attorney David Knoll had rifled my office at HWM and were seen taking out three large boxes of confidential documents. When she went to my apartment, the door was ajar and she spotted my brother Patrick carting out boxes of documents and who knows what else from my residence. He seemed quite nervous about being caught and told Denise he had a right to be in there, which, of course, he did not. I was quite shocked over this! My own brother would do such a thing and enter my apartment without asking me and steal my personal documents and records.

It was late so I waited until the next morning to call the bureau about this startling event. When I did contact them I pointed out what Denise had reported to me about the document raids and that I had quite a lot of needed info which they probably absconded with. The most important ones being the ones my brother took. Besides documents that would additionally help the bureau, there were also Timoney Technology legal papers that showed that I owned 60% of the company. Still, it was my brother and I felt he would never try and screw me. Later on, when I asked him to help my son Joseph, I learned that he wanted the company all to himself and excluded me and my children. Patty was uneducated, having never finished high school. My father always wanted me to take care of him, and I did. He was my brother. I previously told him if anything ever happened to me to use any profits to take care of our other brother and sisters as well as my mother. This he never did and kept it all for himself. It hurt me to see him act like this. We were family and he knows who built the business and brought in the money. I thought to myself, *if you can't trust your brother who can you trust?*

The FBI was ready and besides me, we had numerous witnesses that were ready to testify against the Magaddino Family domain led by Joseph Todaro Sr., as well as the Williams-Reger operations. Alphonse "Little Al" D'Arco, the former acting boss of the New York City-based Lucchese crime family, Angelo Leonardo, the underboss of the Cleveland Family, Salvatore "Sammy" Spano, who himself and his family had been involved with the Buffalo crime family for years, Fred Saia, a key player in the mob rackets, Johnny Sacco, who had a long criminal record but whose testimony could be collaborated by me and the others, and another three others whose names I cannot mention, including a high-level member of the Todaro Family. Together with me we could put these villains away for many years. Equally, we had more than 30 additional witnesses including current and former business associates ready to testify against the Williams', Reger's and Cosentino's illegal business practices.

Before I concluded my agreement with the FBI, I was contacted by attorney Daniel Oliverio. Thinking wrongly that he was sent by the FBI, I decided to talk with him. His opening remarks were that he was "here to help me." After thanking him, he said he would try and get me a good agreement. I told him I did not need him to assist me with an agreement and that I had spent more than 15 years concluding agreements. Rambling on the attorney alluded, "You do need me to represent you when you testify in the John Catanzaro case." I didn't think I did but I said okay.

John Catanzaro was on trial for being a Local 210 no-show labor steward on a Buffalo project. Together with Frank "Butchie" BiFulco they became made men under the Pieri faction in 1981. Both were considered good earners as well as having the ability to kill anyone if were so ordered. When the Todaro-Pieri dispute arose, both secretly switched sides and joined the Todaro faction.

About a month had gone by and the early stages of the Catanzaro case were upon us. Oliverio visited me one afternoon and said that he had first hand knowledge that the FBI was going to screw me and that I should just take off and forget about working with them. This remark sent bells off and I quickly thought, *this guy is not working for me and the FBI. This sneaky no-good is a Vacco plant.* I immediately told him goodbye and contacted SAC Langford about Vacco's deviousness. I further learned from the FBI that Oliverio tried to obtain anything he could discover about me including pulling the lowest of the low (an offense that could have him disbarred) for his useless quest to uncover something illegal I might have been involved in! I called him and told him to stay away from me.

I also learned that Vacco was probably pulling the same gambit with Johnny Sacco and more than likely chose the attorney to represent him. Sacco was a shady character, a mob associate that spent his whole life promoting illegal activity. He carried a lot of baggage, but supported by those that did not, such as me, his knowledge could not be easily brushed aside. With testimony that could damage so many in the Buffalo Family, the bureau knew that it would produce a flood of potential mobsters and shady businessmen that would be looking to make a deal. It possibly would curtail Vacco; and his political future would cease to exist. As a result Dennis "The Menace" openly stated that there would be no "get out of jail" deal for Sacco.

The *Buffalo News* carried an article that said Sacco and I "produced less information than agents expected." Now, who could have leaked a story like that to the *Buffalo News*? It wasn't the FBI, they knew better! I doubt very much that the *Buffalo News* would print an article leaked to them by the mob. Anyone with half a brain, and who had done a little research, knows who leaked it! It is very reflective of what we were up against and the major obstacle in our way, or as the mobster would say, *the stone in my shoe.*

I finally concluded a long term agreement with the FBI which encompassed everything that I needed. The accord did, however, require me to perform additional investigative operations, teaching in-service classes at the FBI Academy, reporting and undercover surveillance assigned to me under the direction of the field offices and supervisors that I would be referred to. I was not opposed to this and welcomed it.

Back in Buffalo, in an effort to try and solve the differences Vacco and I were having, another meeting was arranged by the FBI. This time it would be at the Camp Road Holiday Inn, located in Hamburg, New York. Together With SAC G. Robert Langford, we drove in his car to the hotel and the Vacco engagement. This time he was alone. He started by asking me about my role with the FBI and said it's apparent that it went further than just my being an informant. I told him, "I cannot tell you more than what I have previously alluded to and I didn't appreciate the remarks in the *Buffalo News* stating that I didn't have that much information." I told Dennis, "You became aware of my activity for the FBI from them telling you and they also mentioned to me that you received a letter that stated I was an informant." He confirmed that he did receive such a letter that was addressed to him. I thought to myself that, *that is a bunch of crap, if anyone sent him a letter, he wrote it to himself.*

It was a way for Vacco, even if it was childish, to undress me and have my undercover activity revealed. I forcefully blurted out, "Dennis, this man (pointing to Langford), is not going to bare the activity that I did for the FBI, especially to you. You got your appointment with the help of Jimmy Cosentino, Russ Gugino, Louis Russo and James "Harry" Williams." He was, by now, very irritated with me and said that it was Robert Gioia who presented his name for consideration. I said "Yes he was part of it, together with Jeremy Jacobs, Tommy Reynolds, Sam Santarosa and Larry Reger, but you also know Cosentino, Gugino and Williams were involved." Ironically, instead of saying they are all outstanding business people, he curtly remarked "I am not going to have anyone testify in any case of mine if they think I am a criminal," or words to that effect. I ended the conversation by telling him, "You can't fire me." Without saying another word, Vacco stormed out the door and left Langford with a "well that didn't work out so well" look on his face. I didn't know it at the time, but this egotistical tyrant Vacco had even more power than I could have imagined.

I welcomed work and my years of undercover activity had led me to a new career with the FBI. The FBI Academy is located at the United States Marine Corps base located in Quantico, Virginia. It is a fine facility equipped with everything from a fabricated city (Hogan's Alley) to some of the best classrooms I have ever seen. The food was good and so was the bar (The Boardroom). Rarely did you leave the facility to go out to eat or shop. There was nothing around back then, only a Holiday Inn located in the nearby town of Triangle. I would instruct and lecture agents about my experiences and recommendations regarding undercover procedures.

I enjoyed it, but after my partner, Agent Stan Ronquest, was killed while visiting Kansas City, I, along with others, was required to see an FBI psychiatrist located in Baltimore, Maryland. They wanted to see if the impact of Stan's death prevented me from doing my job. The female doctor told me to stop shaking and I let her know that it didn't have anything to do with my visit to her, but the result of putting down too many beers the night before with Agent Tommy

McDonnell. After the test was completed and I was cleared to go back to work, she told me, "The results show that you enjoy education and should be a teacher."

I was now living in another area of the country and following the burdened schedule the FBI had me on. I was not in touch much with Buffalo outside of helping SA Dave Webster with the no-show Laborers' Local 210 "John Catanzaro, Union Steward Case."

The war between the FBI and Vacco was heating up. In reading the newspapers, I learned that a deal the FBI made with John Sacco had fallen apart; Dennis Vacco threw it out. I think he realized Sacco knew too much, so he ruined a potentially very good witness. Publicly, Vacco berated the FBI and agents Bobby Watts and Jeff McLane for being incompetent and said the bureau should not use such agents on important matters. I personally knew both agents who were hardworking and dedicated to getting at the truth. All this was an excuse for Vacco to eradicate Sacco as a witness. Both agents were transferred and when Langford let Vacco know that he was hanging around too much with Jimmy Cosentino, who was the target of an ongoing investigation, it was just too much for Vacco to bare, so he set his sights on removing the Special Agent in Charge of the Buffalo office, G. Robert Langford.

In a May 8, 2008, interview with the *Society of Former Special Agents of the FBI*, Langford explained what happened.

So I was there two years as SAC and then I had a run-in with the US Attorney. We were investigating a guy who had a lot of OC connections and it turned out he was very good friends with the US Attorney, Dennis Vacco. I'm sure Vacco would have a different take on it. But I said, "Dennis, you do not *need to be running around with this guy." He said, "You don't tell me what to do." I said, "Well, I'm just telling you." And we really had a go at it and it got really nasty and finally he wrote the bureau and said, "I can't work with this guy anymore, he doesn't need to be SAC." The bureau went along with it and I really fought it; so I was transferred out unhappily down to the bureau. Well, they transferred me to the Career Development Section which was just starting up with this consultant to develop a whole new promotions plan for the bureau.*

To me, the only one in the bureau that would appease Vacco and agree to his request had to have been FBI Director William "Concession" Sessions. Unlike other directors, numerous agents would say Sessions had no guts, and only looked out for himself and his wife Alice. If it had been a Louie Freeh, Floyd Clark or a William Webster, this never would have happened.

Under the Justice Department system the FBI answers to the attorney general and the appointed United States attorneys. After J. Edgar Hoover ruled the bureau, no elected official desired to have a strong FBI and since Hoover, its ability to investigate is limited to what the upper management of the Department of Justice allows them to investigate. If the public makes enough noise regarding a given person or situation, or the news is laden with the story of an impropriety, they will investigate. To me, they really are a great organization and have had to try and work through many political restraints as well as being told they spy on too many people. The bureau has a saying "If the public knew the truth" in reference to just how small spying operations on the public really are, then they would not be opposed. It seems that every time someone picks up a phone and they hear some static or other sound, they think the FBI is spying on them. This, of course, is not true and the general public should not be afraid. Sure, they have made their share of mistakes, but as human beings we all screw up once in a while. Believe me, at no time has the FBI, or anyone in the Justice Department, ever asked or prodded me to embellish a story.

One of the weaknesses we do have, or at least did, is dealing with criminal informants. In an effort to limit or avoid a jail sentence, it is a practice to reward those that could help the most. The criminal knows this and will offer even more than what they really know in an effort to cut a better deal. The Henry Hill (*Goodfellas*) testimony deal contained quite a lot of information that he would not have been aware of. I personally knew the Vario's, Mike LaBarbara and the Long Island faction of the Lucchese crime family. There is just no way Big Paulie Vario would get involved with this wannabe.

Today the FBI is inundated with protecting our country from the ever-present threat of terrorism and from those hell-bent on killing Americans and destroying all of us. To me they have done a fantastic job, but as we all know, sooner or later some one or group will slip through the cracks and commit a violent act.

I was shocked after learning that Langford was kicked out of Buffalo, so I contacted my close friend of many years Gene Methvin, the senior editor of *Reader's Digest*, who was a staunch Republican and had connections at the highest level of the White House and Republican Party. I explained the Vacco problem to him and how he was a major deterrent to the FBI's investigation of organized crime in Buffalo. Somehow Vacco had got to FBI Director William Sessions to remove this great crime fighter, Robert Langford. Methvin told me he would look into it. Within a week he called me back and said, "After reviewing the situation it appears that Vacco may be an unsavory character. Unfortunately, unless we can prove that he acted out of malice, there is not much anyone in the administration can do. They did admit that a mistake may have been made with his appointment in the first place."

I wanted to fight back and I was confident that I could get enough signatures of FBI agents from around the country to join me in some sort of protest. Methvin said, "All that will do is hurt you, the FBI and the task you are fighting for. There is one way, however, and that is by following through with the civil *Racketeer Influenced and Corrupt Organizations Act* (RICO) concept that the FBI and the decent federal prosecutors were contemplating to use against the Laborers' International Union." He further assured me that, "The (George H.) Bush administration will never cover up any crimes like you are mentioning and Attorney General Dick Thornburgh would be the first to bring charges against any wayward United States Attorney."

There was no question in my mind that Methvin was a hardworking, honest reporter but I questioned his looking at the situation through rose colored glasses and attacking the problem by way of the upcoming civil RICO action.

While we were implementing the Laborers' International

Union case, not all was well in Buffalo. After the close call with the FBI, James "Harry" Williams and his team set out to derail many investigations that were ongoing at the time. One of these dealt with what is known as *fuel blending* (mixing toxic waste fuel with clean fuel). Envirotek Ltd. was indirectly controlled by Harry Williams and targeted by the FBI for the illegal practice. After substantial information, quality witnesses and a myriad of leads into other Williams's operations was obtained, Vacco decided to curtail the investigations and limit the matter to only a slap on the wrist. In a statement Vacco said, "The ongoing tax investigation was favored because there was a fresher (paper) trail, harder evidence and stiffer penalties."

The bureau was shocked and its agents were openly taken aback. They knew, like most of the witnesses, that the flagrant illegal environmental activities by the Williams companies were being swept under the rug and that we were facing an enemy that seemed to have more power than the bureau. To make matters worse, the FBI had all this documentation, witnesses and informants lined up to address the criminal activities involving Buffalo Mafia boss Joe Todaro Sr., mob members and associates Danny Sansanese , James Cosentino Harry Williams, Russell Gugino, Victor Sansanese, the Cardinales and numerous others.

A chill ran down the backs of many and the mob, as well as their controlled companies, knew that the bureau finally had a means to wreak havoc and mangle their operations.

As I noted before, FBI headquarters wanted nothing to do with creating a rift between the bureau and the Western New York US Attorney. Everyone knew that without the support of headquarters, the Buffalo office was in a losing battle. John Sacco eventually died in jail. I later learned that while attending a conference of United States attorneys, Vacco stated he did not have a Mafia problem in Western New York. Another US Attorney said to Vacco, "Then you do not need any funds to fight the Mafia, so why don't you send the money to me because in my area we have a major problem."

On February 26, 1992, US Attorney Vacco announced the conviction of the Williams-Reger owned Frontier Chemical Waste Process Inc. The company pleaded guilty to falsifying EPA records in 1986, based on the EPA "Landfill Ban" which prohibited the placement of certain type of wastes in landfills.

Vacco said the plea agreement was the result of the intervention by a Colorado corporation called Eagle Vision Inc., under the direction of Dr. Gerry Norton. Norton's companies bought control of the Frontier operations while simultaneously seeking permission from the New York State Department of Environmental Conservation for the transference of the Frontier permit.

Vacco hailed the close cooperation among the responsible government agencies including his office and the FBI. What a damn joke this was! Everyone knew it was going to happen and Williams, Reger and the mob would get off. Even Dobiesz was given a pass. Without ever mentioning their names they received just a $100,000 fine and a five-year ban from staying out of the ownership of Frontier Chemical. What a fucking deal they got! On top of all the swill Vacco had the nerve to call it a win-win situation. What he failed to mention was that Eagle Vision was owned by noted scam artist Alan S. Lipstein, who lived in Tampa, Florida and allegedly had a relationship with Francis Williams and Kimmins. He was also a close associate of noted stock swindler and manipulator Louis Pasciuto and Genovese Family Capo Allie "Shades" Malangone, who controlled the stock broker Hanover Sterling. Dr. Gerry Norton and Lipstein, it is believed, first teamed up in 1986.

More disturbing was that by December 1992, the New York DEC issued a order showing that both Frontier and Eagle Vision were violating the agreement regarding the facility at 4626, Royal Avenue, Niagara Falls, New York. They were ordered to clean up 4,000 drums of leaking hazardous waste.

The companies responded by saying (in an affidavit by Neil M. Gingold, who was also the attorney for many of Williams-Reger operations), "they did not manage the day to day operations at Frontier."

Here is a clear and precise order that clearly points out the scam that Vacco called a "win-win" deal. Where were the news reporters and the investigators? Why didn't anyone investigate Eagle Vision? Why is Dobiesz still working the site? If they did cover this story, as well as the continued leaking of the Love Canal project, the public would, I am damn sure, demand an investigation of all these back room deals and the continuous leaking chemicals. Personally, I cannot believe how someone can or could act so blatantly and get away with it. I know they bought a lot of people, but they can't buy everybody! When the enforcers of the law don't enforce them, this is a clear example of what happens. These are cancer causing mutagens. How can somebody be so inhumane and not care about the mutilation and death that is resulting from their "money first" mentality? All I can say is shame on you and may you never get another good night's sleep.

The Williams brothers, et al., needed someone in New York State to curtail or, at the very least, implement the same type of Hooker Chemical settlements to overcome all the scrutiny that was befalling them. Vacco had to have known that Eagle Vision owner Alan Lipstein was the subject of a securities fraud lawsuit filed in July 1992. In a typical pump-and-dump stock swindle (artificially inflating the price through false statements), the stock was selling at $11 a share with a $7 commission paid to the sellers. Louis Pasciuto was one of those pushing the over-valued stock. He was arrested in 1999, for securities fraud and wound up broke and spilled his guts to federal agents investigating organized crime.

In 2000, Lipstein pleaded guilty to laundering money through fraudulent stock transactions. In 2002, federal regulators shut down one of his companies and in 2006, the SEC permanently banned Lipstein from trading penny stocks.

In 1993, Dennis Vacco was removed as US Attorney by the incoming Clinton administration. With the support of the Williams-Reger-Cosentino-Mob team, he ran for the office of, and became, the New York State Attorney General in 1994. As attorney general-elect, word was sent to Ronald Goldstock that the state Organized Crime Task Force that he headed for 13 years was going to be dismantled and he dismissed. Not waiting for his dismissal, Goldstock resigned on December 12, 1994.

Vacco didn't like that Goldstock's unit was autonomous and out of the attorney general's control. *What an evil move this was*, I thought; everyone in the mob as well as his Buffalo pals knew and feared Ronnie Goldstock. This was a great day for the mob, James "Harry" Williams and all involved, plus payback for all the trouble the crime fighter had caused them. They must have been overjoyed.

I talked to Ron Goldstock about this but he didn't want to discuss it. In conversations with other great crime fighters, such as my friend Bob Stewart, the former Department of Justice Organized Crime Division specialist, who mirrored that Vacco was more interested in his future and politics and it can be a dirty game. Only the people of this country can change it.

Vacco's wrath didn't end with New York State; his relationship with New York City-based US Attorney Mary Jo White was one that was acerbic, at best.

The *New York Times* carried a story September 11, 1996, on just how reckless and ruthless Vacco really was. He hired numerous lawyers for his staff with little or no experience, based purely on political party affiliation and their recommendations, even if their attributes were below average and not qualified.

Several judges complained publicly about the competence of his staff. Vacco's judicial record, in fact, is filled with reprimands from federal and state judges about missed deadlines and frivolous motions. One federal judge in 1996, referred to "a series of unending failures by the Office of the Attorney General."

As an example, Vacco allegedly, pressured Buffalo Mayor Jimmy Griffin to help the Williams-Reger team with city contracts, by spending more than $200,000 in probing and eventually convicting the former City Parks Commissioner,

Robert E. Delano. Vacco was quoted as saying the money was well spent. He chastised Mayor Griffin and said the mayor should accept the responsibility for the parks scandal instead of blaming others. No one I know had courage like Mayor Griffin and I am sure he held out to the bitter end before he was compelled to place prominent James "Harry" Williams lackeys in city hall positions.

Now Vacco was going after bigger fish and in January 1996, his office "opened an investigation into payments allegedly made by a nonprofit, state-financed organization based in Rochester to Hillary Rodham Clinton and her Arkansas law firm between 1990, and 1992." Unable to supply any evidence to support the allegations, the charges against Senator Clinton were withdrawn.

When it became public knowledge that Vacco's wife inappropriately obtained classified personnel documents about lawyers from his Buffalo branch, Vacco denied the charge until unmistakable evidence came out against her. Vacco apologized, but the nonpartisan citizen's lobbying organization Common Cause and outraged citizens wanted an investigation. Of course nothing happened and the matter died.

Vacco took credit for the 1997, arrest of 59 members of New York and New Jersey crime families, for work that had mostly been done by his predecessor Robert Abrams and Ronnie Goldstock. Vacco reduced the criminal charges to civil, so taxpayers could seize the bookmaking operations. Anybody with an ounce of knowledge about the mob knows that profits are disbursed immediately and hidden far from discovery. The cost of filing and trying to collect hidden assets far outweighed what could be gained. The mob doesn't care about coughing up some of their vast millions; they do it every day with kickbacks. What they do care about is lengthy prison sentences. There is no doubt in my mind that Dennis Vacco let the bad guys off again.

The Oxford case stands out brightly, because it reflects Vacco's way of easing the burden for those that contributed to his campaign. Oxford Resources, who had agreements with the state, constantly overcharged its customers for car rentals and leasing, implementing deceptive practices to eke out every dollar they could. Vacco recommended the matter be settled by mediation. This was how Vacco circumvented legal problems for his friends and contributors. During the investigation Oxford, directly and indirectly, gave $8,500 to Vacco's re-election campaign. After the investigation was closed in November 1997, his campaign received an additional $37,500 from nine Oxford subsidiaries, all on the same day.

By March of 1998, Dennis Vacco had obtained more than $80,000 in contributions from 97 of his appointed staff. The previous New York State Attorney's General banned this practice because it would politicize the office. Contributors to Vacco in 1998, included my ex-attorney Paul Cambria, who is well known for his representation as the chief counsel for the porn industry. Numerous organized crime figures and undesirables have benefited tremendously from Cambria's' acumen and knowledge of the law. Paul and his law firm have and still represent Laborers' Local 210. They gave more than $5,000 to Vacco's campaign.

Of course the James "Harry" Williams-Larry Reger myriad of operations and employees gave over $100,000 directly and indirectly. Even Freddie Randaccio's (the deceased underboss of the Magaddino Family) son Albert kicked in. Looking a little closer I found a company that Victor Sansanese and Joseph Rosato secretly have interest in, De Rose Marketing Inc., which contributed one thousand dollars.

There were so many mobbed-up companies and fronts that gave close to a million dollars to Vacco. These people and companies don't just put up that kind of money because they think a candidate is going to do a good job for the citizens of New York! There is no need for me to explain why, the answer and what damage was done is self evident. If the people of the state of New York were aware of this man's abuse of his power, they would have tarred and feathered him long ago.

I know that under our electoral system it takes a lot of money to get elected. Promises are made and the big contributors always seem to be taken care of at the expense of the rest us. This topic has already been covered by better heads than mine and heard by everyone before. It should not be me that repeats the need for revamping our electoral process to make it fair for each and every citizen.

I personally feel that I don't deserve to deliver this message because I am guilty of this implacable practice as well. When I was with the Laborers' Union I would try and direct contributions to those candidates that would go the extra mile and help the union at the expense of the ordinary citizen. I was wrong and knew it at the time, yet did it anyway. I don't know how to undo what has been done except to admit my sins and suffer through my internal hurt and pour out the truth as best as I can.

I remember my constant chatting with my good friend and University of Buffalo professor Norm Goldfarb (as far back as 1977) about this and always sought his opinion and guidance. He knew I was cooperating with the feds and was a little leery of them, he expounded, "You are following the best path to stem mob control of the union." I was not as questionable about the Justice Department's role, but I did agree with him, even though I didn't like it; especially having to play it out as long as I could, rid the union and the good employers from the cancer that was devouring the industry. Goldfarb was a very decent guy who was always fighting for the little guy and would listen intently as I spoke. More than anyone else, it was Goldfarb that prodded me not to quit the union and to stay in there and fight, otherwise I would have quit long ago, that is, if they would have let me.

In September of 1998, only two months prior to the presidential election, the US Justice Department and the states of Pennsylvania and Florida joined Vacco's office in filing a massive anti-trust lawsuit that aimed to block Waste Management Inc. from going ahead with a $1.2 billion deal to buy a smaller trash company. Vacco lost his re-election bid for New York Attorney General to Eliot Spitzer and on his last day in office, December 31, 1998. Waste Management reached an out-of-court settlement. Vacco signed off on an arrangement with Waste Management (a company that had hired him as the vice president for government affairs in New York, New England and Canada). He claimed there was no connection between his new job and the settlement.

Waste Management had strong ties to the Williams-Reger operations. Vacco would have caused too much fanfare if he appeared directly on the Williams-Reger payroll. His dealings at Waste Management were strewed with alleged illegalities and corruption. With no formal degree in business management, Dennis Vacco was promoted to president of Waste Management of New York, LLC, and a subsidiary of the $750 million parent company.

John F. Haggerty Jr. was the constant companion of Dennis Vacco when he was New York State Attorney General. Adept at fund raising and endeared by many in New York State, on June 14, 2010, Haggerty, who was now working as a trusted aide to New York City Mayor Michael Bloomberg, was charged with stealing more than $1 million from the Bloomberg campaign coffers. While awaiting the trial, my Bishop Timon High School classmate, Carl Paladino, engaged Haggerty and his services. Paladino was the 2010, Republican Party nominee for the New York State Governor. I see Carl at school reunions and elsewhere when I am back in Buffalo. Even though we differ on many political and social issues, including his pouring money into the coffers of Dennis Vacco, we remained friends. That friendship didn't extend to all of Carl's professional and political associates, including the Williams-Reger team. It was probably just business and politics. Carl is a pretty savvy guy and I am sure he knew how to fight them.

During his trial Haggerty was represented by his dear friend Dennis Vacco, whom many thought did a terrible job. On December 19, 2011, Haggerty pleaded guilty and was sentenced to jail for his crimes. Vacco is currently in private law practice.

Mason Tenders Sting

I decided to concentrate on my hazardous waste business as well as work a new FBI sting that was poised to go after the New York-based Genovese Family. After the Onyx-Sam Pieri-Tommy Giammaresi fiasco, Carl Mastykarz had no place to go and wanted out of the Buffalo area. The Pieris, with whom Mastykarz remained close, sent word to Gaspar Lupo, the president of the Greater New York Mason Tenders District Council.

I knew Gaspar quite well and I was also mindful of his being a made member of the Genovese Family. Quite frequently he would travel with Mike Lorello and other high officials of LIUNA. He was very quiet but his presence was felt by all. Respect from the union hierarchy was continuously bestowed on him and that included respect from me. I can tell you from personal experience that whatever Gaspar wanted, Gaspar got. It was no secret who controlled the union and even the non-Italian "for show only" officials would humble themselves in the presence of Lupo. Mastykarz was given plush jobs and was looked after by Genovese mobsters and union representatives that were dominated by Gaspar Lupo. (The Mason Tenders District Council represented Laborers' Locals 13, 23, 37, 51, 59, 66, 78,

108, 279 and 1261 in New York City and Long Island. Local 23 was a Gambino Family-controlled and Long Island-based Local 66 under the Lucchese Family's stranglehold).

The Genovese Capo that Gaspar Lupo answered to was James "Jimmy from Elizabeth Street" Messera. At the time I didn't know who he was and asked Mastykarz, "Who is Gaspar Lupo's Rabbi?" He didn't know either but I was soon to learn quite a lot about the potent Jimmy Messera. For many years I have been asked, "Who is the most powerful mob family in the United States and Canada?" My answer has always been, by far, the Genovese Borgata. They share and work almost as one with the Chicago Outfit, and many others such as Pittsburg, Cleveland, etc.

Carl Mastykarz mentioned that he could obtain asbestos removal from building projects for Hazardous Waste Management through a Genovese made man named Lou Casciano (an employee of the Mason Tenders District Council). I discussed it with the FBI and met with New York City-based FBI agent John S. Pistole (who later became well known as the deputy director and second in command at the FBI; later nominated by President Barack Obama to serve as administrator of the Transportation Security Administration).

I clearly grasped that Pistole and the New York City FBI office badly wanted to nail the Genovese and other families.

It was arranged that prior to each meeting with the wiseguys I would be prepped and wear a body microphone. A team of six agents was assigned to the sting.

Mastykarz arranged for a get-together with Lou Casciano at the Grand Hyatt Hotel on East 42nd St. Before traveling to New York and attending the meeting Victor Sansanese insisted that I bring Ron Cardinale along because the Buffalo Borgata needed a well-connected Mafia associate to be involved in the effort to obtain hazardous waste removal business in the Big Apple.

On October 13, 1988, Lou Casciano along with Ron Cardinale, Carl Mastykarz and I assembled at our Grand Hyatt Hotel meeting; Mastykarz remarked that Casciano, as an employee of the Mason Tenders District Council, and the spokesperson for the contemplated projects.

Casciano elaborated that all asbestos removal in the New York City area was controlled by the Mason Tenders District Council and that no asbestos removal companies can do business there without their approval. After discussing our proposal, Casciano liked the prices but stated before a decision could be made "Your people will have to contact my people to get final approval." From my experience in having dealt with many Mafia bosses, I knew that he was telling me that his Mafia superiors would have to contact my Mafia superiors before we could do any business together.

On October 31, 1988, Ronald Cardinale and I again ventured to New York City where we met up with Carl Mastykarz and Lou Casciano at the same Hyatt Hotel. Casciano secretly let me know that he had checked me out with "his people" and that he secured approval to steer some asbestos removal contracts to HWM, provided that in exchange we kickback $25,000 up front, then pay him $5,000 per month and 50% of the profits *for each contract* HWM was awarded. In addition, he muttered that he was representing Gaspar Lupo and that Lupo would be getting a share of the money HWM paid. I resisted these amounts and Casciano ultimately agreed to accept $15,000 up front, $3,000 per month and 50% of the profits from each contract. Casciano outlined the manner in which the payments would be made and for us to show false rentals of equipment from a company to be designated by him. Any union problems we encountered would immediately be taken care of.

On November 5, 1988, I was back in Buffalo and while sitting at my desk, Carl Mastykarcz unexpectedly walked in and mentioned that the New York City deal was approved by Genovese Capo "Jimmy Messera." I replied, "Carl, is this the only reason you flew here, just to tell me that?" "No," he said, "I have been lectured on how to communicate with you from now on and not to have anymore telephone conversations with you or anyone regarding these contracts. A meeting has been arranged on the 10th of this month at the Frontier Coffee Shop on 3rd Avenue and 39th Street at 9:30 a.m. and you have to be there."

On November 10, 1988, while Ronald Cardinale was resting somewhere on a Florida beach, Don Larder, Carl Mastykarz and I flew to NYC and sat down with Lou Casciano at the coffee shop. The mobster grabbed me on the side and affirmed that I was well accepted because of my relationship with Lupo and the Todaros. Casciano was in his late fifties or early sixties and still in fairly good shape for his age. He went on about how HWM would be getting a contract with a company called Zeckendorf Construction Company and we would be removing the asbestos for a Mays Department store located near Park Avenue and 14th Street. He reiterated that we would have no Laborers' Union problems with the asbestos removal project, even if we decided to use non-union labor. "In the event you opt to use non-union workers, Jimmy Messera will handle any potential union problems relating to the Mason Tenders and other labor unions. Any problems which Jimmy cannot fix would be handled by The Chin." Casciano apprised me that the man he called "The Chin" and sometimes "The Robe" was the boss of the Genovese Family that he was a member of. I knew that The Chin was Vincent Gigante. At the end of the meeting Casciano requested that the next time I am in the city we would meet again with Richard Kelly, head of the Mason Tenders Asbestos Removal Training Program, to discuss how contracts for HWM would be handled and that Kelly would be getting a percentage of the kickbacks agreed to under our arrangement.

Another meeting was scheduled for November 16, 1988. I met with Lou Casciano, Richard Kelly, and Carl Mastykarz, at the Midtown Coffee Shop. Casciano and Kelly described the magnitude of the contracts that we could obtain, including asbestos and hazardous waste removal work in the New York City area and in New Jersey. The New Jersey work would be performed in collaboration with DeCavalcante Boss Johnny Riggi, who controlled the Laborers' Union there. Casciano let me know that later that day we would meet with a representative of the Zeckendorf Construction Company. Kelly related that 10% of the total amount of the contract would be kicked back to this person, also mentioning that Casciano would form a fictitious company and use this as the vehicle to obtain the payments from HWM, a procedure they had used in the past with other contractors. They also spoke of the commonly used practice of employing no-show workers and stewards to generate cash for kickbacks.

After leaving the coffee shop we all walked over to the

offices of the Mason Tenders District Council located on 37th Street in an effort to see Gaspar Lupo. Frankie Lupo greeted me and after exchanging a few words and his elation of having me on board with some of the asbestos removal projects, he said his father wasn't in. After leaving the Union Hall we went to another restaurant and met up with a man named Pat, who was introduced as the person representing Zeckendorf, and his friend Donnie. Pat, Richard Kelly, and I discussed the cost we estimated for the asbestos removal at the Mays Department Store; Pat agreed that the prices were in line and that the contract would be awarded to us. Pat openly conversed that he was going to receive 10% of the contract price as a kickback which he'd have to share with persons at Zeckendorf.

On December 1, 1988, I made another trip to New York City. Under the watchful eyes of the FBI who had a surveillance van parked outside the coffee shop, Mastykarz, together with Richard Kelly, reported that Zeckendorf was not yet ready to let out the Mays Department Store job, but it would soon. Casciano then joined us and made known that he could guarantee us the Mays Department Store job. Al Soussi another partner in the scheme was introduced to me as an employee of the Mason Tenders District Council Trust Funds and that he will also be involved with us. As we departed the coffee shop, Casciano in private said that it was safe to talk in front of Kelly and Soussi because "they're okay."

After we left the coffee shop, Casciano, Kelly, Soussi, Mastykarz and I again proceeded to the offices of the Mason Tenders District Council. Kelly called someone at Zeckendorf with whom he had a connection with, to inquire about the Mays Department Store job. Kelly also asked me for the telephone number of Joseph Facenelli, who they were going to use to do the truck hauling for the enterprise. After a few other telephone calls I left the offices of the Mason Tenders District Council.

My trips to NYC were now quite frequent and, probably out of sheer laziness, Victor Sansanese allowed me to see our new partners alone. Once again, on December 20, 1988, I returned to the Frontier Coffee Shop to see Casciano, Al Soussi, Richard Kelly and Carl Mastykarz. Kelly stated that he was going to call Pat about the Mays Department Store job. At one point, Casciano asked Carl Mastykarz and Richard Kelly to take a walk. Lou Casciano then asked me, "Can you speak on your own behalf?" I responded that I had to answer to the people in Buffalo. Casciano then said, "I can speak for myself." From my experience with the Mafia, I took this to mean that he was telling me that he was a made member.

The FBI wanted me to get together with Casciano and others to give him some of the kickback money. On December 29, 1988, while sitting at the same coffee shop I handed an envelope which contained $3,000 of FBI money to Casciano in an envelope. Casciano went into the men's room and on returning said "That's all, where is the rest?" I let him know that I would have the remaining money within two weeks; he responded that will be fine. Returning to the table, Richard Kelly gleefully announced that he already possessed the confidential bid numbers for the May's Department store project.

At various times during my many meetings with Richard Kelly during the months of November and December 1988, he rattled on about the 50% profit of HWM that I had promised to pay Casciano as a kickback. Kelly also bragged that non-union workers from New Jersey were available to work on our projects and he would take care of any licensing requirements.

The FBI had them, and armed with what I provided it would lead to numerous arrests and include a vast array of New York City mobsters.

In 1990, the Mason Tenders sting operation led to plea agreements by those involved. In November 1990, Lou Casciano pleaded guilty to RICO conspiracy charges involving loan sharking and receiving labor payment by participating in a scheme whereby he, and others, illicitly obtained asbestos removal work for Hazardous Waste Management and ensured that the work could be performed without union labor. Casciano used Trust Fund assets in violation of statutes by virtue of his no-show job as a field representative with the Trust Funds. At his allocution, Casciano admitted to spending many of the days for which he was being paid for this job at Jimmy Messera's social club. In 1993, he pleaded guilty to RICO charges involving the embezzlement of Pension Fund assets and admitted to his involvement with the Genovese Family.

Al Soussi, who is Messera's brother-in-law, was also convicted in 1990, of RICO conspiracy involving loan sharking and aiding and abetting the receipt of illegal labor payments. At his allocution he admitted to accepting money from me, in exchange for a promise that non-union labor could be employed at the job-site. The government alleged that Soussi was an associate of the Genovese Family and a close associate of Messera and they presented evidence that Soussi was present at the Messera social club on at least 79 occasions in the year prior to his criminal conviction, during which he and Messera coordinated control of the Mason Tenders District Council and its affiliates.

FBI National Academy

While working at Quantico I was contacted by James Moody, who was the chief of the Organized Crime Section, Criminal Investigative Division of the FBI. Even though he was based out of headquarters, he frequently visited the FBI education center. He apprised me that besides my duties at the academy, I was going to be assigned to the newly formed Civil RICO squad. I was working with my close friends Stan Nye, Stan Ronquest (who I previously mentioned and was killed) and Supervisor Michael Ross. Our office was located in the sub-floor of headquarters and was very small. Justice Department Attorney Kenneth Lowrie was assigned to the squad and I soon found him to be dedicated and cut from the same cloth as that of my friend Robert Stewart.

It was truly a great team to be part of and soon we were traveling all over the country and lining up witnesses for what we considered to be a sure-win case against the Laborers' Union. I must have spent more then 50 hours a week with the hardworking Lowrie, drafting and incorporating every bit of knowledge I had as well as to what I could obtain from future witnesses. My new code name was "The Teacher," most likely because of my constant presentations for in-service agents as well as for the National Academy. I was also traveling to other FBI field offices located in the United States as well as meeting with Canadian intelligence agencies, lecturing on undercover techniques, the Cosa Nostra and the rising risk from the Russian Mafia.

It was decided by higher-ups that the RICO complaint would be filed in Chicago and a meeting was called for all of us involved to attend a collaboration meeting at McDonald's restaurant training school commonly known as "Hamburger University" which is located in the suburbs of Chicago. Chicago-based FBI agents Peter Wacks, Thomas Woodby and Ernest Lurera joined me and Ken Lowrie in compiling the Civil RICO Squad. In addition, Chicago-based Assistant US Attorneys Craig Oswald and David Buvinger would be assisting Lowrie and representing the government and its claim against the Laborers' Union. Many within the FBI organization consider Wacks as someone that knows the ins and outs of the Chicago Family. Ernie Lurera was new to the organized crime field. The expertise he gained from working in the intelligence-gathering field proved to be extremely beneficial. Our work together, as well as our friendship, helped tremendously in finalizing the draft complaint. I would put together a list of questions and ask Pete and Ernie to visit jailed prisoners, informers and numerous other sources who might cooperate. Many of them did, in fact, agree to cooperate.

I was told that Ken Lowrie had an antipathy for porn and had previously and successfully prosecuted one of the nations largest and notorious smut peddlers. I anonymously sent Ken a poster of a noted female porn star and wrote on it, "Dear Ken, I understand you are one of my fans and enjoy my work." At a later date, forgetting that I did it, he mentioned the joke and figured out I was the one that sent it.

In November of 1994, just after we completed the draft complaint, I received a call from Pete Wacks, who angrily mentioned, "There is talk that the DOJ may reach an agreement with the Laborers whereby the DOJ would allow the Laborers' International Union to be involved in the cleanup of itself." Pete was outraged and could not believe it. "Ronnie, this stinks and I am pretty sure that there is substantial political pressure being placed on the DOJ." I was somewhat confused and did not fully comprehend what to make of Wacks' remarks. This was the first time I had heard of this and I couldn't figure out what the rationale behind it was.

In January 1995, the rumors were turned into reality and everyone in the bureau was caught off-guard by the scandalous deal. On February 13, 1995, an announcement was made that a consent decree was issued stating that the LIUNA and the United States had been pursuing various courses of action designed to ensure that all locals and other entities within LIUNA were rid of any corrupting influence of any member of organized crime. My sources at the Laborers International Union included former Vice President Ugo Rossini from Windsor, Ontario, General Secretary Rollin P. "Bud" Vinall, and a few others that are still active with the Laborers' Union. Vinall let me know that Arthur Coia, democratic strategist Vic Kamber, Coia's attorney Brendon Sullivan, Harold Ickes (a deputy chief of staff in the Clinton White House and an advisor to Senator Hillary Rodham Clinton), and a former special counsel to the Organized

Crime and Racketeering Section of the US Department of Justice were behind the deal and Arthur A. Coia, would remain in his position as general president.

Later that month, I received another call from Pete Wacks enlightening me that I would be getting a phone call from the DOJ to ask me to join the cleanup team consisting of Robert Luskin as general executive board attorney for the Laborers' Union and former Associate Deputy Director of the FBI, Doug Gow. Immediately after our conversation, Ken Lowrie called and stated that Robert Luskin was going to contact me and ask me to join the team. I was quite upset and told Lowrie that I thought it was a sham and I did not want to get involved. I then remarked that I would have to see if the cleanup was for real before I participated. Ken said, "I think it is, and if your stance is still no, would it help if I have my boss talk to you?" I told him I did not think so. I never did find out to whom he was referring as his boss. It could have been Paul Coffey, Jo Ann Harris, Deputy Attorney General Jamie Gorelick, or Attorney General Janet Reno.

President Clinton and the first lady liked Arthur E. Coia, and personal letters, correspondence and get-togethers were common. In one 1994, memorandum, Paul Coffey, chief of the *Organized Crime and Racketeering Section* of the Justice Department (OCRS) intended to recommend that a civil racketeering case be filed against LIUNA, including its general president, Arthur Coia. Coffey stated, "It might be prudent to recommend that she (the first lady) avoid any direct contact with Coia, if possible, inasmuch as we plan to portray him as a mob puppet." On the very same day that the

Justice Department sent the RICO complaint to Coia, President Clinton sent him his own handwritten correspondence:

Dear Arthur — I just heard you've become a grandfather — Congratulations! Thanks for the gorgeous driver — It's a work of art. Best, Bill.

Most disturbing, this relationship flourished at a time when the White House received repeated warnings and notifications by law enforcement officials of Coia's alleged ties to organized crime. The political intrigue continued and it was appalling to see our top leaders supporting a labor leader who was the target of the Justice Department. All the work that we did went up in smoke and it again showed me that money talks. Coia raised millions for the president and his efforts succeeded. Coia was free. Believe me, I cannot fault the former president for his actions. He was only following the scenario *no money – no job* that inundated our whole electoral process. I am quite sure deep down in his heart that he knows he's a rascal (like me when it came to women) but he would never stoop to intentionally hurt anyone.

Wacks called me again and stated that if I went to work for Luskin and team, my services for the bureau and the Chicago office would probably come to an end sometime in the near future. I contacted Special Agents Stan Nye and Mike Ross who voiced the same frustration as that of the flustered Pete Wacks. Stan also informed me that the CIA wanted me to make a presentation regarding international crime and the rapidly growing menace of the Russian Mafia. I told him I knew very little about it and that I would have to wing it. He also stated that I was scheduled to make a speech the very same day for a Russian-language specialist class being held at the FBI Academy. Nye was a guy who spent 16 hours a day on the job and spent quite a few nights burning the candle and sleeping at night at his desk.

The FBI's Sabreliner jet arrived at Portsmouth, New Hampshire to pick up its only passenger, me! I could always tell when FBI Director Sessions was visiting Maine, because I would get to fly on the jet. Its use at that time was quite concealed under the guise of Idaho Air and later Aerographics. No one seemed to be aware that the luxury aircraft belonged to the FBI. If questioned, I was told to say that Aerographics was involved in aerial photography. Once I was queried by a perplexed questioner who looked at me queerly and skeptically responded, "You use a jet for taking pictures?"

Mike Ross picked me up at the airport and drove me to a Holiday Inn located in Tyson's Corner, Virginia, close to the Gloucester Building an off-site center used by the CIA. The next morning Ross and I met up with a CIA officer who was quite aware of my previous involvement with the CIA and my work for the FBI. I explained I knew very little about Russian crime outside of the former Soviet Union, except for their late 1960s penetration of the Students for a Democratic Society. He explained that he was fully aware of my limitations but my experience with the Cosa Nostra was invaluable and could be applied to Eastern European criminal activity.

More than 200 CIA officers, as well as a few from the NSA, were present. Most were quite well read and inquisitive. Interesting questions ran the gamut from the JFK assassination to John Gotti and reflected their vast knowledge of intelligence-gathering techniques. After lecturing for around two hours I stayed around for about an hour to answer some of the officers' queries. One senior officer, Mary McCarthy, asked me if I was still tied to the bureau. I explained that I was under contract and that the Chicago office had paper on me but that my contract would soon be up. After telling her of my previous work for the CIA she further elaborated that she would like me to come back to work for the Agency and to contact her when my contract was up. I asked her how much pay I would receive and after telling her what the FBI was providing; she said that they could match it. We exchanged telephone numbers and agreed to remain in touch with each other. I then left for the FBI training center and my lecture to the Russian Language class.

Stan Nye was also a good, dear friend and during the ride we discussed the death of Agent Stan Ronquest. We also discussed the CIA job offer and I told him that I was going to consider it. He doubted that the bureau was going to let me go. There was no love lost between the bureau and the CIA. He believed that they might loan me out but I had a lot of knowledge and abilities that the FBI still needed.

I know I already mentioned this but I would like to again. When I first started working back in the late 1960s, I naively believed that the bureau, CIA, DOJ and all federal agencies were one big happy family. I learned in the late 1970s that this was not the case. I saw agents threatened with transfer and later I had a small glimpse of the bickering when Teamsters President Jackie Presser's involvement as an informant was revealed. I always liked the bureau and especially the agents that I worked with through the years; but my mentor Al Hartel's words always rang clear, "Ronnie, these are bureaucracies and in many cases the left hand does not know what the right hand is doing. They do not share information within their own organizations let alone with each other." Through the years, I learned this to be true but I always hoped that circumstances or the need to combine efforts would change this. The FBI Academy was pretty much taken over by the Drug Enforcement Agency by this time and the bureau's in-service program had to utilize outside sites such as the International Center for Training and Management located in Leesburg, Virginia.

In March of 1995, Robert Luskin called me and tried to assure me that the cleanup effort was for real. He also stated that former FBI Associate Deputy Director Doug Gow was going to call me and ask me to join the team. After talking to Gow on the phone, arrangements were made for me to fly to D.C. to discuss my employment. Treated with glamour and fanfare, they put me up in the Ritz Carlton Hotel located near the Pentagon in Crystal City. That evening I met with Gow and his assistant Bill Rice (former Special Agent in Charge of the San Francisco field office). Gow vowed that I would be free to investigate any leads, including those against Coia. My pay would be the same as the other investigators at a rate of $95 per hour. I liked Gow and I did not think he would ever be a party to a fraud. While at the bureau he was considered lily-clean and untouchable. Gow requested that I communicate in the future with Bill Rice and that I was to send the information as well as my hourly billing to him. The $95 per hour was great.

I never in my life saw so much money, although it would later be reduced to seventy-five dollars. Some of the investigators were billing amounts that I knew were not correct and working on matters not related to the investigation in order to boost their paychecks.

At first, everything seemed in order and I started to investigate Coia Sr. and his relationship to Providence Cosa Nostra Boss Raymond Patriarca and his son Raymond Jr. Because of my previous relationship with Coia Sr. as well as my discussions with Arthur A. Coia (Jr.), it was quite effortless to see that they were deeply connected to the Providence and Boston families.

In May 1996, I supplied Doug Gow and Bill Rice with some pertinent Coia information. I figured if the discovery I provided was investigated it would be easy to show that Coia Jr. was directly and indirectly involved with Raymond Patriarca Jr. Coia Jr. vehemently denied having any relationship with the New England Mafia boss. Bill Rice sent me a letter stating that my investigation into the Coia-Patriarca Jr. relationship was closed. I wrote him back:

Dear Bill, I have just completed reading your letter and I am quite concerned. Most of the additional areas of discovery are a result of my review of Doreen Masterson (girlfriend of Raymond Patriarca Jr.). Omitting those areas of my report could subject me, too. (If you learned of this, why didn't you tell us?) I assure you, if I had any knowledge that the Masterson investigation was closed, I would have ceased my examination. Please let me know if my services should be limited to testimony and my personal experiences versus the information I have access to. I will be more than happy to place my discov-

ery into a declaration. I feel that it would be in the best interest of all that we sit down and discuss my activity and my future input before I continue. Respectfully, #0100

I was deeply troubled by this and I told Rice I was concerned about my freedom to investigate these areas. As I did on many occasions in the past, I threatened to quit. After traveling to Washington D.C. to see Doug Gow and Bill Rice, they reassured me this was not a sham and that the areas that I was investigating were already being handled by another investigator. I did not believe this, since the other investigator never checked with my sources and the only activity that was being performed was his standing in front of the various Union Halls and asking the laborers questions. They wanted me to work the New Jersey criminal activity area instead and they repeated that the Coia matter was under control and they had a very strong case against him.

After about four months of this, I was again transferred to working on the Chicago and Buffalo segment of the case. It was necessary for Luskin and Gow to put a good face on the facade. The perplexing question I had was just how was Coia going to pull this off? He knew that the Chicago Family could retaliate against him, but possibly felt safe because he had some of the highest officials of our country on his side, coupled with the U.S. Justice Department. Prior to his becoming president of the Laborers' International Union, Coia received a summons to meet with Chicago Mafia power Vince Solano.

As previously mentioned I knew Solano quite well and through the years became quite close to him. Angelo Fosco died on February 14, 1993, and his position as president was scheduled to be filled by Chicago Family front man John Serpico. Solano told Coia it was a done deal and that he had to go along with the decision. What Solano did not know was that Coia Jr. was now close with New York Genovese Family power Liborio "Barney" Bellomo. A secret agreement was reached whereby Coia would let the Genovese Family have a vast say with the Laborers' International Union. Obviously, I thought that the Genovese Family and Commission must have agreed to it and allowed the Chicago Outfit to take the heat.

Solano was a power and a force to fear, but Bellomo was even more powerful with the Genovese organized crime family behind him. Armed with Bellomo's support, Coia Jr. was no dummy and knew no other family would risk taking on the Genoveses. As a result, Coia defied the Chicago Family and Solano's demand. Coia and Luskin knew they had to put on a charade to show that the court-approved cleanup effort was real and working. With Genovese Family approval they set about to remove certain Genovese Family backed associates such as Sam Caivano and his sons who ran the New York-New Jersey region. He would be replaced with the controlled Raymond M. Pocino.

I knew Pocino quite well, but for the longest time I could not figure out which LCN family his allegiance lay with. When I would get together with him in the late 1980s I knew he was neither with the DeCavalcante nor the Genovese families. The bureau thought it was the Gambinos, which may be correct. He did tell me that he had to answer to The Boys, but I never followed up on who they were.

Coia and Luskin were also allowed to clean up Buffalo and Chicago, but in removing the union officials, the removed officers would be paid large sums to pad their retirement. After the purging of Chicago and Buffalo began, I again started questioning Luskin and Gow about New England. I openly became very critical and Luskin retorted, "Don't worry, Ronnie, it will happen." More absurdity, I thought. Coia would have to clear out his relatives, law partners, and criminal associates. This is never going to happen!

In Chicago I worked with the former SAC of the Cleveland Office, and my close personal friend, Joe Griffin, and his private company (Quest Investigations). Griffin was a lot of fun to be around and he told me he was thinking of writing a book about the LCN and his experiences. He asked me if I could help him by filling in the blanks with the Cleveland and Buffalo families. I said, "Of course I would." Griffin, who has since passed away, had been always jovial and jolly. Even when he accidentally erased more than 100 pages of info not backed up on his brand new laptop computer, he remained unfettered. When his book came out years later, many mistakes remained, but these things, unfortunately happen.

Working with me in Chicago was attorney Dwight Bostwick, whose previous employment was with former DOJ bigwig, Jo Ann Harris. She helped him get a job with Luskin and the cleanup team. When I testified in Chicago, there was absolutely no security for me. After giving evidence, I walked out of the hotel and into the arms of Chicago Family members and their associates. Many of them were charged and scheduled to lose their jobs. Actually, they were not that threatening at all and even came up to me and talked. Donnie DiMaggio asked me how I was doing. Ironically, they were not even opposed to my testimony. They knew that the takeover was a power play by Arthur Coia and told me the Justice Department was only being used by him. I started wondering if what they were saying was true and if my previous doubts had foundation and merit.

Buffalo was another matter; after all, I knew their deepest secrets and spent what seemed like a lifetime under mob control. I sensed that the cookies were in when the so-called independent hearing officer Peter F. Vaira talked with me at the Buffalo airport over a sandwich and a cup of coffee. "Relax, do not worry it's just that we have to go through the motions," he told me.

This is nuts! The case was still going on, how could he make such a statement? This, more than anything, at least at this time, told me that a defense by the local union officials and its officers, as well as the LCN members and associates, was an effort in futility. Outside of my meeting with Judge Elfvin, talks or meetings like this just did not take place; let alone remarks such as this from Vaira. No one hates the Buffalo Cosa Nostra as much as I, but to scheme and prearrange a charade such as this was totally against what I believe in and what I was fighting for.

In a meeting that June in Luskin's office, he stated that he had good news. Coia was going down and they had more than enough to remove him. "I told you not to worry and that Coia, as well as all his cohorts, would soon be part of the past." Foolishly, I believed him. He also mentioned, "Ronnie I know you are worried about your pension and back wages but don't worry." He reassured me that they would have future work for me at the Laborers' Union once my testimony was done. He also asked me to contact John Flannery (an associate counsel for the Democratic Party), regarding my upcoming testimony before the House of Representatives Judiciary Subcommittee on Crime.

I called Flannery at the number Luskin provided and discussed some of my testimony. I did this in the hope that both the Republican and Democrat representatives were equally interested in cleansing the malignancy that plagued the membership of the Laborers' International Union. Flannery stated, "They will not attack you and are equally interested in the truth. You may get lumped up a little, but just a little." I questioned him on this and he went on about how the Republican representatives on the committee were only using me to get at the president.

On July 24, 1996, I testified and thought that the Republicans would be as interested in Coia and how he escaped the wrath of the Department of Justice and the FBI. The Democrats, especially congressmen Charles Schumer and John Conyers, were not interested in the truth. Schumer even went so far as to ask me if I thought space aliens were linked to the mob. I could not believe what I was hearing. Chiding and spinning matters like this was a let down to me and those that wanted to cease organized criminal activity. It reflected just how important the union bosses were and how little the ordinary worker in this country really was. Here I was, a Democrat myself, being vilified by elected officials who clamor publicly that they work tirelessly to create a better life for their respective constituencies.

For me, coupled with all that I have seen, it was a wake-up call and a new realization that many elected officials are only a medium for the haves; the have-nots are relegated to the back burner. Coia was a crook who lavishly implemented his power and wealth. He was supposed to be a representative of the working class but this was not the case; too many innocents lost or were losing their chance for a better life.

When I testified, I supported the cleanup effort based solely on my belief that Doug Gow and his claimed desire to eradicate the Mafia from the International Union. I should have known better. Like many others, I was duped into believing that the clean up was for real. Just before I testified before Congress, I started getting together with *Time Magazine* reporters Ed Barnes and William Thatcher Dowell. Both were great investigative reporters who really wanted to get at the truth. I learned quite a lot from them about the behind-the-scenes activity that took place by associates of President Bill Clinton and his wife Hillary and their involvement in keeping Coia Sr. in office. We would exchange information and delve deeper into the secret dealings. Luskin was getting rich in the name of cleaning up the union.

After I testified, an article appeared in the *Village Voice* newspaper containing confidential information from one of my 302s (FBI reports) stating that I said Jack Kemp was mobbed-up.

Later that week, or the week after, I received a phone call from *Newsweek* reporter, Michael Isikoff, who wanted to meet me over the Kemp revelation. I do not recall if I immediately called him back or not, but I did call the DOJ and complained. I was so upset that he had my private home telephone number. I drove down to D.C. to meet with the hierarchy at the DOJ's Organized Crime Division. My good friend Ken Lowrie greeted me and brought me into a conference room. I told him that the Jack Kemp information that appeared in the *Village Voice* must have come from a confidential file and that someone had leaked my telephone number as well. I thought I knew who it was but wasn't sure. A couple of other DOJ attorneys came in (probably because I was talking so loud).

After calling Luskin I went to his office and told him that this leak could be very dangerous for me and the mob could also have the information. At first, he was quiet. Then he stated that the Kemp story could be big news for the Democrats and the presidential race. He repeated his allegiance to the Democratic Party when he stated, "I am a dyed-in-the-wool Democrat and this could really mean a lot."

I knew that there was not much to the Kemp story; nowhere did I state he was mobbed-up. I was still a friend of Jack Kemp and did not appreciate my remarks taken out of context. As previously mentioned all he asked me was if James Cosentino was mobbed-up.

Luskin pleaded with me to meet Michael Isikoff and I told him okay. Luskin or his secretary called the *Newsweek* reporter and informed him that I was at Luskin's office. While waiting in Luskin's office, Mark Middleton sat next to me. Middleton was the special assistant to President Bill Clinton and at that time under investigation for campaign fraud as well as the export of military technology to China. Luskin noticed that I was conversing with Middleton and quickly had a secretary move the presidential aide to another seat, far away from my probing questions.

About a half hour later Isikoff arrived and we were placed in one of the many conference rooms. I told him my story and he agreed with me that Kemp did nothing wrong. During our conversation my eyes were fixed on an FBI 302 he had in front of him. He left the room for a minute and I looked at the 302, which was one of mine. On the top it had a fax number showing it came from Robert Luskin's law firm. I now knew that my suspicions were right, it was Luskin who leaked the information. I informed the DOJ about what I had gleaned and they did nothing about it except to say they would look into it. I could see I was now playing with the devil! I now knew that the whole cleanup of the Laborers' Union was just a sham.

The Case Against the Laborers' Union and Local 210

After it became public that I would be testifying for the FBI and the DOJ against the Laborers' International Union (LIUNA) and Laborers' Local 210, the Buffalo mob arranged for a meeting to take place. In April 1988, attorneys Paul Cambria, Richard Lipsitz (who represented Laborers' Local 210) and Harold Boreanaz (representing the Buffalo Laborers' Benefit Fund and that of the mob), joined Joseph Todaro Jr. to discuss this potential problem. They decided to have Todaro Jr., leave his position as a business agent. In connivance with the local union officers, they would contact LIUNA and develop a plan to defeat me and overcome my testimony.

In 1993, the FBI and the Justice Department openly pointed out that the local union was the target of an investigation. Paul Cambria advised Local 210 officials that in order to narrow down potential exposure, certain officials, such as Dan Sansanese Jr., should step down because they could expose the remaining officials.

When they learned of the consent decree reached between the Justice Department and LIUNA, Cambria called for a meeting that was to be held at his office located in downtown Buffalo. Present were Peter Gerace, attorney Robert Boreanaz (son of Harold), an attorney from Albany representing Albany business agent Sam Fresina; Victor Sansanese, and an attorney speaking on behalf of the Pieri brothers. Cambria started by saying that he was representing Laborers' Local 210 and Niagara Falls Laborers' Local 91. At this convergence a decision was made to join with Chicago mobster John Serpico in his lawsuit and prepare for LIUNA and its internal investigation. They would also be challenge the constitutionality of the consent decree and the legality of the LIUNA investigative procedures.

Arthur A. Coia was looking to limit the investigation, by putting on a good show and cleansing only limited pockets of corruption, hoping the problem would eventually fade away. They realized that a few Local 210 officials would have to be sacrificed, but that should suffice. The attorney representing the Pieris' interest pronounced that his clients were not about to answer any questions posed to them by any LIUNA examiner and were only interested in receiving their pension; Johnny Pieri only needed one more year and his brother Joey Pieri around two.

Cambria explained that LIUNA investigators could not arbitrarily remove anyone working for the Benefit Funds and that included union trustees. The only way they could be removed was to either find that all the officers were involved in a crime or fiduciary duty violation. The main concern for Local 210, and some other locals, was that it operated a hiring hall, and with the exposure of its officers and agents to numerous hiring hall violations. Even then, they might be able to explain that a given employee was sent out to the job because of some specialized skill.

One of the lawyers asked Cambria how many of the Local 210 officials were involved in sending out employees to the jobs. Cambria responded, "...they all are, but the Pieris send the names to Peter Capitano and Peter Gerace for placement." He said that I was well aware of this practice, but they may be able to limit the ill deeds through Jennie (DeAngelo) and the other secretaries and, of course, Danny Sansanese for the past sins, should they arise. The areas that Butch Quarcini and Local 91 would have to be concerned about was his being involved with some parking lots that he was part owner of, his exorbitant travel expenses, and the possibility that someone would take a close look at the Love Canal cover-up.

This strategy was eventually told to me by two different well-placed sources. I then obtained information that Cambria requested that $500,000 be put aside for a defense fund but that Peter Capitano, following up on Joe Pizza Todaro orders, informed Cambria the amount was too much.

Arthur A. Coia and the mob wanted to do their best to negate what I had to say. I can fully understand this; after all, I would try and save myself also. The difference here, however, was that they were going to use the dues-paying members' money to fight me.

Attorney David Elbaor, who was and is a close associate of the Coias (whom I met on a few occasions), made a fortune working for LIUNA and the Coias, who considered him a reliable ally.

FBI Agents Pete Wacks and Ernie Lurero uncovered a plot to investigate me. On April 5, 1990, Elbaor held a telephone conference with Buffalo mob counsel Harold

Boreanaz. Boreanaz let Elbaor know that he would provide the International Union with 18 confidential copies of FBI 302s (debriefings) that he possessed, in exchange for assistance from the International Union in an attempt to tray and trash me.

Elbaor later advised LIUNA general counsel Robert Connerton that they should join with Boreanaz for two reasons:

One, they thought I may be a "resurrected and improved Joe Hauser;" and two, my accusations could be the springboard for a RICO civil action against LIUNA, its Regions, or its District Councils and bring about further criminal charges.

Connerton and Elbaor flew to Buffalo and went immediately to Harold Boreanaz's office on April 10, 1990, where they obtained a copy of the eighteen 302s that Boreanaz had in his possession. Boreanaz told them that he had obtained the 302s from Paul Cambria, who covertly received them from a prosecutor in an unrelated case. Elbaor then sent the 302s to Coia and Fosco.

After Elbaor received my 302s, he recommended that Connerton's office conduct an investigation of me under the guise of an "audit" to see if my allegations were true.

Elbaor reviewed the FBI 302s and compiled a catalog of the my FBI reports as well as physically monitored my testimony during the Newark, New Jersey trial of John M. Riggi, John J. Riggi, Vincent Riggi, Salvatore Timpani, and Girolamo Palermo.

On March 5, 1991, after completing his investigation of my allegations, Elbaor submitted his audit report to the General Executive Board for its review. Elbaor wrote:

With respect to the methodology of the audit, its intent

was not to destroy Fino's overall credibility, but to neutrally examine his allegations against interviews and records generated contemporaneously with events in question. There proved in this process sufficient information to justify serious doubt and critical enquiry about my credibility, and his motivations for making his allegations in the first place. But delving into that, and reporting on it, would have required an inordinate amount of time and resources, and would have required a far lengthier audit having a conclusion probably identical to that readily extrapolated from the present audit report. The audit as embodied in its report focuses on allegations affecting the International Union, not its affiliate Local 210, nor other affiliates or businesses.

Also involved in the investigation of me was Coia's personal Attorney Anthony Triani, who had previously represented the Coias in the Hauser case in Florida that took place in the early 1980s.

The International Union, on Coia's recommendation, employed Triani to conduct a complete investigation into my background for the purpose of defending the International Union officers in the event the Department of Justice used me as a witness to prosecute a civil RICO case against it.

Triani said, "In light of Fino's allegations against the International Union and of the government's long history of attempting to indict and convict Officers of the Laborers' Union and to take control of the International Union, a need may arise in the future to question the believability of Fino before a jury, particularly in the context of a civil RICO case."

He undertook his research in an attempt to discover facts and circumstances that might be relevant to undermining my credibility. Triani characterized me as "the prime weapon in the government's arsenal against the union." The FBI soon obtained an intelligence report that while in Buffalo, Triani held secret meetings with the Todaros and everyone who possessed any information about me. More than one million dollars of workers' hard earned money was expended and all they were able to come up with was a few meaningless rumors.

The bureau also gleaned that in 1994, Triani, with the help of some of the court-approved corruption investigators, interview members of my family and friends. They were not looking for illegal activity of the mob but were looking to garnish anything that they could utilize to spin and dehumanize me. FBI agent Pete Wacks wanted to file charges for misuse of the Department of Justice-approved cleanup agreement. Pete was so mad and told me to demand a copy of the investigation and that I should sue the International Union and especially Paul Cambria for violating my lawyer-client relationship. I knew there would be little if anything that could tarnish me, but I went along with the request and called Bob Luskin. He told me that because I was still testifying I would have to wait until my testimony was complete. Later on, after I completed my testimony, I again made the request but to this day, I never received a copy. The statute of limitations has since run out and with it any chance of me filing a lawsuit.

On October 22, 1994, James J. Norwood, the general secretary-treasurer of the Laborers' International Union of North America, died. Jimmy was the brother-in-law of

Matthew Trupiano who ran the mob's St. Louis, Missouri operations. Jimmy had a major drinking problem and together with Angelo Fosco indulged it quite often. For many years Norwood was a source of mine and I learned that his brother-in-law answered to the Chicago Family. Prior to the scam cleanup effort, he would keep me apprised of the cover-up and hoped that I could help out if charges were brought against him. Our relationship was secret and I stayed in touch with him until his death.

I also had a noted Chicago Mafia insider whose name I will not reveal. Doug Gow, reading my reports, wanted to know who my source was. I told him that I could not tell him because of my promise to not reveal his name. This, I felt, was an FBI matter and that he had to take it up with the bureau. Doug was quite upset and demanded to know. Again, I told him no, and if he followed the leads I had sent, he would not need any testimony or direct contact with my source. He threatened to fire me. I told him to go ahead, that I was thinking of quitting anyway. I then learned that Gow went around my back and contacted Raymond Maria (former Acting Inspector General for the Department of Labor) and now part of the cleanup team. Maria also contacted my close friend Philip R. Manuel, who formerly worked with Gene Methvin on President Ronald Reagan's Organized Crime Commission as the chief investigator of the Permanent Subcommittee on Investigations for the U. S. Senate. Somehow Gow learned that it was Phil Manuel who put me in touch with the source, who I had turned over to the FBI and was looking to make a deal. How he accomplished this I do not know. I notified the bureau and they were very upset.

Leaving the Cleanup Team

By October of 1996, I had really had it with the whole damn scam that I was involved in. I wrote Doug Gow and informed him I was quitting. I wrote numerous letters to most of those federal officials involved over the charade, but no one would respond except the FBI.

One of the letters I wrote was to Gordon S. Heddell, inspector general of the US Department of Labor, and reiterated everything that had taken place, from ignoring the leads I presented them, to having my 302s released, to having my personal phone number leaked to the press, and more. I explained that because of organized crime's control of LIUNA and Laborers' Local 210, I was unable to obtain my back wages and pension credits owed me. I also learned from a senior official with the AFL-CIO - a personal friend - that no help would be forthcoming to assist me because of my stance against the mob and Coia. Lastly, I requested a copy of the so-called endeavor to damage my reputation, but my repeated requests went unanswered.

There was a time when I believed that Robert Luskin and Doug Gow would do their best to cleanup mob control of LIUNA but that is no longer the case. It is my opinion that Coia may no longer be the president but that his close associates and personal friends run LIUNA on his and his associates' behalf. Buffalo, Chicago and to a limited measure, New York City, have seen some positive efforts but to a large degree these actions are purely to fend off critics and show that something has been done.

◪ The Gambia - The Coup Joseph Wilson - Andrew Winter Ambassador and American Involvement

IN 1996, I RECEIVED A PHONE call from a friend who was a prior, and probably still is, asset to the FBI. He elaborated on his being connected to a number of high officials from the African nation The Gambia. He explained to me that they were the victims of a 1994, military coup that sent them into exile in the United States as well as England and asked if I may be able to help them. I answered, "How can I be of help? All I can do is offer them my personal support." "Ronnie," the caller answered back, "you have a lot of connections and all they want is for someone to listen to them, you should meet with them, it would be greatly appreciated." I told him to go ahead and arrange it, questioning the uncertainty of how in the world I could be of any help. I knew any participation by me would not involve the FBI, CIA nor any other governmental agency.

The next week I met with five former Gambian political officials at the palatial Four Seasons Hotel located in the

Georgetown area of Washington, D.C. The spokesperson for the group was the well-dressed and highly intelligent Ousman Sallah who was the country's former Ambassador to the United States. He elaborated on the coup and said that The Gambia was subsequently one of the few democratic governments in Africa. Sallah went on about the need for someone to open doors and after about two hours of conversation, I mentioned that all I could do was look into it.

Returning home, and before I reached out to anyone, I wanted to research The Gambia and see what really brought about the coup. Just before the overthrow of the government began, Yahya Jammeh, the commander of the nation's military police, returned from a long visit to the United States. During his stay here he received military training and met with a number of our political leaders and allegedly became close to congressional Rep. William Jefferson, from Louisiana. I started to wonder, even though at that time I didn't know, if the United States was in some clandestine way involved in the coup?

Before the coup, The Gambia had a sophisticated democratic constitutional and legal system. After Jammeh came to power, his junta would, on a regular basis, arrest and detain media representatives, former military officials, political leaders, and the people that believed in the democratic process.

After around three weeks of trying to dig up some background and better understand what took place, I agreed to meet with the former ambassador again.

At the same location as before, Ousman Sallah and I discussed what he knew about the coup. I asked him if he had any knowledge about any American involvement in it.

There was a rumor that Jammeh was secretly telling his associates that the USA backed his coup. Sallah alleged that he possessed proof that the American ambassador to The Gambia, Andrew Winter, and the American ambassador to the African nation Gabon, Joseph Wilson (the husband of exposed CIA officer Valerie Plame), were involved or at least aware prior to the coup taking place. At the time, Wilson was also working with the American National Security Council regarding other American interests in Africa and was considered someone who could get the job done.

Wilson held many high ranking positions with the American government which included political advisor to the Commander-in-Chief of the United States Armed Forces, Europe; Deputy Chief of Mission at the US Embassy in Baghdad, Iraq, during Operation Desert Shield; and as acting ambassador responsible for the freeing of several hundred American hostages. He was the last American official to meet with Saddam Hussein before Operation Desert Storm.

Wilson was a player but many of the people working at the NSA purportedly disliked the guy. They felt that he was cold, callous and unsympathetic towards Africa as a whole, as well as the plight of its people.

In December of 2002, White House spokesperson Ari Fleischer announced the United States had solid intelligence that Iraq had kept weapons of mass destruction, a violation of UN mandates. Italian Intelligence was closely watching Wissam al-Zahawie, an Iraq official and Saddam Hussein loyalist who made travel arrangements to visit West Africa. They notified French Intelligence who notified British Intelligence who, in turn, notified the United

States. The Americans and Brits believed that his visit to West Africa was related to the purchase of large amounts of uranium oxide.

Wilson's reports were submitted to the White House and they believed that purchases of the radioactive bomb-making uranium were taking place.

A July 6, 2003, *New York Times* article affirms that under President Bill Clinton, Wilson helped direct African policy for the National Security Council. He alleged that he only played a small role in the effort to verify information about Africa's suspected link to Iraq's unconventional weapons. The Bush administration countered the Wilson claims by reporting that Wilson did believe that the purchase discussions were taking place and that the African nation Niger would provide Iraq with uranium to be used to make weapons of mass destruction, but Wilson denied this.

Because of the falling out with Wilson, the White House started leaking information about Wilson's wife Valerie Plame and claims were made that those involved in the leaks were Vice President Dick Cheney, presidential chief advisor Karl Rove, and vice president Chief of Staff Lewis "Scooter" Libby. In July 2006, Plame sued the three, accusing them and other White House officials of conspiring to destroy her career.

Sallah asked me if I thought a military retaking of The Gambia was possible, not that he was planning or looking to prepare for one. Explaining that to plan one here in the United States would, of course, be illegal and we should not contemplate that type of retaliation. It would have to involve a large enough organization or a nation willing to provide the funds that would be needed for such an operation. I believed that the best way for us to proceed was for him to let the public know about the United States involvement which he believed to be true.

The disenfranchised Sallah was not the type of person to lie and from our conversation about the coup; I knew he was telling the truth. I asked him if I should let the media know. He responded that he did not want to take a chance on losing his right to stay in America, and that he would think about it. The White House would have had to approve the coup.

If the USA was involved in the Gambian coup, then that involvement backfired! The new Gambian government was developing close relationships with Cuba, Libya and other countries who were personae non gratae. The July 1994, coup strained Gambian relationships with many European countries and the USA suspended most nonhumanitarian assistance to the small African nation.

After having numerous sessions with Sallah and the other displaced officials from The Gambia, I let the former officials know what I could do to help their cause. I chatted on the phone with former president Dawda Jawara, who was now living in London. In one of my conversations Jawara confirmed what Sallah had told me about American involvement in the overthrow. I tried to convince him, as well as I could, that "the American people would help if you let them know this because we, as a people, would not stand for it." After listening to me, the exiled former president said, "The American people may not listen and even if they did, their combined voices may not be enough."

I wondered if maybe he was right; maybe the American people would not be strong enough and that the ousted

Gambian leaders would receive a lashing from the spin doctors if it were known that the United States had secretly engaged in the overthrow of a friendly government. We decided to see if we could gain support from other politicians as well as from the United Kingdom.

I helped establish The Gambia Democratic Forum. Besides Ousman Sallah and a number of other former officials, we were joined by a couple of noted Americans who had befriended Sallah. I set up a web site and started sending emails and snail mail letters signed by Ousman Sallah to many of our elected officials, including President Clinton. I also contacted the British State Department. Very few American elected officials answered, but President Clinton did reply with a cordial, but unhelpful, memo.

The Brits, however, did reply and seriously wanted to assist any way they legally could and a number of phone call conversations were made. One of my concerns was why the United States would want to change the government of The Gambia, if in fact they did play a role in the coup d'état? The Gambia is a poor, small nation that's only natural resource is peanuts and is better known as the birth place of Kunta Kinte, in Alex Haley's epic saga *Roots*.

The Brits asked in a roundabout way for me to look at the Republic of China, commonly referred to as Taiwan, and its relationship with Jawara. At first I couldn't understand why but after some research I figured it out.

Dawda Jawara, Ousman Sallah and the other Gambian leaders wanted to develop better relations with the People's Republic of China (communist China). This was something the US and Taiwan did not want because, even though it's small, The Gambia had one thing that was very powerful: A seat and vote in the United Nations!

Eventually Sallah and I visited the Taipei (Taiwan) Economic and Cultural Office located in D.C. and nicely conversed about their relationship with the current leader, Jammeh. We discussed the overthrow and asked if they could rethink their support for Jammeh. The Taiwanese were soft spoken and smiling but did not want to assist us and potentially harm that current relationship.

I continued to denounce Yahya Jammeh and at the very least gain public support from all corners of the world. One afternoon I received a call from someone claiming to represent Jammeh and the Gambian government asking me if I could meet with him and the Gambian delegation. After inquiring why and if it would help, he answered that they would like to point out the true picture of what happened and that Jawara and Sallah were crooks or some words to that effect. I firmly but cordially countered, "No, I will continue my support for the overthrown leadership and not meet with him."

In the end we never really were able, or for that matter capable, of putting together a quality resistance operation, mainly due to the lack of funding. I felt really bad, it was over my head and my limited assistance was just that, limited. In July 2012, I read that a new overthrow was being contemplated by someone named Sheikh Sidia Bayo. He was raised in France and had backing to lead a coup against Yahya Jammeh and end his reign of terror. By October 2012, an armed opposition group based in Dakar had been established.

The Russian Mafia

THE THREAT FROM *RUSSIAN ORGANIZED CRIME* (ROC) in the United States has been a major concern for some time. Most of us in the know agree that increased organized crime activity is widespread and rapidly growing. Its ability to change methods of operations creates a difficult challenge for law enforcement and society as a whole.

Russian organized crime is an area that is increasingly difficult and quite complicated to scrutinize. The crimes they commit after careful planning involve several Russian criminal groups, networks and include some people who are forced to support their immoral goings-on via threats. They have no limitations or boundaries and you will find Russian organized crime benefiting from just about everything, and not limited to, sex slavery, stolen cars, phony charities, false identifications, passports, visas, stealing state secrets, child porn, illegal arms, money laundering, narcotics, fraudulent insurance claims, medical bills, cyber crime and on and on.

Public nescience and the limitation of financial and human resources have and do create a serious obstacle for law enforcement. Equally troublesome is cutting through the red tape involved in obtaining quality information relating to ROC international activity.

Treaties, and dependence on other countries' intelligence and enforcement organizations, severely disrupt conducting a proper investigation.

In Russia, and many Eastern European countries, graft is a way of life and is expected. Many high ranking governmental positions are not earned but bought by the highest bidder. The same holds true for steel manufacturing, medical supplies and just about every industry. What compounds the problem is that the very law enforcement officials that are supposed to protect the public are in many cases also controlled by Russian organized crime.

I have witnessed and am aware just how vast the ROC network is in America and its ties to Moscow and St. Petersburg criminal families. Anyone that thinks that they do not deal with or supply terrorists, or are in no way connected to terror, does not understand the Russian Mafia.

As ROC activity in the USA and Canada expands so does the migration of its members and their criminal associates to these targeted countries. No longer is it confined to NYC, Chicago, Los Angeles, Boston and Toronto. Today their networks operate in each and every state, and Canadian provinces as well as a myriad of other countries.

In my opinion, the key to fighting the real red menace is through quality intelligence and surveillance. Fortunately, ROC operations can be penetrated. It takes hard work and time but their very greed and loose structure (unlike the Cosa Nostra) opens them to infiltration. The next step is to pierce the ubiquitous corporate structures created to show legitimacy as well as confuse the investigator. With most ROC members, a three to five-year jail sentence is not enough to flip them (cooperate with law enforcement) and their preference is to do the time and "take a vacation" as they refer to a jail sentence. If, however, a ROC member or associate is facing a long, hard sentence and believes that his cooperation will remain clandestine, then substantial information relating to ROC networks and its criminal exploits here and abroad can be obtained.

Since the World Trade Center disaster, American law enforcement agencies have had to change their priorities and utilize the limited available resources to combat terrorism and the threat against our homeland and people. Most of us know that America is at war and it will take diligence and many years of hardship before it is won. This redirection is known by criminal groups such as ROC and they fully know how to exploit it. *The Bureau of Alcohol, Tobacco, Firearms and Explosives* (ATF) is now heavily focused on explosives and provides only a few agents to investigate criminal tobacco and liquor crimes. The vast abundance of shipping containers coming here is a burdening problem for customs agents. The same holds true for the bureau that has had to meet the substantial challenges posed by terrorists. We must not lose sight, however, that many Eastern European criminals are without conscience and are involved with numerous terrorist groups throughout the world including those directly and indirectly threatening our nation. Democracies and their basic freedoms afford a prime opportunity for ROC to branch out and exploit an unknowing public.

Belarus – Eastern Europe – Becoming Gorky

I STARTED TO TRAVEL TO RUSSIA AND Belarus (White Russia) more often and it was taking up more of my time. I continued to work with Ousman Sallah, and the other disenfranchised, but not as much.

It was the summer of 1997, and I decided to see Alla Boulynko, who was from Minsk, Belarus and who I first met in 1993, in Germany. She was attending an art show there and is an accomplished painter of portraits.

Alla did not speak any English and we had to speak with my somewhat suspect ability to speak Russian. During my early visits to Minsk and Belarus I quickly noticed that outside of a very few, the only Americans around were those attached to the United States Embassy. Unlike Russia and the influx of American businessmen and tourists, Belarus remained veiled. One time when I was walking down the main street of Minsk, an elderly man, adorned with highly decorated World War II ribbons and medals, asked me in Russian if I knew where an address was. I answered in my limited Russian, "Ya ne govoryú po-rússki" that I do not speak Russian that well. He asked me where I was from and I told him that I was an American. To my surprise he started to shake, cry and yelled, "Spasiba, spasiba, ya ochen' rad, chto vy Amerikanyetz!" (Thank you, thank you, I am so very happy that you are American.) I asked, "Why does my presence make you happy?"

The crying and shaking war hero bellowed, "Because I am so glad. My family and I are afraid that we are going to be bombed by the Americans. Spasiba, (thank you) now I know that it will not happen." After telling him that we were at peace now and friends, I departed from the blissful man who was still yelling out his thanks.

A Belarusian named Anatoly Neverov was a constant companion. I liked Neverov who I called Little Bear (mostly because of his black beard). Neverov was previously connected to the Belarusian KGB and we would visit some of his former associates at KGB headquarters located in downtown Minsk. I think he liked the idea of having an American around to show to his friends. One time, while at headquarters, we proceeded to the sub-floor and entered the KGB club which was basically a bar. Most agents and those present accepted me but there was one agent who was very disconcerting and showed his displeasure by yelling, "This is our club and now for the first time we are letting in an outsider and on top of that, an American." The other agents quickly calmed down the boisterous agent. Other than that one incident, everyone there was very friendly.

At that time I truthfully mentioned that I worked for the FBI under a contract to help rid the United States of organized crime elements. I knew that if I didn't and they found out, my avoiding the subject would lead to trouble and possible expulsion from their country. I mentioned that I was only there to meet with my girlfriend and our son. I did ask some of the older agents about President Kennedy's killer, Lee Harvey Oswald, who lived just a few blocks away. They did not know much but told me, "If you are interested, come back tomorrow morning and we will have you talk to someone that did know him."

When I went back the next day I was escorted to a small office that could only hold a couple of people. After drinking some vodka and eating a little food, a very elderly man entered our small room. He introduced himself as Gennady and I asked him, only out of curiosity, what he knew about Oswald. He explained that Oswald told the Soviet Union KGB that he possessed a lot of military secrets that could help them. After initial debriefings he was sent to Minsk where further debriefings took place. The old-timer mentioned they were all shocked at just how fluent his Russian was! They prodded Oswald about where he learned to speak Russian. Oswald answered back, "In the States." They did not believe him, his Russian was that good, and if he did, the teacher(s) must have spent a long time with him tutoring the proper dialect. The only thing that he could remember was that as a Marine, Oswald was assigned to the Naval Air facility in Japan and did know quite a lot about American operations at the base. He went on, saying that Oswald was under Moscow's control and everything they did or asked Oswald had to be approved ahead of time. He did not seem to know much more or if he did he either forgot or kept it from me. By this time I was feeling drunk. I could not keep up with Neverov and the others present.

Neverov then introduced me to a couple of his friends, Alexander Vanchin and Anatoly Massiuk. Massiuk had his doctorate degree in agriculture and soon became a very dear and close friend and remains so even today. Here was an honest, hardworking and dependable adviser that I would bring with me on many of my meetings. Vanchin was a former Soviet Union colonel who was highly regarded as someone who could get the job done. Not only could he speak fluent English, he was also fluent in French. His military career was quite illustrious and he would be called by many Soviet soldiers and intelligence officers "Otto" in reference to Otto Skorzeny, the famous German who was personally selected by Hitler to rescue Italian dictator Benito Mussolini when he was overthrown.

Vanchin arranged many daring raids as well as rescues of Soviet troops. One of the rescues was in North Korea when the Americans crossed the 39th parallel and were moving fast towards the Chinese border and were closing in on Russian military advisers that were present there. The Russians did not want it known that they were more than assisting North Korea financially and using ground troops and adept advisers. He hated the CIA and said that they almost killed him and his family during his assignment in Africa. I listened intently to Vanchin and even though we were products of the Cold War, we became somewhat cool yet friendly with each other.

One time at my apartment, Vanchin arrived with Neverov and the ever-present vodka. Over conversation the drinks would hit me hard again. I noticed that many Russians and Belarusians would point to their neck or flick their forefinger against it before they drank. I asked them why they did that. Vanchin told me that during the Reign of Peter the Great the great leader fell off his horse and started to drown. One of his aides or soldiers rescued him and for his quick action was rewarded with a life of not having to pay for most anything. A tattoo was prominently placed on the man's neck so that all could see. Unfortunately, he had a drinking problem and would enter the cafes, restaurants etc., and say "Peets" which in Russian means drink and at the same time point to the tattoo that was on his neck and get served free vodka. I do not know if the story was true but it was very entertaining.

In January of 1998, Alla and I were married in a civil and Eastern Orthodox ceremony. We celebrated our marriage at the Orbita Hotel located not far from where Alla lived. I had Neverov serve as my best man along with my new friends Vanchin and Massiuk. Life remained hard for many of the Belarusian's but was improving. The elderly folks liked their president, Alexander Lukashenko, who helped them with their pensions and costs to maintain their respective homes. Alla's younger years were hard and difficult. Together with her mother and sister they had to overcome the problem of a loving man who indulged his alcohol more and more. Like many other elderly men, he served with honors in the Soviet army. As a child Alla's mother Tatiana witnessed the atrocity of the German onslaught and its destruction of Minsk and Belarus. She witnessed her parents captured by the Nazi's, being tortured and hung as partisans for all to see. Even though she was very young, she was also tortured by the Nazi's and her hair was set on fire.

I was now staying at a Khrushchev (the name that was given to a number of apartments built during the former Soviet Union leader's time as president). The rooms were very small and like most apartments did not have screens to keep out the bugs. All in all, I was quite comfortable. Many evenings Alla's sister Sveta and husband Sergei would visit and break bread with us. By this time their father was disappearing for longer periods of time.

After returning to the States I learned that he was found dead after drinking some bad liquor. Everyone has heard something about Russia having many alcoholics. Alcoholism in Eastern Europe does not exist because of some genetic defect but the result of a predicament which existed in the Soviet Union and continues today. I can tell you that the people are extremely well educated and, like all of us, dream to have a family and enough money to take care of them.

The situation started getting worse after the Soviet Union collapsed. They did not have the government support that they were used to having and did not have the means to enter the new capitalist form of government that was being established in many of the countries. Many of them, especially the elderly, became unemployed and could not find jobs. In frustration they turned to liquor which led to alcoholism. I am not writing to defend Alexander Lukashenko and his policies, some of which I am opposed to. However, he and his administration were and are acutely aware of the drinking problem and tried to implement programs that would keep the younger population away from hard liquor.

I have seen the results and even though the dilemma remains, work started to pick up, at least until the United States stock market collapsed in 2008. Many of us in America are not aware of how this crisis affected people all over the world. Like the United States in the 60s and 70s, the college students are rebellious and debase their president for the woes of the country. Belarus is a country of approximately 10 million people with more then 2 million living in or near its capital, Minsk. After the disintegration of the Soviet Union, Belarus tried its hand at capitalism but, like Russia, the carpetbaggers from its own country combined with Americans and Europeans reaped its benefits and corruption was rampant. The populace suffered under the loss of many of its social programs and started to yearn for a return to its former way of life.

Alexander Grigoryevich Lukashenko was born on August 1, 1954, in the quaint village of Kopys in the Vitebsk region of Belarus. Involved in collective farming where he worked as a manager of state and collective farms, he developed the desire to have his country self-sufficient and not depend on outsiders for food necessities. In July of 1994, he was elected as the Belarusian president on a platform of anti-corruption.

When I first visited Belarus, pictures of American President Bill Clinton shaking hands with Lukashenko were everywhere. In my humble opinion, Lukashenko desired a close relationship with the West and the potential it offered.

I do not know what changed his mind but my hypothesis is he felt, at least with the United States, that its representatives were acting more like a big brother and at times belittling. In April of 1998, a rift caused Lukashenko to force western embassy employees from their residences which were near his home and to move them to new accommodations. It was really a bad time and the relationship with the West never recovered.

I really do not know what caused the bad blood but it affected sorely needed human rights programs throughout the country. When the Chernobyl disaster struck in April of 1986, Belarus received more then 70% of the radioactive fallout. Numerous countries and charities rushed to assist the victims suffering from the disaster. Commencing in 1998, I, too, would try to help. Belarus and its people continued to suffer from the radioactive contamination as well as from a shortage of wheat, medicine and housing, and many still do. I met with Deputy Foreign Minister Alexander Popov, as well as with Dr. Anton Romanovsky, who headed up the Belarusian Red Cross. They informed me that the immediate need was for wheat and all their efforts to obtain the staple food thus far were in vain. During one of my follow-up meetings with Julian Kronberg, a Norwegian representing the International Red Cross, he told me "Do not count on American support, they will not participate in any food assistance." I asked him, "Why not? We are always giving a helping hand to those in need." Kronberg then remarked that he had a previous meeting with United States representatives and they put on a political price that would have to be met before they would assist in the relief effort.

This was hard for me to believe, so I took the next step and appealed to Department of Agriculture representative Heather Lintz who said that aid was available but that the Belarusian government must be the entity that makes the request for the assistance. After hearing this I had Deputy Foreign Minister Popov send a letter to Agriculture Secretary Daniel Glickman. Department of Agriculture administrator Timothy Galvin responded by stating that Belarus must change its ways and become more democratic before any assistance would be given. Galvin also stated that aid may be given if the situation warranted it by having the Belarusian Red Cross request it. I then met again with Romanovsky who sent a letter to Glickman and Galvin on just how important the need for assistance was. Unfortunately, my own government would not assist, and our requests fell on deaf ears. After many phone calls and applying much pressure, the International Red Cross based in Switzerland sent a representative who assured us that they would find the needed wheat and food stuffs from other countries.

It seems like every day I read that claims of dictatorship are made against Lukashenko and that he is now being called Europe's last remaining dictator. The claims that he is violating human rights and freedom of the press are found throughout western newspapers and media outlets. Personally, I see this as a struggle between the United States and Western Europe in conjunction with Belarus. I can only deduce that if both sides gave a little, I think the final result would be positive. Belarus must join us in freedom of the press, allowing those who dissent the freedom to speak. But let's face it— we need a little self-cleansing also. Stop all the corporate carpetbagging, the misuse of our government by some of our elected and appointed officials to personally strive to make their political contributors richer via illegal means here and abroad. I don't like saying that, but it is true. We all know that. Before we can rid the undemocratic problems of another country, we must address our own problems of democracy.

It's unfortunate, but until we fix the political contribution process we will never have the government our forefathers envisioned. The little guy or gal doesn't stand a chance. Sure, we are told you can always get together and voice your opinion because we do, thank God, still have free speech.

The people of Belarus are no different than us and want peace and happiness. I have read so many articles about Belarus that say it is a place of doom and gloom! This, however, is not the case. They are a happy and jovial people. Most of them that vote for Alexander Lukashenko do so because they want to and like him. I know because I have talked with thousands of them. The students, however, want him out; they see him as a blockade to their future and they are publicly arrested when they march to support another candidate.

The problem as I see it is that Lukashenko, his government and a large number of the people fear being taken over by Russia or another foreign country. I know after serving as an international election observer during a presidential election that the people simply like Lukashenko.

Before, I mentioned that there are a lot of his policies I do not like, especially his support of Iran, North Korea and some other countries. If President Lukashenko wants the people of America to support him, he in no way can obtain their acceptance without removing his support for these wayward-thinking countries. He must join most of the nations of the world in their condemnation of terrorism and those threats of nuclear proliferation. In the past, I knew that he desired help from us and thanked me for my trying to help them with humanitarian needs. I know we did not help as we could have, but I do believe that at least both countries should try just a little harder to repair our differences, curtail the sale of weapons that are used to harm others and join those that want a more peaceful planet. I have heard from some people that say and tell me I'm wrong! My desires are only that, just desires that can never be achieved. Maybe they are right and mankind has not changed enough to stop the madness. I hope that's not the case. As I sit here and ponder what I just wrote, I think we all know that friendship and world peace is the only solution, yet its accomplishment, at least at this time, is an inaccessible illusion. It's regrettable, because unless we achieve it, eventually the outcome will be one of mass destruction. Albert Einstein was once asked how World War III will be fought. He answered, "I know not with what weapons World War III will be fought, but World War IV will be fought with sticks and stones."

Vodka

NO ONE SEEMS TO KNOW WHERE vodka originated. Russia, Poland and other countries laid claim to its origin, but, in my opinion, it was probably created in Persia.

The Kryshtal Distillery in Minsk, Belarus was one of the few buildings not destroyed by the Germans during World War II. Once when visiting Minsk, it was arranged that I visit the distillery. Even though the Soviet Union was gone, pictures and statues of Vladimir Ilyich Lenin were everywhere. Vodka was cheap here and export to Western Europe and the Americas had not yet been made.

In the opinion of Russian imbibers I learned that the best vodka came from wheat, and only in desperation would they make it from potatoes or another vegetable. Multi-distilling a product does make it softer but it also removes natural wheat-flavor congeners. When I departed, I took along some of the best vodka they made including a product called Belovezhskaya, which is an excellent drink. In Minsk and in Moscow it is a custom, I discovered, and even though I normally have a local beer, on a few occasions I toasted some high quality vodka.

When I returned to the States I let some associates and friends sample some of the Kryshtal Distillery liquor products. They all thought they were superb, so I sent some on to experts and they equally thought it was some of the best they ever tasted. My friends wanted to see if we could open up an export company and import the Kryshtal products to the States. I told them that I thought the best thing was to have an established importer handle it together with all the costs of marketing and shipping. I started to study the vodka industry and quickly learned that it is not the best quality that gets the kudos but the product that is advertised and marketed properly. There are many poor quality products that are marketed so well, the public thinks they are the best, but they really are not.

Soon, importer Austin, Nichols & Co, Inc. showed interest in handling the Kryshtal line of products and we would make thirty-five cents for every bottle sold in the States and Canada. My friends and associates wanted to import the products themselves so more profits could be made. I was opposed to the concept but went along with their idea. The American Belarusian Import-Export Company was formed and we obtained a liquor import-export license.

I returned to Minsk and this time they showed me a new product which was called Charodei (wizard or magician) and the bottle it came in was something to behold. I knew it would be hard for a fledgling company such as ours to introduce a new vodka product to the already overcrowded market in the USA. I told Nikolai Belko, who was the director of Kryshtal that we would need to have exclusive rights to Kryshtal products and the rights to the decorative bottles. He stated that the bottle was made in Beaune, France by Belvedere S.A. (possibly best known for Sobieski Vodka and Triple Sec) and they would have to sign off on the bottle.

I flew to Frankfurt, Germany, rented a car and drove to Beaune where I was greeted by company chairman Jacques Rouvroy and Chief Executive Officer Krzysztof Trylinski. After a good night's sleep I toured the famous Burgundy vineyards and the Rouvroy-Trylinski bottle manufacturing facility. After concluding an agreement allowing for the use of their trademarked bottle, I returned to America. After our attorney reviewed the legal documentation we hired a couple of people that had experience in the industry.

After a few months we hit a major snag. Belvedere Vodka of Poland and its founder Ed Phillips (the son of "Dear Abby" columnist Pauline Phillips) sent us a legal notice to cease distribution. The reason behind it was that on the Charodei bottle was the name "Belvedere" in small letters. Even though it had nothing to do with the contents it did appear on the bottle and was a trade-name violation. My associates and I were beside ourselves over this news. Here we were ready to start what could be a profitable business and we were stopped dead in our tracks.

I contacted Krzysztof Trylinski and told him of the problem. Trylinski said, "Do not worry it is our name and it has nothing to do with the bottle design." I explained that we could not purchase any more bottles until the name was changed or removed. He then said he would try and remove it by putting a black line over the thousands of bottles already made. We ordered a new container load, but when it arrived less than half of the bottles we looked at had the name Belvedere blacked out.

We then learned that the French company had a long running feud with Ed Phillips, who had won a number of court battles here in the States and Canada, and the French company was previously warned and knew that they could not use the name Belvedere on the bottle. The only possible remedy left was for us to sue the French company. We hired a Washington, D.C.-based attorney to commence an action against Krzysztof Trylinski and Jacques Rouvroy. I was contacted by Ed Phillips who had already initiated a suit, and he wanted us to join him in the legal action.

Belvedere and Chopin vodkas were being sold all over the world and Eddie Philips was looking to recover the damages caused over the exploitation of his trade name Belvedere. Phillips (who would later become a close friend) and I agreed to meet in Warsaw, Poland and start drafting a joint lawsuit. While our American attorneys were going over what we had agreed to, Phillips called me and asked if I could meet him in Paris. He was there to appear before a French court and answer charges levied against him by the French bottling company.

I had just resigned from the so-called LIUNA cleanup team and went back to work for the FBI working freelance and had to attend a scheduled meeting that I could not miss. I called our D.C. attorney and we agreed that he would go in my place. All his costs and travel expenses were picked up by Eddie Phillips. After arriving in France, our counsel discovered that Eddie Phillips and his attorney were arrested and placed in a Parisian jail. After their release Phillips was compelled to conclude an agreement with the French bottle producer Belvedere. The name "Belvedere" could stay but it had to read Belvedere SA. We were on our own again and would have to file a suit and pay for all the costs involved. We didn't have the money and searched high and low for someone to financially back us, but to no avail. The French bottler refused to return those from the Kryshtal Distillery. We didn't have the money to bring a lawsuit and the chance to recover our losses was gone.

The Belarusian Ambassador

WHEN WE FIRST STARTED IMPORTING THE Belarusian vodka I was introduced to the sociable and highly intelligent Belarusian Ambassador to the United States, Valery Tsepkalo. Tsepkalo and I soon became close friends and together with his lovely wife, Veronica, he would join us on trips to Vermont and when in Massachusetts he and his wife would stay at my modest rental home. He enjoyed his stay in the United States very much and truly did want his country and the United States to have better relations.

Once he asked me, "Why is the United States trying to put up a fence around Russia and Belarus?" (He was referring to the expansion of NATO.) I expressed my feeling that it was wrong. NATO was a military treaty established to counter the military threat from the Soviet Union. As we all know, the Soviet Union is no more, and I know just how deeply the people of these nations question the need for it anymore. I know that today NATO is used as a counter balance against terrorism, but if that is the case, why don't we expand it and invite countries like Russia, who are also fighting terrorism, the right to join?

Vladimir Putin had, and most likely still has, a dream

of resurrecting the power that Russia enjoyed during the Soviet Union period. He knew it would take time and he did not want to appear to be an antagonist to the West.

One of the foremost problems facing Putin and his new Russian order was Belarus. Under Boris Yeltsin, Alexander Lukashenko agreed to closer ties but Putin was a different story. Putin disliked the Belarusian leader and Lukashenko didn't like his Russian counterpart. Belarus feared and opposed Putin's Russia. Without Belarus it would be extremely difficult for Putin to bring about his plans to move forward.

The one enemy we have in common is terrorism, and some sacrilegious Muslim fundamentalists believe that the only way to heaven is to kill us off.

As we know all too well, terrorism is for real and deeply rooted throughout the world. I, for one, believe in a strong military as well as the strong commitment to obtain needed intelligence and covert ops. Thugs under the name of religion or any other cloak will stop at nothing to destroy the United States, Russia and every country that does not accept their way of life. Their hatred for us runs deep and every problem that has ever befallen them is blamed on us. I wish I had an answer but I don't. I do know that dropping our guard will lead to millions of our citizens being killed. Please don't get me wrong, in no way do I blame Islam or its followers. It is a beautiful religion that does not preach violence. Like any group of people you will find some nuts that twist their religious teachings to benefit their cause. I have been to many Muslim countries, and I know the vast majority of them hate the terrorists and only desire peace and the ability to raise a family without fear. Look at what the Taliban did to the young Pakistani girl Malala Yousafzai who just wanted the right to an education.

Acquiescing to terrorists or trying to negotiate with them does not help and only makes them feel that we are weakening, and gives them more hope to continue their deplorable ways. I have heard, as a result of some of my overseas enterprises, that many so-called friendly Muslim nations secretly fund "Al-Qaeda" and other terrorist groups.

Probably, the best solution is to curb their money stream by not buying their oil and its related products. Why this practice continues is exasperating and funds the terrorist ability to continue their acts of malice!

Valery Tsepkalo left his position as the Belarusian Ambassador in March of 2002, and became the Assistant to Belarusian President Alexander Lukashenko. In 2005, he became Chairman of Belarus High Technology Park located in Minsk and he continues to promote the values of doing business in Belarus.

By 1999, the American-based Cosa Nostra was in disarray and their members and associates were transmuting to appear to be legitimate businessmen. The onslaught of FBI and other law enforcement officials was taking its toll and forcing the mob to devise new means to hide their criminal activity. Mobster attorneys, such as Buffalo, NY-based First Amendment expert and pornography industry counsel Paul Cambria, made a good portion of his fortune and celebrity status representing the mob and its controlled unions. In their heart these mouthpieces think that what they are doing is okay.

Our Constitution allows that everyone is afforded the

right to have the best representation possible. As most of us, I do not in any way want this amendment changed. However, it does not give the right to have any counsel set out to cripple a prosecution by making false statements about the case and its witnesses that they know are in fact bogus. We all know that this is wrong and a damning thing. The price we pay for this right is high!

By the 1990s, the FBI started to focus more on Eurasian crime and its new peril that was burgeoning endangerment. I was asked by the bureau to learn what I could about them and what some of their weaknesses were.

Russia itself is unfortunately encumbered with the Mafia and

while in Moscow I became quite close to Igor Masteranka, who is well connected to many Russian Mafia families there as well as in St. Petersburg, Kiev, Ukraine, Latvia, the former Soviet empire, as well as in Israel and North America. Day by day I was learning and meeting Mafia heads and members. Unlike the Cosa Nostra, these criminals were well educated and creative. They would not hesitate to kill and the streets of Russian cities were plastered with victims. These were tough sons of bitches and they knew it.

While in Moscow, Igor and I would stay at the home of Maxim, a powerful bigwig who was involved in the smuggling of diamonds and precious gems from Africa. His expensive and luxurious apartment was within walking distance of the Stary Arbat neighborhood and one of the more popular shopping and entertainment districts located in Moscow.

My FBI undercover name was again changed, this time to Gorky. All my correspondence with the agencies I worked with rarely ever contained my real name. There are other names I used, but for security reasons I cannot mention them.

The Oligarchs and Rise of the Russian Mafia

According to my dear friend, former Soviet Intelligence officer Alexander Orlov, who erstwhile worked as a reporter for the Kremlin newspaper and is now an assistant to President Putin, it was the powerful oligarch Boris Berezovsky who selected Vladimir Putin to become Prime Minister of Russia.

Berezovsky had urged Russian President Boris Yeltsin to have the former KGB Lt. Col. Vladimir "The Moth" Putin as the fall guy for the floundering situation in Chechnya. The Russian leadership needed to respond to the expanding criticism, especially those in the intelligence community, military and police. His initial victories in Chechnya bolstered Putin's popularity with the public and played a major role in his becoming a successor to Yeltsin. Berezovsky's plan backfired and "Boris the Builder" (as he was known) suspected that he had an adversary on his hands.

Putin did help Berezovsky set up a car dealership in St. Petersburg and a few other money grabbing ventures. Berezovsky said, "Our relationship was based on mutual interests and mutual goals." Berezovsky still felt that because he was the one who promoted Putin to succeed the ailing

Boris Yeltsin, Putin would never forget this favor.

At a meeting arranged by Putin, the newly elected president told Berezovsky, Peter Avin, (president of Alfa Bank and former minister of Foreign Economic Relations), the ultra-rich Vladimir Gusinsky (an associate of US Congressman Tom Lantos), Alexander Smolensky and others whose names I don't remember, that they were going to have to contribute substantially more to "people-come-first programs" that were going to be established. Berezovsky chided Putin for his request and that he would never go along with it. All but Peter Avin echoed Berezovsky's retort. Berezovsky then lucidly let Putin know that he was personally responsible for Putin becoming the president of the Russian Federation and would not bow to the new leader.

Vladimir Putin and his advisers were quite mindful of the power the oligarchs had and their desire to control his administration. Smolensky and Berezovsky were part of the "Sparrow Hills Club" which was named after a district located in Moscow. They controlled a vast media empire which could be used as a tool to tarnish and manage the wayward-thinking Putin.

The Sparrow's developed a plan to remove Putin from power and to start winning the public over by using their media empire to condemn the Moth.

Putin responded by having the KGB successor *Federal Security Service* (FSB) and other intelligence networks commence an investigation which eventually led to criminal indictments of Gusinsky and Berezovsky, forcing them to speedily leave Russia.

This did not sit well with the Yeltsin holdovers that still held their positions and worked for the Putin Administration. Popular Chief of Staff Alexander Voloshin threatened to resign after learning of Putin's fight against the oligarchs whom he supported. Peter Avin was one of the few that tried to maintain some influence with new president.

It was only after Yuri Scheffler (Berezovsky associate and pupil) became a target for the absconding of the rights to Stolichnaya Vodka, that he and other oligarchs realized they all may become victims of Putin's wrath, and so he departed Russia.

Scheffler was previously utilized by Berezovsky to privatize and head up the Russian government export of liquor operation called VVO Sojuzplodoimport, of which former President Boris Yeltsin allowed them to get away with. Surreptitiously, documents and orders were drafted on legal stationary granting ZAO Sojuzplodimport (with a missing "o") and the illegal transfer and privatization of Stolichnaya Vodka. After Putin was elected and in concert with his operations against the oligarchs, the FSB conducted an investigation which led to the indictment of Scheffler, his theft of Stolichnaya, Russkaya and other noted Russian liquors.

While attending a trade show in Washington, D.C. in early 2002, I was introduced to Timothy Borodin who was a Russian trade delegate. We discussed American-Russian relations and the Stolichnaya Vodka problem and how the Putin Administration wanted it back. He addressed the widespread corruption that took place in the Yeltsin administration and how connected paupers would be made instant millionaires. After hearing the story and offering any assistance I could give, it was arranged that a telephone conversation take place between me and the Russian company that handles all Russian production of alcohol and its export. After letting my bureau contacts know, I made arrangements to get involved. I must note that neither the bureau nor CIA ever asked me to spy on Russia or Belarus. Their interest lay in finding out anything they could about the growing Russian Mafia problem. I was always told, "Just keep your eyes open." We had treaties with these countries and we were told not to do anything that would violate those treaties.

On May 23, 2002, while at a wine and liquor show in London, England, I was approached by man who wanted to sample some vodka which was also available for sampling at the nearby booth. He asked me who I was and I gave him my business card. He then identified himself as an associate of Yuri Scheffler and stated, "I heard you were here and you had better watch your back or else!" He then brought up an article that appeared in the media which showed a company (Kryshtal International) I was associated with in concert with the Russian government to create a profit-sharing program with the original Russian distilleries and their employees that produced the renowned vodka. "You know that type of program may work in the States but you will never get the chance to implement it in Russia." I told him that I did not appreciate his threats and frankly I didn't give a damn. I asked him how he was associated with Scheffler. He, surprisingly, said, "Together with my girlfriend I handle their public relations and media programs. Yuri Scheffler is a close, personal friend." In a condemning voice I responded that threat tactics will not work, at least with me, that Scheffler was nothing more than a wealthy thief and that I was quite sure that the Russian government will handle him.

In response he bellowed that they have plans to fight anyone that tries to take Stolichnaya away and that includes Mr. Vladimir Loginov, the chairman of Sojuzplodoimport (the Russian government company responsible for liquor exports) and another person whose name I was unable to catch.

I told him that I believe that Putin will protect his government representatives. He answered, "You do not understand Russian politics nor do you understand just how powerful Yuri Scheffler is and we have people in Russia that have Putin's ear and he will listen to them. We also have a public relations team that is worldwide and well-placed friends in the media who will aid us if we need them. If I were you, I would get out of this Stolichnaya situation now." Again I answered, "I do not appreciate your threats and you can go fuck yourself." As we parted I watched him as he shook hands with another man. When they broke company I walked up to the man that he was talking with and said, "I know him (referring to the guy that threatened me), what is his name again?" The man responded, "He is Willem Borst, and he is in London working with Boris Berezovsky." I then answered, "Yeah that's right, I just forgot his name." I informed a personal friend that was with me that I was just threatened over the Stolichnaya matter.

About 30 minutes later Borst revisited me and told me that I chose the wrong side and that he could arrange a meeting with Scheffler. I told him to tell Scheffler that if he wants to meet me it would have to be with VVO Sojuzplodoimport Chairman Loginov in attendance. He then left. After leaving London, I traveled to Moscow for a meeting and I informed friends who were associated with President Putin and eventually the authorities there of the threats made against me.

By 2001, the Russians and their government wanted their product back, and who can blame them. Stolichnaya Vodka was reaping millions and everyone in the know knew that it was Berezovsky and Yeltsin that arranged the transfer to Scheffler. After it was announced that the Russian government had filed criminal charges against Berezovsky for this and other reasons, as well as Scheffler for his role in the theft, Berezovsky started swinging back from his base in London by using his Moscow-based newspaper *Kommersant* to write derogatory articles about me and Loginov.

I was having a news conference at the Tverskaya Marriott Hotel located on Moscow's main street and within walking distance from the Kremlin. Besides my dear friend Alexander Orlov accompanying me, I was escorted by five Russian government officials. I explained the Willem Borst confrontation and his working for Berezovsky and Scheffler. Every one of the news outlets and their investigative reporters carried what I said with the exception of *Kommersant,* who tried to put a negative spin on my remarks.

After returning to the States, I, together with my attorneys, believed the only way to get our courts to cancel Scheffler's patents and trademarks was for us to enforce the Russian court decisions here and in Canada. Unfortunately, Scheffler already had lobbyist Jack Abramoff (who was paid with cash to his private Cyprus account as well as an overt token payment showing $25,000 for his services). They were prepared to fight us if we ever brought the ownership matter to court. IRS documents show that Cyprus-based SPI Spirits Ltd., the Scheffler-owned company importing Stolichnaya Vodka, gave $25,000 to Abramoff's Capital Athletic Foundation in 2002. SPI was a client of Representative Tom DeLay's aide Tony Rudy's at Greenberg Traurig LLP, where he worked with Abramoff before joining the Alexander Strategy Group.

Another problem we had was that the American representative of Sojuzplodoimport, Suren Santurian, did not want to follow the lawsuit route in the United States. From Santurian's Valhalla, New York-based Plodimex USA Inc, which was an import company, he told me that he did not want to use that strategy. It was rumored in Moscow circles that if Santurian went along with a recapture of Stolichnaya Vodka lawsuit that Scheffler would then publicize some illegal activities of Santurian that had and were currently taking place. I was never able to find out if these allegations were true.

In July of 2012, Yuri Scheffler was having a party on his $330 million, 440 foot megayacht "The Serene" which was docked in St. Tropez, France. Among the guests were Rihanna, Chris Brown, Swizz Beatz, Ludacris, Leonardo DiCaprio, Kanye West, Kim Kardashian, as well as members of the Saudi royal family and the night's host, Crown Prince of Dubai, Sheikh Hamdan.

Once, I was introduced to Scheffler's wife by a Russian Mafia leader at a Moscow Mafia-controlled club. We were enjoying the music and numerous intros made to Russian officials. His wife knew about me and said, "Why are you, Loginov, and the Putin Administration looking to destroy my husband?" While staring at me with daggers in her eyes she turned her back and went back to the group she was with. Yuri Scheffler was living in London and the Russian oligarch was relishing the high life in a multimillion-dollar mansion. In March 2003, the Russian authorities convinced the Brits and Interpol to find and arrest Scheffler who fled to either Switzerland or Sardinia.

In February 2012, the world's ninth largest superyacht arrived in Venice, California with Scheffler on board.

After a long battle, on July 24, 2012, the Hague Court of Appeal ruled that trademark rights to the popular vodka brands Stolichnaya and Moskovskaya belong to the Russian Federation and not the Dutch-based Spirits International company, part of the Luxemburg-registered SPI Group, owned by the Russian tycoon Yuri Scheffler.

In August 2012, I received a phone call from an American-based representative of Sojuzplodoimport, thanking me for all my help and for me to join them in Moscow. The caller said, "Ronald, we do not forget our friends."

Growth of Russian Organized Crime

EVEN THOUGH CRIME EXISTED FOR MANY years, it was only after the collapse of the Soviet Union and the Boris Yeltsin presidency that it was able to blossom. Unlike the Italian Mafia and the Cosa Nostra there is no definitive structure. The highly structured Cosa Nostra's first and foremost rule is the perpetuation of the family followed by financial gain.

The Russian Mafia knows that in Russia the key to obtaining money is to control elected officials. There are no boundaries to the areas of exploitation. It has established numerous legitimate companies throughout the world as fronts and to cloak their members' prohibited goings-on. It continues to try and maintain close relationships with clandestine allies in the Putin Administration. Boris Yeltsin associates and the oligarchs used them to further their illegal operations. It reflects just how entrenched and powerful they are and shows their resiliency.

Most ROC activity in the United States is through a vast network of hubs in NYC, Chicago, Atlanta, L.A., Miami and Boston. Like the Cosa Nostra, Russian organized crime normally does not bother small businesses until such a time that they become successful or unless they are stepping on the wrong toes. During the 1990s there were numerous turf wars and killings but today that atmosphere has given way to a more mutual respect and a working together attitude.

Igor Masteranka was involved in numerous illegal activities. He did not like Belarusian President Alexander Lukashenko and his cracking down on Russian Mafia activity. Russia, however, was ripe and crime ran rampant.

Even with the Lukashenko crackdown crime still remained in Belarus and Igor took full advantage of the vast amount of money it brings in. One of these areas was child pornography. Masteranka had a hand in it and was allegedly having funds sent to an offshore account he had in Cyprus from a company called Regpay. On July 4, 2004, Regpay and its officers were charged with distribution of child pornography and eventually convicted. Igor somehow escaped being indicted even though the bureau was aware of his involvement. I thought to myself that the only way he could escape the charges was if he agreed to cooperate with the FBI or some other agency. This makes total sense because Igor would be a great conduit for the Russian Mafia's daily activity. ROC was making inroads everywhere in the United States, Britain, France, Spain and numerous other countries were being flooded with these master schemers.

Back in 1995, the FSB (Federal Security Service) became the successor to the KGB (Committee for State Security). It handles mostly internal affairs and leaves external spying to the SVR (Foreign Intelligence Service). In many ways the FSB is like the FBI and its agents are extremely well trained and highly intelligent. The major problem that the FSB has is that its agents and officers are poorly paid. This by itself can lead to corruption, quid pro quo deals, and involvement with ROC and criminal activity. I know it has happened but while I was with the FBI, every agent that I dealt with was dedicated to finding out the truth and enforcing justice.

In November of 2006, Alexander Litvinenko was poisoned while in England. Immediately the FSB and other Russian intelligence agencies became the main suspects. Litvinenko, a former intelligence agent himself, had defected to Britain and was granted asylum. I do not remember if I ever met him but there was quite a lot of talk about his defection. Litvinenko made quite a few accusations against the FSB including that they prearranged the Moscow theater hostage crisis that took place on October 23, 2002, where 129 of the 850 hostages were killed. I do not believe this because the FSB was just as shocked as all of us were. I am sure that some of what Litvinenko reported may be true, but his story also contains many falsehoods. It was rumored that he secretly provided British Intelligence with information and his personal insight regarding the Russian Mafia and its ties to high officials in the Putin Administration. Was he killed by Russian special services? I would have to say yes but not for the reasons that many of us believe. He was most likely killed because he knew too much about the Russian Mafia and its ties to the FSB and some its agents that were corrupt and he may have threatened to reveal their names as well as some international goings-on. This, more than any other reason, was a gross violation of the trust he developed when he was working for the FSB. According to some close friends in Russia who are in the know, Alexander Litvinenko was also suspected of aiding known Muslim terrorist elements in the Middle East and Chechnya.

In a meeting with a possible terrorist whose name I

cannot remember, he stated that Alexander Litvinenko was indeed working with the Brits as well as supporting Muslim fundamentalists and, at the time he was killed, arranging for Russian military arms to be shipped to them.

Arms Smuggling

In April of 2003, I was in Moscow and after arriving at my hotel I was contacted by Igor Masteranka, a ROC leader named Vitali and Alexander Orlov. Masteranka told me to check out of the hotel and that we would again stay at Maxim's palatial apartment. Maxim arranged for us to meet two close friends of his who are high ranking Russian Mafia leaders, Andrei and Mikhail who had substantial input in the Putin Administration as well as in the arms, precious gems, seafood and liquor industry, and probably a lot more.

We went to the office of Rosspirtprom to talk about the Stolichnaya Vodka situation. We waited outside and Mikhail arrived escorted by two military bodyguards. Igor and I were introduced to him by Maxim and we were told that Andrei would be along shortly. While waiting, the two military bodyguards checked all the nearby cars as well the general area for any suspicious-looking people. Andrei arrived with three or four military bodyguards in tow. After our introduction, Andrei said he was already aware of our needs and escorted all of us into the Rosspirtprom building. We entered the office of a young man (23-28 years old, whose name I do not remember) and I could see that he answered to Andrei. Later I learned from Igor that he was the son of a high-ranking Russian Mafia member. The young man informed us that he could assist us with the vodka problem and be able to pressure Scheffler but he did not know about Berezovsky. After leaving Rosspirtprom I talked further with Andrei and Mikhail outside the building about a request I received from a representative of Gorton's Inc. who wanted me to check out the pricing of king crab legs. Andrei informed me that he could assist with Kamchatka Crab legs, as the Russians refer to them, and that he owned six ships located in Magadan, Siberia. Masteranka and I were then invited to dinner by Andrei.

Maxim drove us to a restaurant located near the center of Moscow and after parking the car we were escorted by a plain clothes security guard to a private dining area. We met up with Andrei and Mikhail and eight or nine of their associates. After we sat down, a conversation started about the *United Arab Emirates* (UAE) and the needs of its royal family. I believe the arms dealer Victor Bout sat across from Masteranka and together with a Muslim man who stated to Masteranka and Maxim that the UAE royal family was looking to move $30 billion US out of the Mitsubishi bank in Japan and convert it into Euros without the US government becoming aware of it. The UAE was willing to pay 1% for having this done. After hearing this, I asked Masteranka to go over what they needed again because I missed part of the communication. The Muslim, overhearing my remarks, then spoke in English restating the UAE matter. He also said that the proposal was very new and that he would have more info later in the week.

Because these people are normally quite secretive about their operations I think they thought I was an associate of

Andrei. After dinner we were then invited to a private club which was owned by Andrei and located off of Tverskaya, near the statue of Yuri Dolgoruky. Igor and I were joined by Mikhail, the young man from Rosspirtprom and a number of Andrei's associates. Maxim, the Muslim man, and Bout did not join us but many Russian celebrities and government officials did. We stayed until 4:00 a.m. and were driven back to Maxim's plush apartment.

The next morning, I talked to Igor about the meeting and asked if he knew the family names of Andrei and Mikhail. He responded, "I don't know, but Maxim told me that Andrei was the boss of one the largest Russian Mafia families and even has Putin's ear. Later that day he mentioned that Andrei spent a number of years in France and assisted Maxim with his precious gem and gold business in Africa. "Ronnie, Maxim wants to know about the American marketplace for gems and gold and if we have the means to move any for him. Maxim also let me know that his current Swiss banking relationship would soon be ending because the Swiss were asking too many questions about the origin of the gold and gems." I responded by telling him I would look into it. Igor went on about these guys (referring to Andrei, Mikhail and Maxim) by saying that they have more money than I could possibly imagine and their current objective is to create nonprofit charities as legal business fronts.

Later in the day a low-level Belarusian government official came to Maxim's apartment to spend the night before he traveled home to Minsk. He had just returned from Africa and he was in the precious gems business as well. He stated that he was aware of me and my closeness to Valery Tsepkalo and the others in the Lukashenko regime. He stated that Tsepkalo was now very high in the government and asked when I would be traveling back to Minsk. I think I mentioned not then, but soon. Later that day, Mikhail called Masteranka and stated that he was going to come over to Maxim's apartment to chat with us. When Mikhail arrived he said that Andrei liked us very much and could help with our endeavors. He also wanted us to meet with Vera Shevshenko, who, together with her husband, handled most of the protocol affairs for Vladimir Putin and his wife Lyudmila. We eventually met with Vera, as well as a number of Mikhail's associates, at the Monolith Club. My conversation with her was of a legal nature desiring and needing help with a charity called For the Health and Spirit of the Nation. During the meeting the director of a distillery that Mikhail owns located in the Ukraine sat with us and wanted to know about the liquor industry in America and that they had sent small amounts of liquor to the USA (eventually Atlanta). Mikhail also stated that he was going to Canada with Agriculture Minister Aleksey Gordeev whom I already knew and liked very much. Later he said that if I needed him I could contact him there.

Later in the week Andrei invited us to dinner again, this time at a Japanese restaurant located near, or in, the Golden Ring Hotel. He was surrounded by a number of bodyguards and a number of his associates including Dr. Andrey S. Peshkov who is the director of the All-Russian Research Institute for Nature Protection and is also an official with UN-Habitat, an organization who provides shelter-assistance to people around the world. Igor later informed me that Peshkov works with Andrei. At this meeting Igor had a private chat with Andrei and after the meeting; I asked Igor if Andrei discussed the UAE deal. He replied that it did not come up but repeated that Andrei is looking to establish legal businesses around the world and wants to use a nonprofit organization as well. Masteranka stated that, "We have to show them, including Mikhail, that we have the ability in the USA and Canada." He also explained that he was a partner with Maxim and had been for some time and that these are the very people that run Russia and decide who gets appointed to government positions. I asked Masteranka if he knew a man by the name of Wesley (Wieslaw) Michalczyk who wanted to join me in trying to resurrect Charodei Vodka.

He told me that he didn't and asked where Michalczyk's operation was based. I said he operated out of Warsaw, Poland and Chicago and is also involved in the illegal arms business. Masteranka responded by saying that if the weapons are coming directly from Russia then all sales would have to have through government or ROC approval. Masteranka further stated, "Ronnie, forget the vodka, we need a nonprofit organization, not only to show good faith to Andrei and Mikhail, but for power and for you and me to make money. My friend has started a nonprofit organization called North Star in the USA and he now has a lot of power here as well as a lot of money." I later learned that the nonprofit is based out of Framingham, Massachusetts.

Masteranka said, "I have only $10 million left in the USA from the $20 million I made and I have to find a legal front as well." I asked him about the money he was making with Maxim and Masteranka said, "It does not go to the USA outside of a few watches and rings that I wear and if you can help Maxim find a way, it helps me as well as you." I responded, "Igor, you previously told me that right now people are trying to get money out of the USA and offering 15 percent if they can." "That's true Ronnie, for some, but people that live there permanently like Suren Santuryan, they have to show an income otherwise the IRS or another agency will question their lifestyle."

I learned that Andrei is related to the royal family in the UK via his sister or a cousin. He allegedly maintains close ties to the FSB and has strong ties in the UK as well as in Cyprus. According to Alexander Orlov, whom I believe, Andrei is one of the most powerful figures in Russia today. Masteranka confided to me that he learned that Andrei used someone else with the UAE deal but that we could still gain his confidence if we show him our ability and connections.

I have been told by Orlov and others that Vladimir Putin does not like the Russian Mafia and personally would not approve of anyone who is a known member or associate from becoming involved in his administration. But, like the United States, Russia has the same problems that we do. Money talks! Organized crime is the same all over, whether it is Russian, Italian, Chinese, Albanian, etc.

Wesley Michalczyk

Wesley Michalczyk was born in Poland and immigrated to the United States in the middle 1980s but initially did not find his new home to his liking. Working at a metal machine shop in Chicago, Illinois did not offer him much and his dream of wealth and prominence seemed hopeless. Opening a hotdog business equally seemed a dead end and the despondent Pole entered a phase of depression. He did, however, open the door to new friendships and opportunities.

The desperation did not prevent him from dreaming and knowing that he would have to travel the illegal path he pursued. Michalczyk knew that the illegal weapons trade business was very lucrative and seizing the moment he nurtured and became quite close to some international arms dealers. One of them was Emmanuel Weigensberg, a Canadian, Iran-Contra figure and a close associate of former US General Richard Secord. Weigensberg was already operating out of Eastern Europe and felt that Michalczyk could be an asset with his connections in Belarus and Russia. The friendship blossomed, money soon poured in, and the errant Pole relished his new-found status.

He turned his back on his principles, friends at the machine shop and his oath of allegiance to America. In order to maintain an appearance of legitimacy, he purchased a Chicago restaurant that was featured in the 1989, movie, *Roadhouse,* with actor Patrick Swayze, but the limited business proceeds could not cloak his vast sums of illicit cash that were pouring in. After consulting with his accomplices in the United States, Poland and Eastern Europe, he opened up offshore shell companies and offshore bank accounts in Cyprus, Switzerland, Bahamas, Barbados, Virgin Islands, and in the United Kingdom. This answered part of the problem but he still needed to address his need for the millions he desired to bring to America to support his high living lifestyle. He used his Polish friends Paul "Pawel" Podedworny, Jack (Jacek) Wypych, Jacek Dabrowski and Zbignew "Zig" Skirucha as fronts for American operations and the myriad of corporations he owned here and abroad. His Chicago-based attorney, Robert Prorak, represented his American operations and London, England based Steven Daultrey, was one of his numerous European legal representatives.

Michalczyk knew that the best way to hide his sources of funds from the prying eyes of the enforcement agencies was to make it almost impossible for them to pierce the corporate veil. Companies such as ERA Industries Inc. of Franklin Park, IL; Cracovia Inc., Harwood Heights, IL; American Speedy Printing Centers, Harwood Heights, IL and numerous others were utilized to avail Michalczyk to his desired cash needs. His overseas corporations and their holdings were even more immense. Heat Engineering Poland Sp. z o.o., located in Warsaw, Poland, became the center of operations and included MP Consulting, Amron International Management Services of Gibraltar, E.E. Company Ltd Sp. z o.o., Lodz, Poland; IZAO "Eurotransenergo," Minsk, Belarus and fronted by Vladimir Manatin; Ekkar 98 Limited of Malta, The American firm ATOS International Acquisition Ltd., Velcom Telephone of Belarus, Teasdale International Ltd. with offices in Gibraltar SEN Group of Companies, Belarus; Stolibet Trading Ltd (Cyprus), and Gordes Co. sp. z o.o. (Poland) to name just a few.

Early on, in order to avoid conflicts in Belarus and in Russia, Michalczyk partnered with Vladimir Peftiev of Beltechexport of Belarus, a large supplier of arms and military goods working their way around the world. Podedworny, Michalczyk's Chicago associate, was originally in favor of the Peftiev deal and the riches he was receiving from the arrangement, but later opposed the joint operation and he let Michalczyk know his feelings. He did not trust Peftiev and his secret connections in Belarus. He felt that eventually Wesley would become a minion and have to answer to the powerful Peftiev. Michalczyk responded by telling his associate that his connections were stronger.

Podedworny also feared that if they didn't get out of Belarus, Lukashenko would find out that a large portion of the arms that were being purchased and shipped out of Belarus, under the guise of legitimate sales, was really being shipped to undesirables and terrorist organizations. Michalczyk and Peftiev both knew that the West, especially the United States, would be watching their respective operations closely. They also recognized that it was wise to play both ends and cooperated with Russia and Belarus on one hand and the United States and United Kingdom on the other. The United States and the UK were considered easy and could be bought off more cheaply. A little accurate information here and there, together with a lot of misleading information as well, became the norm.

With the development of the Russian SA-300 air defense system and the claim that it could surpass stealth technology, they did everything possible to help get United States hands on the system. The United States and its western allies wanted it and had Wesley directly and indirectly try to ship the air defense system to them. Eventually Russian authorities found out and stopped it. Both arms dealers would directly and indirectly provide information to the West, just enough to keep the wolf away from the door to show their worth and placate efforts to stop them from achieving their goal. Wesley was a master at this and just about everyone in the know in Belarus and Russia became aware of his game.

Peftiev, on the other hand, did not like the USA, in fact, he hated it, but he did enjoy visiting Florida and arranged to purchase a home in Hobe Sound. Today, the arms dealer has a few of his money laundering corporations located there. Unlike Michalczyk he did at one time provide pertinent information via an American associate but then stopped in an effort to avoid discovery by the Russians and Belarusians.

Prior to the Iraqi war and the downfall of Saddam Hussein, Michalczyk and Peftiev were major suppliers of military equipment to Iraq including the S-300 anti-aircraft system. They were selling so much equipment to Syria, Iran and Iraq that some of their equipment ended up in Chechnya and was used to kill Russian soldiers and its loyalists.

At an Orlov-arranged party I was introduced to Gennady Troshev the former Commander of the Russian Army in Chechnya. We talked for about two hours while drinking vodka, joking and covering many subjects. In talking about Chechnya, the highly decorated General said to me,

"How do I fight an enemy that is constantly being supplied with technology and weapons by people here?! In my own country! How do I fight that?"

Michalczyk and Peftiev also knew the power of the Russian Mafia and that if they were not taken care of properly that they could be a potent adversary. The payoffs and bribes to Russian and Belarusian politicians and the ROC were necessary and a price that had to be paid. So much money was being made that it didn't matter.

Their major weakness was their growing egos and looking down on the citizenry. My friend Anatoly Neverov was a strong supporter of Alexander Lukashenko, but he disliked Wesley Michalczyk and publicly made statements against the arms dealer. One evening he went into a tirade in front of many people, yelling that Michalczyk was an American spy and that he had a penis implant and a hand pump that would bring stiffness to his manhood. One of the former KGB agents present told him to shut up and that he didn't know the full story. I even told him to be quiet or he could get hurt. On September 11, 2001, Neverov was shot and killed by assailants while he was home with his family. His murder has never been solved.

I was asked by my friends in the States to learn what I could about Michalczyk and that I could utilize an interest in importing Charodei Vodka in a new bottle which would be made by one of Michalczyk's companies. He also owned a liquor distillery in Belarus which was being run under a corporation named SEN. I discussed the matter with my close friend Anatoly Massiuk who told me to be careful of Wesley, that he was also a major weapons dealer. Of course I already knew that but for King and Country I figured that

I would give it a shot and only keep my eyes and ears open. The boss of the Kryshtal Distillery, Nikolai Belko, made arrangements for me to meet the mysterious arms dealer.

This was not my first trip to Warsaw; I have been there quite often. Warsaw is quite lovely and has totally changed since the fall of the Soviet Union. I was picked up at the airport by one of Michalczyk's associates and driven to my hotel to freshen up. That evening, a dinner and reception was held for me and my traveling comrades Nikolai Belko and his deputy Victor Posnikov (former director of Wesley's Distillery and secretly on his payroll).

While at the restaurant, Wesley was surrounded by approximately 20 bodyguards and associates and our ability to chat was quite limited. He asked me to come to his home the next day where it would be quieter. His home was quite large by Polish standards and was bristling with security. Everywhere you went you found a security guard as well as police dogs who seemed quite confused by all the people present. It was difficult for Wesley to navigate the corridors and doorways because he was in a wheelchair as a result of previous accident that crippled his legs. Close friends of Wesley would say it was the result of a dare when he was quite drunk. Supposedly Wesley climbed the side of a building and a fell leaving him paralyzed. Others alluded that he was thrown off a second story building in Jakarta, Indonesia as a result of an arms sale gone bad.

We reached an agreement whereby Wesley would manufacture the bottles for a new vodka called Charodev (to see if we could get around the problem with the French Belvedere company), and my company would pay him only for the vodka and not for the costly, new fancy bottle. I departed the plush residence realizing that I never would have done it but for the fact it gave me great access to the arms trade industry and would be beneficial to those Americans secretly fighting our battles all over the world. I didn't believe that it would violate my standing orders of just looking and listening. I may have stretched it a little, based on additional instructions I was given, to find out what I could about the mischievous arms dealer Victor Bout who was now a subject of FBI scrutiny. Equally I had learned from so many sources in the know that Michalczyk was playing a triple agent game.

The pact I just made was with the devil himself and I knew it.

Vladimir Peftiev

VLADIMIR PEFTIEV LIVED IN MALTA, BUT also enjoyed his Belarusian residence, the nightlife, and the beautiful women that were everywhere. A close asset of mine, who had access to the Peftiev complex located in downtown Minsk, brought me to the Peftiev abode on quite a few occasions. Peftiev was never around and my source would shower me with information about Peftiev and Michalczyk. I would also meet my asset in Geneva, Switzerland, Genoa and Torino, Italy, where Peftiev and Wesley had additional residences. While in Geneva in the summer of 2003, Wesley and his close associate Rafael Farid, the president of Continental Traveling Center, and an Austrian by the name of Norbert Furst, president of the Redway Holding Corporation; Sharif al-Masry (who I believe is Egyptian and an Al-Qaeda operative) and Farid Rafiee, president of the American-based R&G International, Inc. were also were also present. They would be joined by additional Muslim representatives looking to purchase illegal arms and have them transferred via Victor Bout's various cargo planes or, as it was referred to, The Flying Circus.

By 2004, Wesley and Peftiev had dissolved their relationship. Wesley started operating out of Moscow from a yacht parked in one of the rivers running throughout the Russian capital. Vladimir Peftiev maintained his operations in Belarus but because Malta had joined the EU he had to relocate his operations there or subject himself and his myriad of companies to Maltese investigators. Previously Wesley was involved in the Iran-Contra arms trade and at that time was the vice president of ATOS Corporation which utilized Belarusian and Russian arms to aid the Contras. It is almost impossible for me to remember the names of the players and the corporations they were involved with.

Fadi Darwish

FADI DARWISH WAS BORN IN LEBANON and was a clandestine member of the terrorist group Asbat al-Ansar (the League of the Followers). The Lebanon-based, Sunni extremist group's goal is to establish a radical Sunni Islamic state in Lebanon. Unlike some of the other members, Darwish wanted to maintain close ties to Al-Qaeda and Osama bin Laden, who he believed to have the right answers on how to defeat the West. Darwish stated that the West and especially the United States must answer for their sins and its people must accept and convert to Muslim if they do not want to see their children die.

Around 1992, Darwish first traveled to Belarus to locate and purchase weaponry for the terrorist group but was thwarted in his efforts by the Belarusian KGB. Making Minsk his base, Darwish learned that even though illegal arms could not be purchased in Belarus, the same was not true of Russia and the Ukraine. Darwish was educated at the American University of Beirut where he learned to speak English as well as Russian. While at the university, he hooked up with extremists who brought him to the attention of a terrorist group. He mentioned the name of the group but I cannot remember it. He did say that he received training in Syria and later in Malaysia. Darwish was then sent to Eastern Europe to procure needed weaponry.

In July of 2005, while talking and enjoying the evening over a bottle of wine at the Café Grip in downtown Minsk across from KGB headquarters with my close friend Giorgio Adrimis, a man walked over to our table and Giorgio introduced me to Fadi Darwish. After chatting for a few minutes, Fadi went to another table and joined some Arabic-speaking people. At first Fadi seemed quite cautious of me and Giorgio told me to be careful around him. He said Fadi was a low-level associate of some very big and bad people. He seemed to know quite a lot about Fadi and my inquisitiveness kept me asking questions.

I first met Adrimis in 1996, and I truly enjoyed his company. Giorgio, whose parents were of Greek decent, was born in Sicily and in 1976, he left there for the USSR. I never did learn the reason. His political views were not communist but more like a capitalist. He was always picking up the tab and people like Fadi would show up for a freebie. Giorgio did not speak English and I did not speak Italian, so we had to communicate in Russian. I wanted to know all I could about Fadi so Giorgio put me in touch with a former PLO representative and close associate of Yasser Arafat who only went by the name of Michael. At Michael's home in Minsk he spent more than three hours telling me about the threat that Fadi poses and how he remains quite active with Al-Qaeda and its affiliates. Michael was a really nice guy who I could tell did not believe in extremism and violence. In the following years he introduced me to numerous Muslim residents of Belarus. The only bad words they had for my country dealt with our military being involved in the Middle East and Afghanistan, and attempting to turn those countries into capitalistic states, and, of course, their desire to see Palestine as a united country and a member of the United Nations. We had our differences, especially over Israel and my support for its people.

I still wanted to know more and the only way I could do this was to get close to Darwish. At first I visited the clubs where he hung out. It seemed that his main interest was picking up young girls for sex. After a while, I invited him to have a drink with me. For being a Muslim extremist, he obviously did not adhere to the Muslim teachings. He drank quite a lot and one drink led to another and after about two weeks of nurturing the extremist, I finally got him to open up. I started slowly, and gradually got to the point where he told me that he wanted me to convert to Islam. I told him I was interested but would have to think about it. (When I brought this up with my American-based handlers, they responded by telling me emphatically no. It would be considered an insult to the Islamic people if my hidden agenda became known.) Little by little, he started to open up about the arms trade and his connections in Russia, Ukraine and how he would use a Latvian bank that helped him funnel cash from an offshore account in Cyprus to pay for the illegal arms.

Fadi never seemed to have money and lived a modest life. He married a Belarusian girl and had two children. Even though he loved his children and probably his wife, he put his cause first. He expressed this on numerous occasions. One time I asked him if he could arrange for the purchase of five T-72 tanks for shipment to Nepal. Within a week, I was escorted to a hotel room where three Russian men told me they could arrange it. After seeing the price, I told them that I would have to get back to them because the price was too high. After discussing this with the bureau after I returned to the States, I was told to return and find out more without carrying out any purchases.

At one meeting with Fadi he enlightened me about the killing of former Prime Minister Rafic Hariri of Lebanon, who was assassinated on February 14, 2005. Darwish pointed out that his associate Syrian General Assef Shawkat who received his orders directly from Syrian President Bashar al-Assad who approved the assassination. I didn't know if this was true or only an effort to increase Darwish's status. He talked quite a lot about Syrian General Assef Shawkat and how their relationship began. He constantly berated Iran and the Shiites, who he really hated. Recently, separatists killed Assef Shawkat in a daring raid in Syria and based on what I gleaned about him, he probably deserved it. When I called the Iranians 'Arabs' he would correct me and say they are not Arabs, but Persians and not true believers.

Fadi was like a bug, between his seeking women and arranging arms shipments, he was always looking for a quick buck. One time in 2006, a group of American businessmen desired to export products from Belarus and they asked for my assistance. Fadi, who was nearby, overheard one of our conversations and seized the moment. He was affable and told them he could find everything they need and could act as a translator. I told the Americans not to do business with him and to be very careful. After one of the Americans became involved with a Belarusian girl who did not speak English, the errant businessman arranged to hire Fadi as a translator. Again, but to no avail, I could not convince them to stay away from him. By this time I had learned enough and broke away from Fadi.

Eventually the FBI and other agencies started to fear that I had placed myself in a position where I might get killed and they wanted me to cease my work overseas. I do not know if they had information, or if it was just out of concern that I placed myself in a discoverable position. Back in the States, I was transferred to the FBI Chicago office to assist them with a new investigation.

ULLICO – Global Crossing Union Labor Life J For Jobs

WHILE I WAS WAITING TO BE transferred to the Chicago field office, FBI Special Agent Greg Naples wanted to know if I could assist the *Washington Field Office of the Bureau* (WFO) and its ongoing investigation of a number of labor union officials who had inside information and were on the board of directors of the *Union Labor Life Insurance Company* (ULLICO). ULLICO was founded by Samuel Gompers in 1924, to provide cost-effective insurance for union members. In 1990, Building Trades President Robert Georgine was named chairman, president and chief executive officer of ULLICO.

In the late 1990s, a telecommunications company known as Atlantic Crossing was formed. Soon after that its name was changed to Global Crossing. An associate of the Genovese Family, Gary Winnick, became the chairman of the company and alerted Robert Georgine and Laborers' Union President Arthur A. Coia that they could reap millions from the company's public offering. Georgine and Coia then let their cronies, as well as the other union officials, know of the great opportunity that had been laid at their feet. To help make sure the stock price rose they had union-controlled insurance company ULLICO pour close to $8 million into Global Crossing and realized an after-tax gain of about $305 million. Robert Georgine, together with Arthur A. Coia, their mob colleagues and other union officials, overtly and covertly netted millions in profit. Georgine, whose salary at ULLICO was $650,000 per year, netted more than $20 million in stock profits and benefits over a three-year period.

Jake West, president of the Ironworkers International Union, who was already under a federal investigation, was also a director of ULLICO. During the investigation his stock trades were discovered as well as some of the sources of money. West was eventually charged with embezzling from the Ironworkers Union and pleaded guilty in October 2002, to charges of embezzlement and falsifying a financial report. He was sentenced to three years in prison and fined $125,000.

LIUNA President Arthur A. Coia, a director at ULLICO since 1993, on the other hand, was more creative. Allegedly with his law firm and LIUNA partner, Armand E. Sabitoni, they hid their investments in the ULLICO-Global Crossing scheme, which by all accounts reaped more than $2 million in profits. In January of 2000, Coia pleaded guilty to fraud for evading taxes on the purchase of his $1 million Ferrari purchased with some of his illegally made profits.

A very high former public official may have also profited from Global Crossing. It appears that he may have been paid in stock shares in lieu of cash for a public speaking engagement. Just four months later the company went public and the public official went on to make more than $4.5

million dollars in profit. Like the other insiders, he allegedly knew when to sell and sold his stock just weeks before Global Crossing went bankrupt.

In May 2003, ULLICO shareholders elected a new board of directors and installed Laborers' International Union President Terence O'Sullivan as its new chairman. O'Sullivan had to dance a little to avoid digging too deep in an attempt to clean up the scandal-ridden insurance company. It was believed by many insiders to be a sham and an effort to curb the ongoing investigations. He appointed former Federal Judge Abner Mikva to explore the bad behavior of Georgine and some of those that publicly were known to have been involved.

The ULLICO scandal wasn't the end of the union bosses and politicians personally benefiting at the expense of their respective memberships and constituencies. It has gone, and continues to go, on.

Our investigation team was small and consisted of only three of us. My first step was to let them know that I was aware of previous nefarious criminal activity that took place with ULLICO.

I recall that early on, there was not much financial involvement of the Mafia and its controlled unions with ULLICO. Later on, ULLICO became an appealing investment division for local unions as well as for their parent international offices to invest in-union construction projects. It was called the J for Jobs program and it started by lending out union and fund assets in the late 1970s. The first person to approach me (probably in the middle 1980s) was the previously mentioned Sam Cariola, president of the Western New York Maritime Trades. The longtime mob associate informed me that the Hotel Restaurant Workers' Union and some of its affiliates had already invested and he wanted me to have Local 210 and its benefit funds do the same thing. He explained that we all could make a lot of money and that Joe Todaro Sr. and Sammy Frangiamore approved his request and that I should go along with the proposal. At that time we had just started the Western New York Building Trades Investment Foundation. Cariola knew this but felt we should look at the J for Jobs program as well. I let him know that I would contact Joe Todaro Sr., his cousin, and or Joey LoTempio (Fred Randaccio's nephew and the person who secretly ran the real-estate investment operations behind the scenes and under the cloak of Russell Lipsitz's Buffalo-based company the L&M Agency).

In one conversation I had with Arthur E. Coia, on a date that I cannot remember, he informed me that his son was working with Terry O'Sullivan Sr. and the ULLICO's J for Jobs program. I asked him what O'Sullivan was doing after the LIUNA battle with Chicago and Angelo Fosco battle for the presidency of the union position. The elder Coia made it quite clear that O'Sullivan Sr. was back and now playing a major role with ULLICO and another company named World Wide Insurance. We discussed Mike Lorello and his dislike for O'Sullivan Sr. I was told that Coia Sr. felt the same but that O'Sullivan was a stand-up guy and made quite a lot of money for Santo Trafficante, Bernie Rubin and many family members.

At one time, Arthur E. Coia had a project he wanted me to finance in Central New York but I informed him that our ability to invest was limited to the western part of the state. I discovered that the project was eventually funded by his son Arthur A. Coia. I later uncovered that there was a Daniel O'Sullivan who was a prior president of ULLICO in the late 1970s and still remained close to Coia Jr. and probably, in my opinion, remained involved in additional illicit money making operations.

While attending the wake of LIUNA Vice President Mike Lorello in February 1987 I had a conversation with Angelo Fosco and Bob Georgine regarding the J for Jobs program. Fosco whispered loud enough for Georgine to hear that I and the Buffalo Family could make a lot of money if we used the J for Jobs program instead of the one we started locally. I was kind of surprised about Fosco's openness in front of Georgine and I asked Angelo if I could see him alone for a moment. I explained that I could not answer his request; I would have to let Todaro Sr. handle it.

That night I called SA Steven Naum and let him know about the wake and Angelo's remarks. When I got back to Buffalo, I informed Joe LoTempio about Fosco's desire. LoTempio told me that Todaro approved some investments and that a new company with Russell Lipsitz would be involved. As of today I do not know if they did in fact make any investments with ULLICO.

In 1988 Joseph Cardinale clued me in that he had a long friendship with and been in constant touch with his close friend Ironworkers International Vice President James Willis. I knew Jimmy Willis but this was the first time I heard of their relationship. Cardinale went on about how Willis was going to help our hazardous waste company. Cardinale and I visited Willis in his office in Washington, D.C. and it soon became apparent that they were more than friends. They discussed Lackawanna, New York and Willis thanked

Cardinale for helping his son with some legal problems (I later learned it was drug related). We were soon joined by Jake West, who at that time was an Ironworkers vice president, but in reality the real power in the union. West knew of me and was perplexed why I had left LIUNA. He also told me that he was close to Arthur A. Coia. We then went to lunch and had a discussion about ULLICO and the J for Jobs plan. A number of projects in Florida were going to be financed and kickbacks would be arranged for Buffalo and Pennsylvania Mafia members.

The detailed rip-off plans mentioned were secretly being recorded by me.

A project is presented by a developer to a friend (Cosa Nostra member) and or (corrupt) union official. Both parties agree what money or other valuable assets will be extracted, such as controlled contractors or subcontractors, through high insurance costs, percentage of the project profits, service-providing contracts after the project is completed, key jobs for relatives or fronts, political favors, high percentage of closing costs on both construction loan, and permanent financing.

Once the parties agreed, a presentation was made to the J for Jobs representative. The presentation included land and property appraisals, feasibility studies, cost, project potential, potential leases, competition studies, exit strategy, etc.

The next step was to set an interest rate. Because of the *Employee Retirement Income Security Act* (ERISA) and other applicable laws as well as fiduciary responsibility, the trustees involved in the process try to obtain the highest rate of return for their investment. Because of this, the amount that can be illegally kicked-back shrinks and lessens their desire to invest in the project. Creative means of avoiding legal problems have to be used and one of them is called *a kicker*. A kicker is a certain percentage of the "equity" profits of the said project that will be paid to the finders of investors. To make sure that the kicker does not ever come into play, an out-of-reach program is implemented. For example, the developer knows that the project will only generate $10 million a year so the developer or the lender shows a business plan that reflects that $15 million per year is projected. The contract then reads that the investor will receive 20% of all profits after $12 million of business is reached per annum. In return, the lender agrees to set the lending rate at 1% below prime.

After the project is approved, the first financing is the construction loan. The owner or developer has to pay the lender and his attorney's closing costs. In many Cosa Nostra and corrupt union official funded projects these costs are inflated and sometimes even include unneeded charges. Part of these charges is then kicked-back to the Mafia member, corrupt union official, or their fronts.

Many projects are even allowed to use non-union employees during certain phases of construction to keep costs down or to increase the amounts kicked back. A couple cases in point were the Eden Roc and the Diplomat Hotels in Southern Florida.

Numerous projects involve the demolition of dilapidated buildings and in very many cases the demolition contractor is connected or controlled. The demolition industry has been for many years controlled by the Cosa Nostra as well as the Laborers' International Union. Demolition contractors have access to copper, brass, and many cash-producing metals and the mob has always made sure the unions did not bother these people.

After the construction phase is completed, the permanent financing is put in place and additional closing costs are paid.

Unless you have someone secretly cooperating, the trails seem endless and mind-boggling, but there are easy avenues to follow. I drafted an investigative program for the Justice Department and FBI:

Analyze who receives construction financing.

Select certain projects where the likelihood of kickbacks took place.

See what contractors were utilized.

Check the loan packages to see if there is inflated closing or other irregular costs.

Talk to employees of certain contractors as well as other contractors that may have bid on the project.

The investigation is much easier than it appears and in most cases will prove rewarding.

When I was working on the cleanup team back in 1996, I sent a rather lengthy report to Inspector General Douglas Gow that dealt with Union Labor Life Insurance and some of its illegal practices. I also reported the seriousness that the illegal misuse of ULLICO had and continues to have on union members. While attending a United States Department of Labor conference in 1998, I insisted that they must please look into this and do what they could to curtail this foray into the workers' pockets.

Sometime in 2004, I attended a meeting in D.C. with FBI

Special Agent Greg Naples and the FBI agent assigned to the case. We were joined by Stephen J. Willertz, an investigator from the Department of Labor to discuss just what information I may be able to obtain to aid the investigation. I explained that even though I had been away from the labor field since 1989, I still had high-level connections who I could contact. One union leader I reached out to (whose name and union I will not mention because I fear he would be retaliated against), and who is well informed, said that he could provide me with documentation and information that would be of value. I was also in touch with an AFL-CIO representative that also claimed that he could provide me with additional needed documentation that would prove that certain AFL-CIO officials were involved in the illegal activity.

I was in the process of rescheduling a meeting with a source when I was informed by Greg Naples that the matter was being put on the back burner. I asked him why. "Ronnie, I don't know the answer but I am supposed to tell you that your services are needed for a major case that is being developed by the Chicago office." The investigation into ULLICO was not only put on the back burner, it was killed.

After around a year of work, one of the Chicago-based FBI agents and I were in disagreement on how to proceed and my ever increasing dangerous undercover activity started to get to me. The feud between us was probably more my fault. I was by now becoming more irritable as well as critical. Looking back I think this was the only time in my career that I had a dispute with a bureau agent. I decided that I was not getting enough money in the potentially deadly drama that I was involved in. I am not at liberty to discuss this case except that in late 2006, I terminated my position with the FBI on a good note. As for the organization and all those I worked with, we all remained good friends.

Gennady Vasilenko

GENNADY VASILENKO IS A RUSSIAN PATRIOT who resisted America's bid to make him a double agent. Intensely pressured by my close friend, CIA Agent Jack Platt, Vasilenko never caved in and remained loyal to his homeland. At the same time, Vasilenko, who was assigned to the Russian Embassy in the United States, was trying similar tactics by flipping his American counterpart.

The struggle went on for years and after a while both would visit a nearby restaurant, chat and joke and eventually a close friendship developed between the two Cold War warriors.

FBI Supervisory SA Robert Philip Hanssen was a recruited by the Soviet Union in 1979, and provided them with highly sensitive secret and confidential information. Even after the collapse of the Soviet Union Hanssen continued his traitorous ways until he was finally arrested on February 18, 2001. In one of his reports submitted to his Russian handlers, he stated that Gennady Vasilenko was working for the CIA. In January 1988, Vasilenko was arrested in Cuba on espionage charges and sent back to the Soviet Union, where he was imprisoned for six months and expelled from the KGB. Even though this was not the case, the damage to this man's reputation was done. After his release, he started a private business with his now close friend American colleague Jack Platt who had retired from the Agency. In 2005, he was again imprisoned in Russia on trumped-up weapons charges. These new charges were nothing more than a setup to punish the KGB colonel who the Russians still believed was a traitor. Gennady had in his possession 500 rounds of .22-caliber ammunition that he used for hunting.

By this time I had pretty good relations with the Putin Administration and I was asked to see if I could assist the beleaguered and innocent Vasilenko.

In the winter of 1976, I flew back to Moscow and upon arriving at the Sheremetyevo International Airport, I was greeted by my friend Alexander Orlov. Orlov was a good man who had been a reporter for the Kremlin newspaper. Now he held a powerful position as the representative of Russia to the Commonwealth of Independent States. More importantly, he had President Putin's ear. I let him know that Vasilenko was innocent and always resisted American efforts to have him cooperate. I asked him for his help to see what he could do. Meetings were arranged and I met with a couple members of the Russian Parliament (DUMA) who, after hearing of my request to get this innocent man released from jail, said they would get back to me. After a couple of days they informed me that they could not lessen the sentence but arrangements were being made to send him to a much less restricted and more comfortable prison community outside of the Russian City of Smolensk.

In early January of 2008, a cell phone was discovered on Vasilenko and I learned that he was going to be punished and transferred to a strict security prison. I again went to

Moscow, but this time it was different. Relations with the United States were at a low point and I found no one willing to talk with me about the plight of Gennady Vasilenko. I found this very disturbing and all I was told was "we sympathize with you over the situation."

On June 29, 2010, the United States acknowledged that 11 Russian spies were arrested. They used coffee shops, bookstores and street corners to contact handlers to pass on the secrets they obtained. All the suspects appeared in federal courts and one young girl, Anna Chapman, gained notoriety for her good looks. All argued that they were not spies, but the wealth of information and surveillance that the FBI had was more than sufficient. I knew, like everyone that has ever worked the Moscow Circus knew, they were spies looking to garner any secretive information that they could get their hands on.

On July 10, 2010, a spy swap was announced and one of the Russians coming to America was Gennady Vasilenko. I went out and celebrated with a dear retired CIA friend who lives near me in Williamsburg, Virginia. Today Vasilenko lives in the Washington, D.C. area and from everything I have been told, truly enjoys his freedom.

Epilogue

The bureau and U.S. Intelligence agencies are acutely aware of Russian plots to place hundreds if not thousands of deep cover operatives in the United States and Canada. These spies located in North America under the guise of being ordinary people looking for a better life and a piece of the American dream. We are now at least in part aware that their intentions are to obtain military and corporate clandestine information. From their respective geographic locations they seek to uncover everything they can learn regarding military troop movements, new technology, etc. They basically nurture in the know American citizens to become friends and prod them to reveal what they know. This practice is so widespread that most U.S. Intelligence officials agreed that there are more Russians spying now than during the Cold War era. The Russian fifth column is opening up businesses everywhere, working at manufacturing facilities, and even infiltrating our universities and schools.

It is not limited to the Russians alone, many countries such as China and Iran equally support fifth column operations infiltrating and obtaining covert classifications here and in Canada. I am not trying in any way to degrade Vladimir Putin or leaders from other countries. These types of information-gathering practices are a way of life. We practice it as well as many other countries. After the collapse of the Soviet Union, hundreds of thousands of Russians migrated to the United States; the vast majority of them are hardworking upstanding citizens of this country. As with all migration movements, you will always find some bad actors and we have to be ready and prepared to deal with it. We also must better develop those areas that we do have a common problem with such as terrorism.

We all know that terrorism is for real and is deeply rooted throughout the world. As competent as our intelligence and enforcement is, it can be improved. Thugs under the name of religion or any other cloak will stop at nothing to destroy the United States, Russia, and every country that does not accept their way of life. Their hatred for us runs deep and every problem that has ever befallen them is blamed on us. I wish I had a better answer but I don't! I *do* know that dropping our guard will lead to millions of our citizens being killed; our means of communication hacked and eventually destroyed, food contaminated, and so on. Acquiescing or trying to negotiate with them does not help; it only makes them feel that we are weak. It gives them more hope. I have even learned that some so-called friendly Muslim nations have and continue to fund Al-Qaeda and other terrorist groups. The only way to stop them is to stop the money stream and not buy their oil and gas. The continuation of this practice is maddening and nurtures their very being.

By 1999, the Cosa Nostra was in disarray and knew that it had to mutate so as on the surface to appear to be an ordinary legitimate business. Because of the onslaught of the FBI and other law enforcement officials and the number of made men turning informant, they knew their previous way of life was finished. They still, however, maintain their presence and continue to control labor unions, businesses and some political figures. They just go about it differently! Political contributions are now made via labor political action contributions or through controlled businesses. They're still present and are no less visible. In the early 1990s, the FBI started to focus more on transnational crime and the new danger that was rapidly growing. I was asked to learn what I could glean from my perch in Eastern Europe about the Russian Mafia, its activities and movement in North America. Russia itself is seriously encumbered with the Mafia burden. Personally, I believe that Putin would like to get rid of them as well. From my conversations with some of his high-level advisors and representatives, he on numerous occasions referred to organized crime as a deterrent to a more stable Russia and its people.

Russia today is a capitalist country and it takes money to obtain many leadership roles in the government. When you compare the United States to Russia, let's face it, it takes money to get elected here as well. The difference is (even though it happens in the States, too) in Russia the deals are made in secret and involve transferring large sums of money to offshore accounts. The poor in Russia are very poor and the rich are very rich. The Russian Mafia is, in my opinion, the most powerful transnational crime syndicate and its power continues to grow. In America, too many citizens do not think the Russian Mafia is a problem. Many do not know just how prevalent they are and how entrenched they are in our daily lives. We are a people that watch a few movies, read a few articles, but rarely ever try and fight to eradicate these forces that are paving a way for the control of the future of this country and Canada. They are in almost every community and their criminal activity talents are endless. Why is it that we have glamorized organized crime and its criminal activity? This I cannot understand. It perplexes the hell out of me that many of us are enamored with the mob(s) and their activity. Let me tell you, they do not give a damn about any of us. They are self-centered and would steal your last dollar if they get a chance. Believe me, I know! They will only welcome you if you have money or influence that they can reap to line their pockets with. Every now and then I read about some of their escapades on internet forums and I am shocked at the amount of supporters they have. If a mobster came up to one of these supporters and robbed him or her of their cash and savings, what would they do? Would they still support them? I doubt it; but believe me it happens to many of us every day. Gasoline prices, the cost of the war against terrorism, drug trafficking, child porn, enslavement of women, illegal computer software, selling of state secrets. I could go on and on about how they impinge on our daily lives.

I can understand the difficulty in removing this rarely observed force. The problem is that they are here; ever-present and raping North America. Equally, they now are well entrenched in almost every country in Europe, Asia, Africa and South America. Our allowing their greedy grasp just seems to me to trump all enforcement efforts to rid the real red menace from our doorstep. Open societies with basic freedoms are a breeding ground for criminal activity. Maybe it is just something we have to live with? I pray not.

How do we overcome our personal desires? Does anybody

have an answer? Religion and our consciences let us know that it is wrong, yet almost all of us on this planet continue down this path of allowing avarice to fester and spread. Of course, I strongly point criticism at myself. Looking back on my life, which now you know a little more about, you can clearly see it has been filled with moments of greed and the casting aside of my beliefs. Maybe mankind cannot change or rid itself of these undesired emotions. I hope we can, though, and I think maybe if we all took a few moments to really help someone in need... that soon friendship could to some degree replace our hunger for more.

I guess I have seen too much in my lifetime. I have tried to dedicate my very being to the fight against corruption. I personally believe in labor unions but I cannot stand what has happened to too many of them; especially their mutation into becoming big business. Unions were established to look after workers' needs, not to line the so-called leaders' pockets. The labor movement is not supposed to be about getting rich; it acts as a vehicle to create a decent life for their membership and all workers, and not just the desires and needs of a select few. If the membership just took a good look at their leadership with the perks and money they make, they would be alarmed. Unions were never about having their officials fly first class with unlimited expense accounts.

President Obama and many of our elected officials are unknowingly deceived by some union officials by thinking that they are dealing with those that represent the values, dignity and welfare of the membership. Sure they helped raise the wages and benefits of their shrinking membership, but look at the cost. We can no longer compete in the international marketplace. They have forced companies and employers to go non-union and seek employees elsewhere. I am not saying that they should give up their wages and security. There are ways to alleviate the problem. Profit-sharing programs can be established and employers can develop a program where a union member can be placed on the board of directors and review the proceeds. I know many employers would not like this, but it would help them to be more competitive. This concept is not new but many have not tried it or any other savings program. No one wants to give up a dime but in the end, they will have nothing if they don't try.

Elected officials must stop listening to some of the International Union's leadership and realize that there are some who really do not speak on behalf of their membership. Not all union leadership is bad. I know of a few Internationals who really do try to do what is best for their members and equally work hard to keep their respective employers competitive. We know that America is having serious problems with the ability to compete in the world. How are we ever going to pay for the debt we owe? We have lost a generation (our children) to computer games and the television and many are not prepared to enter the workplace. What will it take for us to wake up and regain control of our values? I may not be the best person to push the panic button but I am pushing it; and as hard as I can. The private sector needs to compete internationally and act according to the principles of our founding fathers and to be responsive to the needs of our workers. Far too many corporations have screwed their investors and continue to do so. I'm not saying that in some areas they should not be rewarded for a job well done, but when I read about the millions upon millions that they pay themselves, I wonder. If they took 50 percent of what they are paying themselves and use it to create new jobs for their companies, what effect would it have?! The same holds true for union officials. Besides the law, anyone representing anyone else has a fiduciary responsibility to look after their membership's interest. We all must change and sit down and think how we can help others.

My cooperation and employment with the feds cost me quite a lot. Watching many friends and relatives turn their backs on me was not easy for me to take. I think they mainly did this out of fear and not because of who I am but because of what I have done. People want to be strong yet when it comes down to their livelihood being affected, understandably so, strength tends to give way to an "I just can't do it" attitude.

I could have been a very wealthy person if I went along with the development of the mob rip-off schemes and other illegal activities. Fortunately, I chose the other road. Even though I hated, and continue to hate, the mob, I think I never acted out of revenge. I really tried to stop them and firmly believe that what I did was my only course of action. The FBI, CIA and Justice Department have always done their best to make my life a little easier and for this and I truly thank them.

Are they, as well as local and state agencies, capable of slowing down organized crime? The answer is most likely yes, but only if we as a people yell loud enough! Our screams, if thunderous, will compel our elected officials and those directly and indirectly aiding and abetting the mob's criminal activity.

Dramatis Personae

A List of Some of the Main Characters

Buffalo/Rochester/Upstate New York

Harold Boreanaz: Lead Western New York mob attorney until his death in Sept. 1993

Paul Cambria: Current Western New York lead attorney for the mob and its controlled unions. Updated the "stay out of jail programs" established by Harold Boreanaz which included charity contributions, public assistance, utilizing the media to spin the truth.

John Cammilleri: Mob Capo who was killed on 05/08/1974, by the Frangiamore-Todaro-Pieri faction for trying to have the Bonnano Family of New York City take over the Magaddino empire.

Peter Capitano Jr.: Strong associate of Joe Todaro Jr. and Victor Sansanese. Came from the Pizza gang and was placed into his leadership role by the Todaros. At first fought the takeover of Local 210 Laborers Union International. Today, now that he is back in the leadership states it was a good idea.

Samuel Capitano: Brother of Peter and a member of the Pizza Gang; a confident of Joseph Todaro Jr.

Joseph Cardinale: Son of mob enforcer Salvatore Cardinale; ruthless, just like his father. Status in the family is unknown. He answers to Victor Sansanese.

Ronald Cardinale: Son of Sam Cardinale, brother of Joseph; status unknown. He answers to Victor Sansanese.

Salvatore Cardinale (aka The Priest): Mob enforcer who turned on his boss, John Cammilleri— he answered to Capo Victor Sansanese. Died 09-07-2000

Sam Cariola: Major union official in Western New York who at first answered to mobster Jimmy LaDuca and then to his cousin Joseph Todaro Sr.

Rosario "Roy" Carlisi (aka The Clam Man): Very powerful mob Capo and brother to Chicago Boss Sam Carlisi; Extremely dangerous and ruthless. While in jail, the Fred Randaccio faction was overseen by Roy. He died 04/29/1980.

James Cosentino: Hotel and Restaurant magnate involved in acting as a front for the mob to arrange political elections and favors. He partnered with James Harry Williams.

Joe DiCarlo (aka the Wolf): Strong and dangerous member of the mob who died on 10/10/1980.

Norman Dobiesz: Front man for James Harry Williams and loose associate of Russell Gugino and Joseph Cardinale. He was involved in the Love Canal illegal dumping fiasco, the Rose Chemical scandal, numerous illegal operations and corporate bust outs.

Daniel Domino: Mobster under Sam Pieri and later under John Pieri. He was fired from his union position because of Joe Todaro Sr.'s dislike of him. This man saved my life and if he wasn't a member of the mob, he would have been one of the great representatives of workers' rights. He was my friend.

John Elfvin: Federal Judge for the Second Circuit. He chased his assistant Edna too much; he developed a close relationship with attorney Harold Boreanaz.

Denise Erb: Girlfriend of William Dellamore, the bodyguard of James Cosentino. She was brought into the hazardous waste business by Joseph Cardinale. She eventually became my girlfriend for a short time.

Frank Ervolino: Western NY union leader who answered to Sam Cariola and Joseph Todaro Sr.; involved in numerous scams that cost the members of the union millions.

Leonard Falzone: Enforcer for the Todaro Family. Some say he is the current boss but I believe it is Joe Todaro Sr.

and that Leonard is fronting for him. Strong, but in my opinion, he could have become much more if he was not involved with the mob; much smarter that Joe Todaro Jr.

James Fino: Older brother of Joseph and Nicholas. He was never a member of the family and was limited to numbers and bookmaking collections. He disgraced the family by stealing his brother's money.

Joseph Fino: My father; brought into the Magaddino Family by Sam Pieri and rose to become a section chief for the family. He was then placed as the leader of the faction that overthrew the Magaddino's and their control of the family. He became acting boss for a few years until the Mob Commission in NYC rejected him. In his later years he had lost any power he originally had. My father died on 03/13/1984.

Nicholas Fino: Brother of Joseph Fino who remained a soldier until his death. Outside of taking a little advice, Joe Fino limited his brother's activity to bookmaking. He died 05/02/1982.

Mike Fitzpatrick: International Secretary Treasurer of Ironworkers International Union. He held positions with the Erie County Development Agency and as an Erie County Legislator. He helped me try to fight the takeover of the Dresser Industries property.

Salvatore Frangiamore: Became boss of the family after the removal of Joe Fino. Later, he turned over the leadership to his nephew, Joseph Todaro Sr.

Richard Fumerelle (aka Rocky): Noted boxer and my half-brother. A great man who deserves the recognition he receives.

Tommy Gascoyne: One of the greatest thieves to come out of the area; leader of the second story gang. He eventually turned informant but did not really provide much information. He told me that he once killed someone and put him in the Buffalo garbage incinerator.

Peter Gerace: Married Joe Todaro's daughter, Linda. I was required to give him a plush position at the union which was a rotten shame and I was responsible for his welfare. Today he is part of the Pizza crew.

Thomas Giammaresi: Former police officer and very close associate of Sammy Pieri; his connections to John Demjanjuk (Ivan the Terrible, who was involved in the mass murders of European Jews during World War II.) Thomas Giammaresi remains an enigma in chase of a mystery.

Norman Goldfarb: Professor at the State University of New York at Buffalo. Norm was a very dear friend who became my sounding board. I loved him dearly and he will always be remembered as a fighter for human rights.

James Griffin: Mayor of Buffalo and my friend. His administration fell prey to the James Harry Williams onslaught via Dennis Vacco. I miss him very much. Jimmy had guts and should always be remembered as a great Mayor.

Russell Gugino: Former aide to Congressman Jack Kemp. Very close associate of Joseph Cardinale, James Harry Williams, former U.S. Attorney and Attorney General of New York State, Dennis Vacco. Gugino was a high-level front man for the mob and mob associates. In my opinion he is in part responsible for the Love Canal and other hazardous wastes sites cover-up.

Al Hartl: Former OSS, CIA and Department of Labor officer and investigator. He brought me into the fold and reared me from a young boy, teaching me much of what a learned about clandestine work. Al was like a second father to me and we remained close until he died.

Ronald Jaworski: Former quarterback for the Philadelphia Eagles football team. He allowed his brother Billy, and Joseph and Ronald Cardinale, the right to use his name in the establishment of a charity for helping needy handicapped children. Ron did not know that the Cardinales were ripping off the fund with extravagant expenses and kickbacks.

Jack Kemp: Buffalo Bills quarterback and later a United States Congressman. Jack was a pretty good friend who unknowingly indirectly helped the mob.

Dave Knoll: Western New York Attorney who represented the Todaro's with the sale of their Florida hotel. I was compelled to use him with my hazardous waste business. He was involved in fuel-cocktailing (mixing toxic waste with oil, gas and diesel fuels) in Canada.

Don Larder: Former assistant to James Harry Williams and Norman Dobiesz who was aware of the illegal dumping of toxic waste of which he did not want any part. Unfortunately, under Dennis Vacco, there was no one in Western New York that he could turn to. The FBI wanted to help but their hands were tied by the demonical U.S. Attorney. I told Larder to seek assistance in Toronto and Canada. I do not know if he ever did this.

Richard Lipsitz: Highly regarded Labor Attorney in Western New York.

Stefano Magaddino (aka The Boss, Old Man, Steve, Don): Much more powerful than what has been stated about him. He ran a vast empire from the outskirts of NYC, Middle and Western Pennsylvania, to Ontario Canada and headquartered out of Niagara Falls. The Old Man died on 07/19/1974.

Angelo Massaro: Started as an enforcer under Charles Cassaro and John Cammilleri. He became head of the Buffalo Laborers Benefit Fund. He died on 09/11/1980.

Marshall Miles: The agent of former heavyweight champion Joe Louis, Marshall became a leading figure in the black community and ran the numbers and bookmaking operations there. To me, Marshall is a fond memory and he took care of me as a child. I loved him very dearly.

Daniel Oliverio: Buffalo attorney and formers U.S. Assistant Attorney. He was appointed to represent me by Dennis Vacco. I fired him for good reason.

Robert Panaro: Buffalo Family soldier and related to Joseph Todaro. I testified against him in the Herbie Blitzstein murder trial while he was operating in Las Vegas. He, along with Steve Cino, was acquitted on the murder charge but convicted of extorting money from him.

Rene Piccaretto: High ranking mobster from Rochester, New York. I got along with Rene, and his son Lauren, very well.

John Pieri: Son of Joseph who rose to be a Capo in the family; not very strong, and dependent on Dan Domino.

Joseph Pieri Sr.: Became consigliere of the Buffalo Family and brother of Sammy Pieri. He moved to Buffalo from Youngstown, Ohio around 1968, with his two sons, John and Joe. Highly intelligent and knowing of the Cosa Nostra ways, he went along with Sammy Frangiamore during the war with the Rochester faction of the family. I witnessed him on numerous occasions direct, as well as scream at, his brother Sam. He died 02/10/1998.

Joseph Pieri Jr.: Soldier under his brother John; very strange character.

Salvatore Pieri (aka Sammy John, Archie, or SP): Ruthless and totally corrupt mobster. He would kill you in a heartbeat. Read the story and you will see. Sammy died on 08/04/1981.

Nicholas Rinaldo: Mobster who became the caretaker for Danny Sansanese Sr. while he was in jail.

Federico Fred Randaccio: Underboss of the Magaddino empire. Many people called him ruthless but I always viewed him as a fairly nice guy, at least with me. He was the brother of Victor Randaccio. Just before I was surfaced, I attended a wedding and sat with Freddie. He told me it was a tragic mistake putting me in Local 210. He died 10/04/2004.

Victor Randaccio: As the Secretary Treasure and Leader of Laborers Local 210, he tried to ingratiate himself with my father by appointing me as a business agent. We fought bitterly and I eventually ran against him and won. Later on, I secretly brought him in and we became the best of friends. I miss him, also. Victor died on 11/10/1995.

Lawrence Reger: Married into the Mader family and eventually became a millionaire. I liked Larry very much as I was sorry to see him get involved with Williams and the mob.

Reverend Herb Reid: Minister of the Gethsemane Baptist Church that constantly fought to help the black community of Buffalo. He was a very dear friend that I looked up to.

Edward "Eddie" Rutkowski: Played for the Buffalo Bills football team and a former County Executive for Erie

County. Became too close to James Harry Williams and took care of him by turning over the Dresser Industries facility for free. Millions were made on the scam.

John Sacco: Mob associate who turned FBI informant who could have divulged numerous secrets of mob ties to hazardous waste. U.S. Attorney Dennis Vacco negated the agreement and Sacco was cut loose. He was a major criminal but his testimony could have been verified by me, Angelo Leonardo from Cleveland, Fred Saia, Sammy Spano and four others who I cannot mention. What a shame, we really could have crippled the mob. The two FBI agents who developed Sacco as a source were transferred and the Special Agent in Charge of the Buffalo office was also let go. It says quite a lot about the power Vacco wielded. Sacco died 12/09/1990.

Vivian Sacco: Previously married to Rudy Sacco and owner of a famous restaurant. She then became the girlfriend of Danny Sansanese Sr.

Daniel Sansanese Sr.: One of the most dangerous people I have ever met. He was Capo in the family who made quite a lot of money off of Sonny Mauro and gambling. He died 11/01/1975.

Daniel Sansanese Jr.: Just like his father, an absolutely cold blooded man who didn't care about anyone but his own family. Danny died 06/16/2003.

Victor Sansanese: Youngest son of Dan Sansanese Sr. Sneaky but trusted by Joe Todaro Jr. A Capo in the family. after I left the union, I had to answer to him and his enforcer Sammy Cardinale, who threatened to waste me, and wanted to frisk me at a clandestine meeting. He and his sons severely beat up WNY media leader Billy Delmont for refusing to go along with their requests.

William Sciolino: Billy the Kid was made a mobster around 1968, and was a member of my father's crew, one of the original members of the second story gang. Billy was a born thief. He was gunned down on 03-07-1980.

James Smith (aka Tex): One of my closest friends and unlike some family members, he always remained close. Tex was a black community leader and an assistant to New York State Assemblyman Arthur Eve. He recently died and I still remain close to his widow, Waddell.

Sammy Spano: Like all of the other witnesses we lined up, mob-associate Sammy could have proven to be a great informant after he was flipped by the FBI.

Richard Swist: Former head of the Erie County Development Agency and involved in the Dresser Industries scandal.

Joseph Todaro Sr. (aka JT or The Big Guy): Mafia boss for the western NY Mafia family. He was a wealthy businessman who made a fortune in the pizza industry. I actually got along with him quite well. He died in 2013.

Joseph Todaro Jr. (aka Joe Pizza): Became boss after his father retired and is possibly still the head of the family. Not as smart as his father; he's the leader of the Pizza Gang.

Frank Valenti: Rochester, New York Mafia Capo who helped in developing his area and a leader in the failed break from the control of his area from Sammy Frangiamore, the Pieris and the Todaros. Close associate of Joe Fino. Frankie died 09/20/2008.

Francis Williams: Mob associate and younger brother of James Harry Williams. He made millions on the Love Canal cleanup, as well as in the demolition and toxic waste arenas. Close associate of Daniel Sansanese Jr.

James H. "Harry" Williams (aka Harry): Mob associate well known for his involvement in bribing public officials and getting his man or woman in office to serve his efforts. The American and Canadian mob made millions with his schemes.

New England

Arthur E. Coia Sr.: General Secretary Treasurer of the Laborers International Union and longtime mob associate of Raymond Patriarca Sr. He received kickbacks and worked for numerous mob families.

Arthur A. Coia Jr.: Son of Arthur E. Coia and a mob associate who rose to become the president of the Laborers International Union. Besides answering to the New England mob, he became involved with the Genovese Family. He used his political connections to save his position with the Laborers' Union.

Raymond Patriarca Sr.: Longtime boss of the New England family.

Raymond Patriarca Jr.: Became the New England family boss when his father died.

Armand Sabitoni (aka Mondo): Patriarca family associate and close associate of the Coia's. His son is now the General Secretary of the Laborers International Union and was a partner with the Coia law firm.

Steve Saccoccia: Longtime New England mobster closely aligned with the Coias. Robert Luskin, who became the Laborers' International Union Executive Board, represented him when he was convicted for laundering more than 500 million dollars of drug cartel money. Saccoccia secretly funneled $505,125 in gold bars as well as Swiss wire transfers of $169,000 as payments for legal services to Luskin. Luskin received a slap on the wrist and was ordered to pay back 250,000 of the money received.

New York City

Lou Casciano: Genovese Family soldier under Capo Jimmy Messera.

Joe Colombo: Boss of the Colombo Family and a close associate of Joe Fino.

Johnny Dioguardi (aka Johnny Dio): Member of the Lucchese Family who, more than anyone, led the way and developed procedures for the mob takeover of labor unions throughout the United States and Canada. He made sure that noted crime fighter and reporter Victor Riesel could never see again by throwing acid in his face. He died January 12, 1979.

Sam Caivano: Longtime Genovese Family associate to rise in the ranks to become a vice president of the Laborers' International Union representing New York and New Jersey.

Louis Giardina: Gambino Family labor leader of local 23 in New York City. He was involved in constant fights with the Genovese Family. He and his two sons were, and are, closely aligned with the Todaro Family.

Vincent Gigante (aka The Robe or The Chin): Became boss of the Genovese Family.

Jesse Hyman: New York City dentist involved with kickbacks to mob families in New Jersey, Cleveland and Buffalo. Turned informant to avoid a long jail sentence after my information that was provided to the FBI led to his discovery.

Richard Kelly: Headed up the NYC Mason Tenders District Council. Genovese Family associate. I provided information to the FBI that led to his conviction.

Mike Pagano: Laborers' International Union representative and a Genovese Crime family associate.

Mike Lorello: From Brick New Jersey and a Genovese crime family associate, Laborers' International Union vice president representing New York and New Jersey until his death in February, 1987. Sam Caivano was his successor.

Frankie Lupo: Son of Gaspar Lupo and a Genovese Family associate. On his father's death Frankie took over his position as head of the Greater New York Mason Tenders Union. My information helped lead to his discovery by the FBI and to his eventually becoming an informant.

Gaspar Lupo: Soldier in the Genovese Family who answered to Capo Jimmy Messera and Vincent Gigante. Gaspar was the head of the Greater New York Mason Tenders Union and message deliverer.

Carl Mastykarcz: Mob associate with the Buffalo Family and Genovese Family. Before moving to New York City, he was a banker who helped the Todaros and Pieris. I didn't know him until he was chosen by Sam Pieri to assist Giammaresi and Sammy Pieri. I was compelled to join their scheme.

Jimmy Messera: Powerful Genovese Family Capo who

oversaw labor racketeering; my information led to his conviction.

Angelo Ponte: Genovese Family Capo, restaurant owner, and garbage industry magnate.

Philip Schwab: Genovese Family associate who probably killed and injured more people than anyone else with his illegal dumping of toxic wastes. He made millions for himself, Santo Trafficante, Jimmy Messera, Sammy Pieri, Russell Bufalino, Raymond Patriarca, the Cleveland, Detroit, Chicago, and Philadelphia families. It is really unbelievable how he could get away with all the damage this administrator of death caused.

Al Soussi: Genovese crime family soldier under Jimmy Messera; my information led to his conviction.

New Jersey

Ray Pocino: Mob connected but I never learned to which family. Never could get along with Johnny Riggi. Longtime labor leader and is the current vice president for New York and New Jersey.

John Riggi (aka Eagle): Boss of the DeCavalcante Family. The television show *The Sopranos* is supposedly based on him and his crime family. I was a major witness in his case which led to his conviction.

Chicago

Anthony Accardo: The real boss of the Chicago Family until his death. I always had a good relationship with him.

Michael A. Bilandic: Mayor of Chicago who should have listened to me and he would have remained mayor.

Sammy Carlisi (aka Black Sam or Wings): Rose to become the boss of the Chicago Family. Brother of Roy Carlisi.

James Corporale: Chicago crime family soldier who, as a Laborers' International Union Official, took a criminal rap for the family and Laborers' International Union President Angelo Fosco.

Nick DiMaggio: Became a soldier under his Uncle Sammy Carlisi. When he was in Buffalo, I was saddled with him and he made a lot of money off of me and the laborers.

Tom Donovan: Protégé of Chicago Mayor Richard J. Daley and the real behind-the-scenes power of Chicago Mayor Michael A. Bilandic.

Angelo Fosco: Chicago mob associate who became president of the Laborers' International Union when his father Peter died.

Peter Fosco: Chicago mob associate and president of the Laborers' International Union.

Ernest Kumerow: My friend and the son in-law of Anthony Accardo.

Peter Schivarelli: Chicago mob associate and manager of the singing group *Chicago*. He was also with the Chicago Streets and Sanitation Department.

Johnny Serpico: Mob associate who answered to Chicago Capo Vinny Solano. He was a Laborers' International Union leader and Vice President. We got along quite well.

Vince Solano: Chicago Family Capo as well as a Laborers' International Union representative; he was always friendly with me.

Cleveland

Edward J. DeBartolo: Cleveland Family associate. Born in Youngstown, Ohio, he became one of the richest men in the United States building and operating numerous shopping centers and the San Francisco 49ers football team. He died on December 19, 1994.

John Demjanjuk: Born in the Ukraine. He was convicted as an accessory to the murder of 27,900 Jews while acting as a guard at the Sobibor extermination camp located in Poland. He was connected to the mob in Cleveland and Thomas Giammaresi.

Angelo Lonardo (aka Big Ange): Became the acting boss of the Cleveland Family and an FBI informant. We were going to use him in Buffalo but Vacco got in the way.

Anthony Liberatore: Cleveland Family soldier who was involved in the bombing death of Danny Greene. He also held the position as head of the Laborers' Union in Cleveland. My testimony in his case led to his imprisonment.

Jack Licavoli (aka Blackie or Jack White): Rose in power to become the boss of the Cleveland Family.

Leo Moceri (aka The Lips): Cleveland mob family underboss who was killed during the so-called Greene Wars. He did not like or get along with crazy John Nardi.

Jackie Presser: General President of the Teamsters International Union who became a government informant. The Presser problem, as it was called, led to sever friction between the FBI and the Justice Department Organized Crime Strike Force.

Milton Rockman (aka Mashie): Jewish mob associate of the Cleveland mob. He was always pleasant.

Ontario, Canada

Michael Gargaro: Toronto labor leader under the Coias. He wanted fellow labor leader John Stefanini killed.

Enrico Mancinelli: Mob associate of the Todaros and associate of the Coias. Took over leadership of Eastern Canada and became a vice president of the Laborers' International Union.

Johnny "Pops" Papalia: Longtime Buffalo Family soldier who ran numerous illegal activities in Canada. He was killed on 05/31/1997.

Ugo Rossini: Vice President of the Laborers' International Union until he was ousted by the Coias and Todaros. He was always a good source of mine as well as a close friend.

James Ryding: Canadian mob associate and businessman who fronted for the Todaros.

John Stefanini: Powerful Canadian Labor leader who ran the largest local union for the Laborers in North America. Disliked by the Buffalo, Detroit and Chicago families and considered a thorn. I liked him very much.

Union Officials / Florida, Louisiana, Texas, Las Vegas Criminal Activity

Herbie Blitzstein (aka Fat Herbie): Longtime mob associate of "Tony The Ant" Spilotro and friend of Lefty Rosenthal. He was killed on January 6, 1997, by Buffalo mobsters and their California cohorts who tried to muscle in on his illegal operations. He, along with Rosenthal and Spilotro, were featured in the movie *Casino.* I testified for the government in this murder case.

Isaac Irving Davidson (aka Irv): Mob associate of Carlos Marcello, Santo Trafficante, Pre-Castro Cuban dictator Fulgencio, and Nicaraguan President Anastasio Somoza, Dallas-based oil magnate Clint Murchison, LBJ aide and friend Bobby Baker, and numerous others. I may have played a key role in the failed Bay of Pigs invasion and many theorists believe he may have been involved in the John Kennedy assassination. Much of his dealings with the mob remain a mystery.

Robert Georgine: Mob associate and former president of the International Building Trades/AFL/CIO. Who absconded with millions in the *Union Labor Life Insurance Company* (ULLICO) rip-off.

Johnny Giardiello: Florida-based Santo Trafficante crew soldier, who took the rap for Angelo Fosco and others.

Joseph Hauser: California con who arranged to buy Farmer's National Insurance Company of Florida and to pay illegal kickbacks to the Coias, Angelo Fosco, Chicago Boss Anthony Accardo, New Orleans Family Boss Carlos Marcello, Florida mob leader Santo Trafficante and numerous others. He became an FBI informant and tape-recorded mob conversations relating to the killing of President John F. Kennedy. Former U.S. Attorney General Richard Kleindienst lost his license to practice law for one year for his alleged duplicity regarding his relationship with Hauser.

Alan S. Lipstein: Tampa, Florida-based and noted scam artist, who through one of his front companies took over the Niagara Falls Hooker Chemical ownership from James Harry Williams and Lawrence Reger as well as the illegal cleanup effort taking place by Williams-Reger front company Envirosure. Why no one ever took the time to investigate Lipstein is beyond me. The sale was called a win-win for everyone by then U.S. Attorney Dennis Vacco who only slapped a 250,000 dollar fine down and did not pursue criminal charges against Williams/Reger/Dobiesz, who later helped Vacco get elected as NY State Attorney General. In 2000, Lipstein pleaded guilty to laundering money obtained through fraudulent securities transactions involving two other companies. And in 2002, federal regulators shut down Tel-One, a Tampa video-conferencing company that sold at least $1.7 million of stock after "false claims."

Carlos Marcello (aka The Little Guy): Longtime New Orleans mob boss.

Terence O'Sullivan: Current president of the Laborers' International Union. Very close to Arthur Coia Jr. who utilized him as his replacement in the powerful Union president's position. O'Sullivan has made sure that Coia lackeys and their operations remain in place.

Robert Powell: Laborers' International Union vice president. He was one of only two black men to hold a senior position in the union. He tried to do right by all the working class and was threatened for his actions. He retired after one of his supporters was killed.

Santo Trafficante: Florida mob-head and very close to most Cosa Nostra families in North America.

Sal Tricario: Santo Trafficante crew soldier who also pleaded guilty and who also who took the rap for Angelo Fosco and others.

Washington, DC

W. Doug Gow: Former Deputy Director of the FBI who was chosen by Robert Luskin, Arthur Coia, Vic Camber and covertly by others to head up the Inspector General of the Laborers' International Union. I liked Doug, but I knew he had to be aware of the scam that was taking place within the union. Terrible shame; like I said, I liked the guy.

Lyndon LaRouche: Presidential candidate who wanted me to run for vice president.

Robert Luskin: Graduate of Harvard Law and a Rhodes Scholar at Oxford University. He was formerly Special Counsel to the Organized Crime and Racketeering Section of the U.S. Department of Justice. Luskin was a chief supervisor in the ABSCAM scandal. After leaving the Justice Department, he represented New England mob-member and Coia-associate Stephen Saccoccia in the gold bar payment controversy. Powerful in the DC area, he was chosen by Arthur Coia Jr., Attorney Anthony Triani, Victor Kamber of the then Kamber Group, and AFL/CIO President John Sweeney to become counsel to the Laborers' International Union General Executive Board. He was the main architect in putting together a covert program to keep Arthur Coia Jr., in power and at the same time rid him of his enemies in Chicago, Buffalo, and elsewhere. I was myself duped by Luskin along with former FBI deputy director Doug Gow into believing that they really wanted to cleanse the union of organized crime. I joined the so-called cleanup team and later quit after I realized it was a scam. Luskin also represented Karl Rove who was the senior advisor and chief political strategist for President George W. Bush during the Valerie Plame/CIA scandal. He currently represents bicyclist Lance Armstrong for his doping charges.

Philip R. Manuel: Another crime fighter that belongs near the top along with my friend and author Dan Moldea. Phil acted previously as the chief investigator of the Permanent Subcommittee on Investigations for the U. S. Senate. He also served as a counterintelligence agent assigned to the 902nd Intelligence Corps Group in Washington, D.C. where he was involved with counter-espionage and security investigations in the United States and abroad. Phil is a dear friend and we remain in touch with each other.

Eugene Methvin: Senior editor of the Readers Digest Washington Bureau. When we talk about crime fighters, Gene's name should be right up there near, or at, the top. A great author and reporter; he really was a wonderful man and a close friend. I met with him on more than 100 occasions at his home or, at a favorite lunch spot, the National Press Club. He was a member of President Ronald Reagan's Commission on Organized crime. We remained close friends until his death on January 19, 2012.

Jack Platt: Former Virginia based CIA officer who worked Eastern Europe. He was one super hero who dedicated his life to serving his country and protecting all of us. We continue to stay in touch with each other.

Joseph Wilson: The husband of exposed CIA officer Valerie Plame.

William Rice: Former Special Agent in Charge of the FBI's San Francisco office. He became the number two man under Douglas Gow in the laborers Inspector General's office.

Jack Wilkinson: Laborers' International Union vice president and Mid-Atlantic Regional Manager. One of the best, and he could have been great if the mob and its lackeys did not control the union. I remained close to Jack after I surfaced and he was a great source of mine.

FBI

Stanley Ronquest: Worked with me and the Laborers RICO complaint until he was killed in the line of duty. He was my partner with the RICO squad.

Stanley Nye: A Supervisor who I was very close to. I use to say, "My way or the Nye way." He was an expert on Eastern Europe.

Anthony E. Daniels: Former Assistant Director of the Washington DC field office and a good friend.

Roger Edens: FBI supervisor for Eastern Europe. Always a gentleman.

Ronald Eowan: Great agent working out of DC. Hard-working and dedicated to his country.

Louis J. Freeh: One of the best directors the FBI ever had. The men and women of the FBI liked him very much.

Richard Genova: Worked undercover against the Buffalo mob.

Joseph Griffin: My buddy Joe became the Special Agent in Charge of the FBI's Cleveland office.

Robert Philip Hanssen: A traitor who sold his country out for a fast buck. I never met him.

Donald Hartnett: Buffalo, New York Agent who stood by me.

Ronald Hettinger: My first FBI handler; a good man and a friend.

G. Robert Langford: The best! He wanted to get rid of

the mob in Western NY when he was the Special Agent in Charge of that office. Unfortunately all his efforts which would have been successful became a victim to the Dennis Vacco syndrome that plagued us all. Vacco eventually had him removed from his position.

Ernest T. Luera: FBI agent and dear friend who worked with me on the Laborers' Union complaint out of his Chicago office. We continue to stay in touch.

Charlie Mauer: Stood by me in my darkest hours and worked with me when he was in Las Vegas.

Gregg O. McCrary: Always a great agent and dear comrade of mine. He became very famous in the profiling of numerous killers and serial murderers throughout the country.

Thomas McDonnell: Remains a dear friend and a great investigator. This country needs more like him.

Jeff McLaine: Transferred after a falling out with Dennis Vacco. I have not seen him for years.

James E. Moody: Big Jim was the FBI Section Chief of the Organized Crime Division until his retirement. He really knew how to get the best out of the agents. He became a specialist on Eastern European crime.

Paul Moskal: FBI Buffalo office council and media representative. We were always close until he retired a few years ago.

Dean G. Naum: A good agent that deserves more recognition.

Steve J. Naum: Longtime contact that I worked with, dedicated and hardworking.

R. Gerald Personen: Great agent who I worked with in Cleveland. He died in May, 2010.

John Pistole: My work in New York City was under his supervision. He was really smart and rose to the rank of Deputy Director of the FBI and currently heads the TSA, Homeland Security.

Jack Porstel: My supervisor after Ron Hettinger was transferred. A good agent and dedicated to the bureau.

William Sessions: FBI Director not at all liked by the agents and gave in to political pressure even when it involved what appeared to be improper activity. The agents would refer to him as *Concession.*

Robert Ulmer: Buffalo Supervisor whom I e-mail and chat with all the time. Bobby came to Buffalo at a bad time and also fell victim to the Vacco syndrome even though he does not talk about it these days. He is a great humanitarian and the type of person anyone can call friend if you knew him, excluding, of course, the bad dudes of the world who totally feared him.

Peter J. Wacks: One smart and tough agent that every

mobster in Chicago was afraid of. He worked with me and the RICO squad in putting together the complaint against the Laborers' Union. We were pretty close and enjoyed each other's company.

Robert Watts: Good agent but was transferred after the problem with Vacco.

Arthur "Dave" Webster: Rose to the rank of Assistant Special Agent in Charge of the Atlanta office. I visited the Atlanta office in 2006, and spoke to their Intelligence/ Counter Intelligence units about the Russian Mafia and Al-Qaeda. Dave was a great leader and agent throughout the more than 20 years we worked together.

F. Ronald Webb: Supervisor of the Buffalo division of the fight against organized crime. I only knew Ron for a short time and I can only say he really tried to stop organized crime.

United States Attorneys

Anthony M. Bruce: Buffalo Office attorney and a great defender of the people.

David D. Buvinger: Chicago-based and another one of my friends who I would argue with over procedure and the scam that had befallen us with the so-called cleanup effort with the Laborers.

Richard D. Endler: Former Western New York head of the Buffalo Organized Crime Task Force. Dick is a nice guy and I like him.

J Kenneth Lowrie: The lead council in the drafting of the RICO charges against the Labors' Union. When we were together, the FBI agents that were present would shudder; in drafting the complaint, we were both motor mouths who would talk for hours upon hours. Great guy.

Mitchell Mars: Tremendous prosecutor and head of the Chicago Organized Crime Strike Force. I only wish we had him in Buffalo.

Craig A. Oswald: Chicago-based U.S. Attorney and my dear pal. He would always say that my job is to protect the innocent victims, and he meant it.

Martin Steinberg: Not a nice guy, wanted heads and did not care where they came from.

Robert Stewart: Head of organized crime strike forces in Buffalo and New Jersey; he belongs at the top with his efforts to eradicate the mob. We've remained good friends throughout the years.

Mary Jo White: Great crime fighter in New York City area.

Dennis Vacco: Nobody in the history of law enforcement did more damage that this man. As U.S. Attorney he protected the people involved in criminal activity that put him in office. As the Attorney General of New York State, his rewarding his friends and the mob continued and the industrial waste cohorts reaped millions avoiding any criminal persecution.

New York State Organized Crime Division

Ronald Goldstock: Great New York State crime fighter when Dennis Vacco became New York State Attorney General. I believe Ron was the first person he forced out of office.

Ambassadors/Friends/Political Leaders In Russia/Belarus/The Gambia

Valery Tsepkalo: Belarus, Great man and author. Valery was the Belarusian Ambassador to the United States. After his stint in the United States he became the Assistant to President Alexander Lukashenko and now heads up the Belarusian Enterprise zone. We remain friends and we always get together when he is in the States or when I am in Belarus.

Ousman Sallah: The Gambian Ambassador to the United States and assistant to its then President Dawda Jawara. There government was overthrown in a coup led by American military trained Yahya Jammeh.

Timofey S. Borodin: Currently Russia's trade representative to the United States and a personal friend of mine.

Anatoly Massiuk: A personal friend of mine in Belarus.

Alexander Orlov: Former editor of the Kremlin press and close associate of Russian President Vladimir Putin. I have not seen him in years but we were good friends and I understand that he is a major player with the Russian State Department.

Anton Romanovsky: Former head of the Belarusian Red Cross and a personal friend.

Alexander Vanshin: Former Soviet Union military colonel who worked in the intelligence arena and currently living in Minsk. He stood up for me at my wedding and we remain good friends.

Arms Trade/International Criminals

Wesley (Wieslaw) Michalczyk: Has homes in the USA, Moscow, Warsaw and Minsk. Wesley has made millions in illegal arms trade and to my understanding continues to do so. I visited with him in Chicago, his home in Warsaw, and numerous times in Minsk and Moscow.

Vladimir Peftiev: Major international arms dealer covertly moving both legal and illegal weapons throughout the world. I have spent quite a lot of time at his Minsk residence when he was not around.

Igor Masteranka: Lives in Minsk as well as having a home in Massachusetts.

Dawda Jawara: The first and only democratically elected president of The Gambia who was overthrown in a coup led by the current tyrranical Gambian President Yahya Jammeh.

Russia/Belarus/Poland

Boris Berezovsky: The Russian oligarch who played a major role in the selection of Vladimir Putin as president, thinking Putin would become the fall guy of the Chechnya problem. It backfired and Berezovsky quickly departed his homeland for safety in England. Berezovsky and I do not get along.

Anna Chapman: Russian spy who was sent as part of a spy swap trade back to her Russian homeland.

Fadi Darwish: Lebanese terrorist and graduate of the American University of Beirut who was sent to Belarus to purchase military equipment for Asbat al-Ansar and Al-Qaeda. According to my close friend, and former senior Palestine Liberation Organization representative who I will call Michael, Darwish is as evil as they come. Even though he remains living in Minsk, he was unable to procure the desired weapons there; he did use his Russian connections in Moscow to get military arms. One time in a meeting together, I requested that he see if he could get me T-72 tanks. “No problem,” he said. I then received the cost of the tanks and went with him to see them in person. After picking up some information and fearing for my life, the FBI requested that I cease my contact with him.

Julian Kronberg: International Red Cross Representative.

Alexander Litvinenko: The former Russian KGB officer who was flipped by Vauxhall Cross/MI6 and made his new home in the UK. He was definitely killed by Russian Special Services but not for cooperating with MI5 and MI6, as most people think, but for aiding and abetting terrorist cells in Chechnya and elsewhere.

Vladimir Loginov: The chairman of the Moscow-based Sojuzplodoimport which handles all liquor exports. He is a good friend of mine.

Alexander Grigoryevich Lukashenko: President of Belarus. Right after he was elected, pictures of American President Bill Clinton who had visited Belarus were all over the place, and he was well liked by Lukashenko. One of the problems that surfaced was that American, Canadian and European businessman started to rape the country. Trying to contact American officials regarding this proved futile. Lukashenko, fearing hidden agendas by the United States and a number of European countries as well as Russia under Putin, suspected every move these entities made. When his country was in need of wheat, the United States demanded that they would not give it unless Lukashenko changed his ways and followed our concept of democracy. More and more he started to use forceful means to keep the United States, Western Europe, Russia and, what he perceived as twisted, journalism at bay. Any one Belarusian that protested was subject to incarceration. Fear of outside rabble-rousing has changed him. This is a classic case that could have been avoided that most of us have seen before and will probably see again. I honestly believe that if Lukashenko had been handled as an equal, the situation in Belarus would be different today.

Yuri Scheffler: Russian oligarch who currently purchased a 75 million dollar estate in Malibu, California. He, together with his mentor Boris Berezovsky, stole Stolichnaya Vodka from the Russian people and now reaps the rewards of the theft. I cannot believe we let him into this country. There are European warrants out for his arrest. We do not get along with each other.

Gennady Vasilenko: Former KGB colonel assigned to the Russian Embassy in Washington. FBI Agent and traitor Robert Hanssen told his Russian handlers that Gennady was secretly providing CIA officers with information; this was not true and Gennady spent many years in a cold Russian jail. I tried to help and, at first, succeeded a little. Gennady was part of the American/Russian spy swap and now resides in the United States. The Russian people should know that, in my opinion, Gennady is a Russian hero who never turned his back on his country.

Boris Yeltsin: His presidency was the worst thing that could have happened to Russia. I refer to it as *The Time of the Oligarchs* and the rape of Russia and its assets. A friend of mine in Moscow was writing his memoirs and asked me what I thought of Yeltsin. I am sure my remarks about him will never appear.

Krzysztof Trylinski: Polish born and now living in Beaune, France; a close associate of actors Jean Reno and Bruce Willis.

Ed Phillips: The son of "Dear Abby" columnist Pauline Phillips, owner of Belvedere and Chopin vodkas; he was a good friend.

Willem Borst: An associate of Berezovsky who threatened me.

Ronald Fino

author

Ronald M. Fino was born in Buffalo, New York.
His extraordinary life story as the son of a *made man* who became an FBI undercover operative both in the U.S and around the world, inspired 'The Tringle Exit' - Mr. Fino's first book.
For more information visit *www.ronaldfino.com*

Michael Rizzo

contributing author

Michael Rizzo was born in Buffalo, NY and has authored five books on Buffalo history, with another four to be released over the coming years.

CPSIA information can be obtained at www.ICGtesting.com
Printed in the USA
BVOW040758260613

324366BV00006B/44/P

9 789655 501933